A JOURNAL OF CONTEMPORARY WRITING

IRISH PAGES

DUILLÍ ÉIREANN

IRISH PAGES is a biannual journal (Spring-Summer, Autumn-Winter), edited in Belfast and publishing, in equal measure, writing from Ireland and overseas. It appears at the end of each six-month period.

Its policy is to publish poetry, short fiction, essays, creative non-fiction, memoir, essay reviews, nature-writing, translated work, literary journalism, and other autobiographical, historical, religious and scientific writing of literary distinction. There are no standard reviews or narrowly academic articles. Irish language and Ulster Scots writing are published in the original, with English translations or glosses. IRISH PAGES is a non-partisan, non-sectarian, culturally ecumenical, and wholly independent journal. It endorses no political outlook or cultural tradition, and has no editorial position on the constitutional question. Its title refers to the island of Ireland in a purely apolitical and geographic sense, in the same manner of The Church of Ireland or the Irish Sea.

The sole criteria for inclusion in the journal are the distinction of the writing and the integrity of the individual voice. Equal editorial attention will be given to established, emergent and new writers.

The views expressed in IRISH PAGES are not necessarily those of the Editors. The magazine has no editorial or financial connection to the Linen Hall Library or its Directors.

Submissions are welcome but must be accompanied by return postage or an international reply coupon. No self-addressed envelope is required. Reporting time is six months. If work is accepted, a copy on disk may be requested.

Your subscription is essential to the independence and survival of the journal. Subscription rates are £16stg/€26/$24 for one year, or £24/€39/$36 for two years. For postage outside Ireland and Britain, add £4/€6/$5 per year for Europe, or £6/€9/$8 per year for the rest of the world. Visit our website at www.irishpages.org for a subscription form. Credit cards are welcome.

IRISH PAGES
The Linen Hall Library
17 Donegall Square North
Belfast BT1 5GB

IRISH PAGES is designed by Tonic and set in 12/14 Monotype Perpetua.
It is printed in Belfast by Nicholson & Bass.

This issue has been generously asssisted by Foras na Gaeilge
and the Arts Councils of Northern and Southern Ireland.

ISBN 978-0-9561046-5-6

IRISH PAGES

CHRIS AGEE, *Editor*

CATHAL Ó SEARCAIGH, *Irish Language Editor*

SEÁN MAC AINDREASA, *Managing Editor*

EDITED IN BELFAST
VOLUME 5, NUMBER 1

IRISH PAGES

DUILLÍ ÉIREANN

VOLUME 5, NUMBER 1

CONTENTS

Language and Languages

IN OTHER WORDS: IN THE SPANISH

PORTFOLIO

FROM THE IRISH ARCHIVE

Boatmen, The River Suir

By Michael Coady

POEM-SEQUENCE & PROSE

Michael Coady

VOICES OFF THE RIVER

1. New Year's Eve

i.m. *Bernadette Quehen and her children Alain, Nathalie, Bernard and Mary who died in the River Suir at Carrick-on-Suir, 31 December 1979*

That sunny morning after hard frost
on the last day of the year
I had just gone down the town
for bread and milk and the paper
when I heard the terrible news
going through the place like a knife –

the car, the mother and children
gone into the flood after slipping
from Carrick Beg Quay.

Half of the town was rushing
to crowd on to bridge and quays.
The sight of a little drenched slipper
left on the floor of a boat
was enough to bring tears

with the people's grief becoming
blind anger that turned
on the cold heart of things –

how strange that seems –

people who live by a river
helplessly raging

against the flowing
force that brought
their settlement into being.

Nothing worse than this horror
had ever happened
in the memory of those still living,
although this place
two hundred years back had seen
scores of terrified women
and children drown within minutes
when their boat capsized in a raging
flood at that bridge.

In time to come
this morning's story also
would be buried
and almost forgotten
along with its tears,
for that is our only way
to go on living.

That frosty morning of New Year's Eve
the sun shone down
on women and men
of my town gathered in grief,
their tears flowing together
by the river and the bridge

while four swans in alarm
beat up off the water,
rose above quays and houses
and circled high over
the human commotion
then headed upriver
towards Dovehill.

2. What Paddy Doherty Remembers Mundy Hayden Telling

They were coming back
after making a haul
when he heard
the voice of a woman
humming and singing
out on the river

and then they saw her
in the half-light
coming along

sitting up and floating
on the water, her clothes
ballooned around her
and keeping her up
as she hummed along
to herself on the tide –

the mind gone on her
when she went in.

They pulled across
in the cots
and humoured her home
while she was still
humming away
a song her father
used to sing to her
when she was young.

3. Titanic

The man who lived
in the house that used to be

there in Oven Lane
was called Titanic because
he was supposed to sail on her
out from Queenstown
to meet up with the brother
in New York.

He changed his mind
on the morning
he was supposed to go
because he was feeling so bad
after the big farewell
of the night before.

4. The Wobbler's Tale

He swore by the holy
jingos and
the high cross
of Kilkenny

that his father was all
his life on the river
but couldn't
swim a stroke –

lost his balance
once in the cot,
and took a header
into the tide

then walked
underwater
to get to the bank

and surfaced
with a salmon
in his arms.

5. *Dream Country*

She dreamed
that she dived
one summer's evening
from the bridge

and into a full tide –
then turned underwater
and kicked back up
to light and air

to find herself
in another time,
another place.

6. *The Stranger*

We were out for most of the night
after making three or four hauls
without a pull of a fish.

Before dawn we drew into the island
to light a fire and boil up the tea
before packing it in.

A man stepped out of the dark
and into the light of the fire,
a stranger, maybe a traveller, and stood
over us like he owned the place.

– Any luck with the fishing? He asked

and we said no, not a thing.
– Try it again, he said,
as soon as the light
shows over the hill.
Two hours ago in the Long Reach
fish were breaking in shoals
on the first of the flood.

Sure enough we put out again
and met up with a big flock of salmon
that threatened to sink the cots.
We dragged a few netfuls in on the mud
and had to get help in bringing them home.

I think the count was fifty-three.
John Toms the Waterford buyer said
the likes of that haul of salmon
seldom if ever was seen.

We never found out who the stranger was
who was gone as quick as he came.
My brother Tommy was inclined to believe
he wasn't a flesh and blood man
but maybe one of the boatload of all
the women and children and soldiers lost
long ago on a raging flood
after a blizzard of sleet and snow

when the barge bringing more than a hundred
down from Clonmel
tried to pull in above the town
but swung sideways-on in the torrent
and couldn't be stopped
till it whirled around and tipped over
then shattered with all the people
against the bridge.

They say the bodies
and ghosts and bones
of all those drowned
were coming to light
below in the islands for years.

7. *The Scales of the Salmon*

for Eugene O'Callaghan

There was no fishing that early spring
on account of the floods that lasted beyond
St Patrick's Day. Cupboards were bare

but my grandfather Dan wouldn't lie under anything
and word came to the house to be out for a haul
one morning at seven above the New Bridge.

My father was sick so I had to go
before school in his place, along with Dan,
Paddy Foran and old Paddy Meagher.

Making the haul that morning
the water was terrible strong and it looked
like we'd have to give in

but then old Dan pulled on
the net ropes with a grunt
and was drawing in two big salmon.

They were so powerful he had to wrestle them
down on the floor of the cot. One was
twenty-nine pounds and the other twenty-seven.

When they were killed and Dan raised his head
I started to laugh to see his moustache
and chin all covered in scales –
I can see it still –

and as I looked on I also took in
my uncle Willmo just then above us
crossing the bridge on his way to work.

Willmo looked down and saw the cots
the men and the fish, old Dan with the salmon
scales decorating his face

and myself
the young fellow
laughing.

That morning we were all thankful to God
as we pulled into the bank
below the bridge.

I doused my face
in Tobar na gCrann
then headed off a bit late for school.

In the years to come my grandfather Dan
went blind as a bat but still fished on
and used go on batters now and again.

A WINTER'S NIGHT, A GERSHWIN SONG

He'd set out to locate and photograph a holy well but went astray on unmarked roads deep in June greenery. Go on to meet a sign, he thought, until he found himself entering a small town where something vaguely tugged from his deep memory. He parked the car in the square and then in sudden rush recalled one winter's night a world ago.

Here's where he'd played at his first dance. The first of all his nights and times as a musician, the recollection fused with a particular song, remembered even to its key of E flat. He was going on seventeen, a learner on trombone, making a nervous debut with his uncle Peter's band. *Orchestra* rather: the musicians wore tuxedos and could read music scores. Two saxophones, trumpet, piano, bass and drums. And on that night, tentative trombone as well. His initiation among elders, all of them now gone.

Standing in sunshine in that small town again, he remembered an archway and a tunnel-like entrance to a spacious dance hall and stage, with a supper room off to the side. Coloured lights and Christmas decorations. It was Saint Stephen's night. Tea, cooked ham, tomatoes, cream buns and cake and sherry trifle. Music and warm bodies weaving, touching, holding. Perfumed women, sleek-headed men. All subsumed within a winter past.

Here and now, an old-timer sitting in the sunshine on a window sill. Cross over to greet him and enquire.

–You must mean the Arch, the man said. That was in my hair-oil days for sure. The Arch Ballroom. And cinema that was. Across the square behind you.

A man is summoned from the bookie's. Hugger-mugger about keys. And then he's led to a bricked-in archway between shops. A door set into it is unlocked. Under that arch he steps again as once before in time, into a long roofed-over passageway like a cave. And there, through swing doors at the end, the hall itself, now a community centre but essentially unchanged.

Lights flicker on in its windowless and haunted space of memory. Spacious; silent; eloquent. Sound of his own breathing. How mysteriously can chance resolve between intent and outcome. Setting out to find a well, unmarked summer roads return him to this space one winter's night long past.

Look towards the darkened stage.

There they are, who are no more. His mother Dora, still with her good looks, sitting side-stage at the piano. The saxes up front, his uncle Peter standing at the single microphone to sing *The Way You Look Tonight*. The brass behind, with bass and drums. That shy teenager seated at a music stand, in a badly-fitting dress suit, jacket borrowed by his mother from one source, trousers from another. New white shirt and black bow-tie for his debut, from Bourke's Drapery, Main St., Est. 1806.

– Put it down in the book until I settle after Christmas, she said to Hughie Ryan. We have a dance to play for on Saint Stephen's night.

The trumpet player beside him there. Joe Carroll, who would be friend and mentor to his coming out. Heart of kindness and innocent excitability. Sometimes his embouchure might act up, or his hernia erupt if he overstretched on a high note. Tales of circus bands, brass bands, dance bands, pit orchestras.

Deep into that distant night, Joe will lead through the first chorus of *Love Walked In*, then take the trumpet from his lips, lean quickly towards him and above the music shout *Take it!* No time for nerves or backing off. With the next downbeat he's thrust into the lead on slide trombone; breath and lips and pulse of Gershwin song –

Love walked right in and drove the shadows away
Love walked right in and brought my sunniest day,
One magic moment and my heart seemed to know
That love said hello, though not a word was spoken…

One winter's night of going on seventeen. Upstream were all things still to come that would in time be gone. While Joe sat back, the trumpet in his lap, and smiled to hear and see a youngster coming on.

Michael Coady was born in 1939 in Carrick-on-Suir, Co Tipperary, where he has lived all his life. He is the author of five books published by Gallery Press, most recently All Souls *(1997) and* One Another *(2003), which integrate poetry, prose and photographs in an innovative form he has made his own. He is currently working on a new collection in the same vein.*

OLD JERUSALEM

Gerard McCarthy

Uncovenanted surplus.

Dawn was breaking on the road to Jerusalem. The sherut from the airport carried me in, through the new city to the old city walls. It dropped me at the Jaffa Gate. From there it was predictably a short walk in to the Jaffa Gate hostel where I had booked a room. The alley was deserted. The door of the hostel was locked but there was an envelope with my name on it. In the envelope there was a key with which I let myself in. Inside there was silence. I stood, taking it in. The silence was broken by the shuffling of footsteps, followed by the appearance of a man of about my own age, who introduced himself as a fellow guest, a Scotsman. He said the proprietor would be along later, and showed me where I could recline on a couch. He told me he was a born-again Christian. I lay on the couch, in a twilight between sleeping and waking, until eventually the proprietor arrived and I was let into my room. Outside the room was a small outdoor landing with a prospect of the roofscape of Jerusalem, more modest than the roofscape of the capital of the old empire, Istanbul. As I stood there a church-bell rang. Suddenly, a loudspeaker was turned on nearby, and the sound of the church-bell was drowned out by the loud call of a muezzin. Soon the voice was joined by voices from other mosques, filling the air above Old Jerusalem.

In the late afternoon I ventured out, through the narrow crowded alleyways of the souk, in the general direction of the Temple Mount, the Haram Esh-Sharif: one of too many sacred places in the world that have more than one name. It is the mount where the Jews had their two temples, and which has held the Dome of the Rock, the Muslim heart of the city, since the seventh century after Jesus. Soon, I found myself at one of the gateways to the Western Wall, the Wailing Wall, one of the retaining walls of the second Jewish temple that was destroyed by the Romans a few decades after the death of Jesus. I looked down at the bowed heads of the crowds in the plaza in front of the wall. The golden dome glittered above them. I headed back into the souk in the direction of the dome, but an Arab man stopped me and said the way was closed. He said I should go to the Christian Quarter. I acquiesced to his assumed authority and walked back the short distance to the Church of the Holy Sepulchre.

In Jerusalem, there is a greater concentration of holy ground than anywhere else on planet earth. The Temple Mount was probably a holy place for long before the Jews made it theirs. The Muslim shrine of the Dome of the Rock now stands on the same site, along with the El-Aqsa mosque. It is perhaps fortunate that by definition the crucifixion would have taken place away from the temple mount, and not in competition for that sacred space. But the Church of the Holy Sepulchre itself has such a concentration of holy ground that it has been fought over for centuries by the various Christian sects, centimetre by centimetre. There has been a precarious balance between them since the status quo was meticulously codified in 1757, by the edict of a Muslim Emperor. In contrast to the abstract space of their Jewish and Muslim cousins, the church is filled with icons, idols. Inside it I found myself in throngs that were more pilgrim than tourist. Many were fervently kissing the sacred spots that are more myth than historical reality. Legend implausibly has the church as the site of both the crucifixion of Jesus, and his tomb. I joined crowds filing up the stairs past the place that has been deemed Golgotha. On the stairs there was a cowled figure sitting motionless, turned away from me. I couldn't tell was it human or statue until, as I descended the stairs, I turned back to look and saw the coal-black living face of an Ethiopian. Downstairs was a slab said to be the slab on which the body of Jesus was laid, which my book said was put there in the eighteenth century. One of the crowd, a schoolgirl, was spreading out a pack of biros onto the stone and rubbing each one on its surface, presumably to bring back to her fellow students as a good luck charm for their exams. At the putative tomb there were crowds queuing. An Orthodox priest was herding them like children, reprimanding any who stood out of line. I retreated from the church, outside into the courtyard beneath a ladder that has remained unmoved in some obscure political balance for centuries. I saw with relief a quiet door, but when I went inside I was followed quickly by a voice behind me of an exotic cleric who emphatically said, "private". He gestured towards the church, indicating that I should go back in there to join my fellow pilgrims. I didn't obey his injunction. I left and wandered back through the alleys. Suddenly, a Muslim man pushing a heavy cart around a corner almost glanced its wheel off me. A very young woman Israeli soldier began berating him. I carried on, lost in the labyrinth, until eventually I found my way back to the openness of the Jaffa Gate. I sat outside the walls for a while, wondering what in god's name had brought me here.

I had been there before, en famille, on a day-trip to Israel from Cyprus, way back in the last millennium. Our tour-bus had skimmed along a pre-ordained itinerary. We had been shepherded around Jerusalem for a few hours. I had hardly seen it.

In the intervening years, my memory had become less memory than imagination. All that remained were shards: for example, the sudden loud call from an unseen mosque at the centre of Christendom that our guide did not seem to hear as she marched us at great speed through the alleyway of the souk that she said was the Via Dolorosa. Periodically, over the years, the shards of memory were augmented by images on television: most were of conflict, of carnage, of lamentations. But these images, as almost invariably with images in the media, seemed to be skimming along the surface of the unknown *what* that is going on: the turbulent passage of the human world whose direction, if any, is perhaps unknowable to our finite minds.

Meanwhile, Jerusalem has continued to be a place of pilgrimage for three religions: a centre for those who have through the generations made the extreme gesture of committing their all to their imagination of a beyond that they see as far more real than the flood of the finite world. For the pilgrim the name of the city is less the name of a physical place than a metaphor whose meaning is beyond us. As for this infidel, ever since the brief shepherded visit, I had had in some place in my mind the intention to return: this time to follow where my own feet took me, to loiter in the hope that I might begin to see.

On old maps the classical Roman world is little more than a coloured margin around the Mediterranean. Jerusalem is at the eastern periphery. Although so close to the Mediterranean world, in contrast to the world of the Greeks and Romans, the world of the Bible is the desert: a place of religious fervour: the place where the one God was born: the God that was divided into three faces. If the Romans had not maintained a garrison in Jerusalem, this God might have remained a little known god of the desert. As it was, a few centuries after they destroyed the Jews' second temple, the Roman emperor Constantine had converted to Christianity, and a century or so later the religion born in Jerusalem had reached beyond the western periphery of the empire, as far as the holy mountain on the west coast of Ireland that became known as Croagh Patrick. Sixteen centuries later, names from that eastern desert world had gained for an Irish imagination the deep mythic familiarity of names from a child's story-book.

On Friday morning I went to Bethlehem. I took a taxi from underneath the walls at the Jaffa Gate. When I asked my driver was he a Palestinian he said "yes, I am an Arab". He said he was born in a hospital on the Via Dolorosa. On the way I asked him to show me Jerusalem's infamous twenty-first century wall. He went around the long way, along the Israeli side of the wall; his Israeli number plates gave us an easy journey. Then as we came into Bethlehem he stopped for me to take a photograph of the wall from the Palestinian side. The wall had many graffiti including one I was able to translate for him: *tiochfaidh ár lá*: the old catch-cry of the Irish republican movement: *our day will come*.

In Bethlehem he introduced me to my guide, who brought me through Nativity Square that I had remembered from the previous visit as claustrophobic with pilgrims, tourists and hawkers. This morning there was a subdued quiet. We went into the church. My guide was a quiet Muslim man with a modest dignity. He explained he had been educated by Armenian Christians, and he quickly got permission to bring me down into the grotto where an Armenian service was just ending. The priest indicated for us to go in. The guide and I were the only congregation, and, at the end of the service, to my amazement I found myself kneeling, and paying my respects at the putative spot of the birth of Jesus. I tried to listen to the silence. Afterwards, my guide showed me around the rest of the church, and, as we were leaving, I asked about the siege that had taken place six years before, when Palestinian fighters had retreated inside the church, and had stayed inside with Christian Orthodox clergy, with the Israelis surrounding it. It had been yet another episode of the human drama that has drawn the children of Abraham together in conflict, across the generations. My guide seemed to flinch at the memory of the episode that did much to inaugurate Bethlehem's current misfortunes. I asked him about the man who had been shot a few days into the siege as he crossed the square on his way in to ring the bells in the church as he did every day. My guide said that of course he had known him: Samir Ibrahim Salman: my guide said he was a simple man, too innocent to know that he should not have headed out that morning as he had always done to ring the bells of the Church of the Nativity. By what seemed to me an uncanny coincidence, the day was his anniversary. It was six years to the day from the day at the dawn of the third millennium when a shot rang out in Nativity Square and killed the bell-ringer of Bethlehem.

Back outside in the square, my guide told me that he almost never visited Jerusalem as it had become too difficult. He spoke about the problems of living in Bethlehem: he said that tourism and pilgrimages had been their lifeblood and that few visitors had been coming since the beginning of the century. He told me that many of his associates had emigrated, to Europe and America. He brought me to the edge of the square and showed me the road with the dumbfounding wall snaking across it. Samir Ibrahim's innocent eye would not have comprehended it: the vision of a wall blocking the way from Bethlehem to Jerusalem.

Back in Jerusalem, I paid a visit to the Holocaust museum. At the door of the Hall of Remembrance I was instructed by an attendant to wear a Jewish cap made from light cardboard. At the centre of the hall is a flame, such as one might find at the centre of a religious shrine, but on the floor surrounding it are dark placenames from the centre of Europe. For a few moments I was its sole occupant. I tried to listen to the silence. I thought of Franz Kafka: child of Zion: one of its finest, and most sensitive. Harbinger of the terrible fate of his people at the hands of Europeans. There is no boundary in any of his writing between the literary and the personal. He called himself a Western Jew, saying that meant that not one moment of peace was granted to him. He dreamed at times of emigrating to Palestine, in order that he might live; but, as he wrote in a letter, "the temptation beckons, the absolute impossibility replies". If he had gone he might have lived to see the foundation of the state of Israel. As it was he stayed, and his voice belongs to the soul of Europe.

I came back through the new city. The streets had a Mediterranean European atmosphere that seemed a world away from the world within the old city walls. I walked through a loud busy market. It was near closing time on the eve of the Sabbath. I lingered in the bustle of buying and selling, drinking it in. As I came near the old city walls I passed the King David hotel, and read the plaque outside commemorating the day in 1946 that a bomb was planted by terrorists, targeting the British headquarters there. The sign expressed regret that, as the advance warning had not succeeded, many were unintentionally killed. Two years later the British withdrew from Jerusalem, cutting and running, leaving behind them war.

In the dark of the evening, again I wandered the streets of the souk. Again I made my way in the direction of the Dome of the Rock. Again I was stopped, this time by a boy, and again I was told it was closed. The boy said "I have roof", indicating he would show me a place from where I could look down on the Wailing Wall. Uneasily I followed him down an alley, but there was no need of uneasiness: he brought me to a platform overlooking the plaza. On the eve of the Sabbath there was a surprisingly festive air. A crowd of young people were dancing and singing in a circle, while above them on either side the two Muslim domes were so close to the wall as to form part of the one scene. Then the call came out from the mosque; and the images of the people, the wall, and the domes above them, seemed as they might to the innocent eye of one such as Samir Ibrahim, as if they were rising towards the one God. I looked up through the glimmer of the roofscape of Jerusalem into the darkness above us all and could make out just one star floating in the profound silence.

On Saturday morning I walked the old walls of Jerusalem that, unlike the new one, however brutal their past, seem to have mellowed with history. I loitered in the souk, following where my feet took me. In the afternoon I found myself in the Christian quarter. Suddenly I came across a young man carrying a huge cross with a crowd following him. Via Dolorosa: I didn't linger on it long. I carried on into the Muslim quarter as far as the Damascus Gate. Hawkers had spread their wares on the steps outside. I lingered in the bustle of buying and selling, drinking it in. As I came back inside the gate, down the steps, suddenly there was a clattering noise and somebody pushed me from behind: it was a man pushing me out of the way of a cart careering down with a man barely controlling it. I carried on until I found myself again at the entrance to the Western Wall. This time I went in. At the bottom of the steps there was a table with cardboard skull-caps. I put one on my head and went down to the wall and sat in front of it. Around me there were various groups, each pursuing their own ritual. Some were unrolling large scrolls. Some men were sitting alone reading the Holy Book. I went up to the wall and touched it for a few moments to pay my respects, filled with incoherent thought. I retreated to the back plaza, and carried on sitting, waiting to see if I would hear the call from the mosque. A flock of swallows suddenly appeared and circled above the worshippers at the wall, but the call didn't come. I went up the stairs to the exit. Then, as I looked down from above, the call came. I gradually returned down the steps;

gradually the sound from the mosque receded. By the time I was at the bottom again I couldn't hear it.

I left the Jewish worshippers behind me and within minutes I was once again among my fellow Christians in the Church of the Holy Sepulchre. It had an evening quiet. There was a singing service going on at the putative Golgotha. Some people were making noise on the stairs. A cowled nun at the back turned round and hushed them, but then smiled a sensuous angelic smile to soften it. The putative tomb was quiet. At the Coptic side there was almost nobody. There was a young priest tending it, who handed over to a woman who began cleaning it. She scraped wax from the floor before diligently sweeping it. The priest then took away the day's takings. I thought they were closing up for the night but I saw him nearby afterwards talking into a mobile phone.

The Haram Esh-Sharif was closed to infidels on Friday and Saturday. On Sunday morning I was up early to go to it, but there was already a long narrow queue there when I arrived, just to the side of the main entrance to the Wailing Wall. A young woman from Germany was beside me, who told me that on a visit to Ireland she had climbed Croagh Patrick in the rain. Meanwhile, the Jerusalem sun was rising, glistening in the golden dome above us. As we climbed the narrow ramp to the gate we could see beneath us Jewish men and women praying separately at the wall. Then a small gate gave us an entrance through it to the Muslim sanctuary: the golden dome and the El-Aqsa mosque across from it. It was surprisingly spacious and quiet. I met the young German again, sitting on a low wall, sheltered by trees. There was a group of American tourists beside her. One of the group was an old woman, who stayed on after the others had left, who had a fit of coughing, and who looked at me disapprovingly before she left to follow her companions. Before the young woman left, on her request, I took a photograph with her camera of her standing alone in front of the Dome of Rock. Then there was just the Dome of the Rock. I tried to listen to its silence.

The Dome of the Rock: is it Art that saved it? It has stood since it was built in the seventh century at the centre of that volatile place. It could be seen as a cousin of Istanbul's Aya Sofia and was built soon after it. Its architecture is as much Byzantine as Islamic. Like the Aya Sofia it has had both Muslim and Christian periods of its history. Unlike the Aya Sofia, it has emphatically not become a museum. It is believed that it was built directly on the ruins of the Jews' Second Temple, around the rock on the mount where, legend has it, one morning Abraham climbed with his son Isaac to make sacrifice. As they climbed, Isaac asked in all his childhood innocence where the sheep was for the sacrifice, and Abraham answered with the terrible words, "God will look after the sheep".

Jerusalem: the mount of the ruined temple is at the centre of the question of it. That place which for millennia has been seen as the human world's opening to the transcendent. Its subterranean passions: fault-line between Christianity Judaism and Islam: its history is at the centre of the conflict between them. The place where the One God was born. The God that was divided into three faces. The very personal God of Genesis: a figure of authority and unpredictable power, like Kafka's father.

How long before there comes a generation that will not be willing to sacrifice its children?

In the afternoon my feet took me without knowing back to the Damascus Gate. I went outside and walked up the Nablus road. By then the sky that had clouded earlier had begun spitting rain, and there was a strong wind blowing. There was a Palestinian girl walking up in front of me, putting out stickers saying Jerusalem is my city. Some of them came unstuck in the wind and billowed off, joining the other detritus blowing down the street. I passed a Palestinian bus station. There was a bus for Ramallah just leaving. There was a feeling of having crossed a boundary to a poorer world. But then, further on, I passed the fortified American consulate, and a short distance beyond that was the American Colony Hotel. The doorman welcomed me in. There was an atmosphere of discrete gentility in the foyer, with just a scattering of people around. In a small lounge beside it there was a western journalist with two well-dressed middle-eastern men. (I couldn't tell their nationality or persuasion.) There was a television camera on a stand beside them waiting, presumably for an interview with some important personage. I found my feet retreating out the door.

I walked back the road I had come. There was little sign of human activity, and it was disconsolate in the wind and drizzling rain. A man appeared, coming up the other way, and he approached me drawing out a concertina of postcards. I could see the gleam of the golden dome among them. So used had I become to such approaches I said "no thanks" and walked on. But then, there was something about the man's immediate acceptance of my refusal – a thin poor man with his goods in a black plastic bag, perhaps returning home from the old city with the day's meagre takings. I called him back. He said they were five shekels. I had already paid twice that for less. I gave him the money and he reached into his bag and handed me a selection of cards held closed with an elastic band. Then, as he was turning away, looking down, he said, haltingly: "because – you know – they are for Old Jerusalem". I put the cards into my bag and as I walked back down the windswept road to the Damascus gate, suddenly, without warning, for the first time since I came ... what am I saying? For the first time in a long time ... I wept.

That evening, I paid my final visit to the Church of the Holy Sepulchre. Upstairs at the putative Golgotha there was a Greek Orthodox service. There was then a procession downstairs, and my way was blocked by one among them, an acolyte, only a boy, as they performed their ritual at the putative stone. Then they carried on to the putative tomb. There was a Catholic service in an oratory close by. I stood between their separate musics. They were not singing from the one hymn-sheet. Then as the Orthodox moved away it seemed as if they raised their voices to drown out the voices of their Catholic counterparts. None of them seemed to be aware of the scene in the Gospels on Easter morning: when the women came to the tomb to anoint Jesus and were met by a stranger who asked them why they had come to seek the living among the dead – that the man they were seeking was gone.

I returned for my final night in the hostel. In the room I glanced at the book I had brought with me. Marcus Aurelius: *Take it that you have died today, and that your life's story is ended; and henceforward regard what further time may be given you as an uncovenanted surplus* ... Outside the calls from the mosques were beginning again. I stood out on the landing to listen until their concordant cacophony died away. I lingered on awhile, letting the sounds drift up to me: church bells, birdsong, Arabic music coming from a radio, the noise of traffic from outside the Jaffa Gate, a continuous stream of random voices coming up from below.

The next morning, as I was preparing for leaving, I was engaged for the last time by the Scottish man who had greeted me on my arrival. A few times during my stay there he had approached me helpfully, in a Christian way. Each time he had taken the opportunity to express his religious conviction, despite my ambivalent responses. This time he seemed to be making a point of giving me his valediction. "You don't believe in anything, do you?" he began. I mumbled, "Nothing that I could put into words". Then he gave his synopsis of how Jesus had saved him: he said his life had gone astray: he called himself the last card in the pack and told me how he had been laid lower than anyone else he knew. He said, if he could be saved by Jesus anybody could and looked at me intently. As he was showing me out the door we looked at the sky in which the clouds were once again threatening. The previous day's rain had been no more than a drizzling. He said it looked like there'd be a deluge today.

I went back out for the last time to the Jaffa Gate and took a taxi to the bus. The driver was a droll man: when I asked him would it rain he said words to the effect that he didn't make conjectures about matters that are in the hands of The Almighty. When he asked me where I was from, I said Ireland, and then delicately asked him the same. He said that he was an Arab: "You are Irish, I'm an Arab, that's the way it is". We agreed it was a pity about the plight of his native place. I didn't ask him did he call it Israel or Palestine. He said he had heard that Ireland had had its troubles too. I told him about the outbreak of peace there: of the day that came that, by an inexorable law of history, was utterly unlike the day that any of the antagonists had conceived.

In the bus to Telaviv I was sitting beside a man who couldn't speak, who for a while engaged me in accentuated communication with his face and hands, but it didn't last long. For the rest of the time I looked out the window as we left the desert hills behind us and made our journey down through the land of Israel to the city that is as yet only lightly weighed down by history: Telaviv. It is a twentieth-century city, but is an outcrop of the old Arab port of Jaffa which it has now assimilated into a suburb. (After I returned home I saw on television an interview with an Arab man from Jaffa who spoke about the time the Israelis had uprooted his father's orange trees to make way for development. He said his father had said it was like his heart was being ripped from his chest.)

When the bus arrived in Telaviv the sun was shining. Outside the bus station I put my nose into the sea breeze and walked down until at last I saw the open blue of the Mediterranean. The waves were rough and the breeze was cooling. I passed a young couple on the sea wall, dressed in Orthodox Jewish clothes. They were sitting beside one another in front of the waves, and the tender image transcended the clothes of the particular faith that they happened to be wearing. I spent the rest of the day ambling slowly along, stopping at various stages, with the sun on my face, breathing it in. The beach was punctuated with signs saying go in peace that could not evoke anything other than heartfelt agreement. The sea did not seek to proselytize me. The breakers just kept rolling in. On my way back I stopped at a beach café for a bottle of beer which I drank as slowly as the sun descended to the western horizon. There was a fusion of east and west in the pop music on the radio. In front of the café people were doing their beach things. Surfers were rising and falling in the waves. I watched one distantly small figure persistently heading out through the waves, before a brief riding, before a fall, before heading back out persistently again into the immensity.

When I walked on I saw a man with long grey hair and beard looking out to sea. Unlike the western garb of the others around him, he was dressed almost like an Arab, or a follower of some obscure religion. It seemed as if he had come out to pay his respects to the setting sun. I imagined Jesus after his resurrection, leaving the desert at last, making the short journey to the coast, and living out the rest of his time as an uncovenanted surplus, in silence by the sea.

I walked back up to the bus station in the darkening day. The bus headed out into the darkness. When it arrived at the airport I sat for a while outside in the fresh night air, close to where I had sat on the night of my arrival, thinking that there was nothing to prevent me boarding a bus back to the Jaffa Gate, and heading back inside the walls to make another attempt at Old Jerusalem. But that was just a passing idle thought. However unknowingly, by whatever mix of chance and intention, the path followed was the one that was taken. The past is inexorable. My feet made for the departure door. On my way in I was stopped by a young security man who looked doubtfully at me and my bag as he asked me the question which I already knew I would be unable to answer: "what was the purpose of your journey?"

Gerard McCarthy works as a social worker in the West of Ireland. His first published essay, "Old Istanbul", appeared in an earlier issue of Irish Pages *("The Home Place", Vol 3, No 2).*

FOUR POEMS

Paddy Bushe

E-MAIL

for Ang Wong Chhu Sherpa

I would not, in the same breath, join *email*
With *serene*, but on my screen your message
Breathes equanimity, and I am touched
By your condolences, and I will honour
Your request to *please don't make bad feelings*,
Your prayer *that her soul will be getting Nirvana.*
I finger the texture of your words as I fingered
The texture of the lama scarf you draped
In sad benediction around my shoulders,
A moment before the shuddering helicopter
Gathered itself, and lifted itself up to drop
Abruptly from that terrace near Annapurna,
And veer dizzily towards my mother's deathbed.
And so, my guide, my friend, I join my hands
Then touch the keys in *namaste* to you.

SAFE PASSAGE

Dear Mother, since that the lodge's radiophone
(the first since we came from the high altitudes)
Crackled with that time-lapse in the voice
That you are without doubt dying; and since
That if there is no cloud the helicopter
Will come for us at first light for Kathmandu
And God knows through where else to home,
And the sky is now a hushed dome of stars;
And since that I left before all clouds had cleared
And since that, after all, we may not make it,
What can I do this sleepless night but cling

To the throwaway kindness of the lodge-owner:
When is big trouble, is no need to tell sorry,
And pray safe passage for you and for us all.

JANUARY

That is no season for the margins, the thin
Cries of seabirds along an empty shore,
The exhausted light turning a haggard face
To the overwhelming clouds, and the sodden clay
Of the retreating cliff falling in dribs and drabs.

I will go inland awhile, accept the shelter
Of woods, the texture of bark and knotted twigs,
Ease myself into the dark of leaf-mould, nut-mast,
And become familiar with warm, hidden stirrings
Among the blind, white protuberances of bulbs.

RINCE FADA THULO SYBARU

Taiscigh seo: gile réalt agus ré os cionn sléibhte,
Mar a bhí is mar a bheidh, anseo, faoi láthair.

An t-ainm freisin, taiscigh é, ós gurb é
An Rince Fada is ainm don bhaile, agus féach

Slabhra fada na mbeann mórthimpeall, céim
Ar chéim stádmhar, sneachtúil i ndiaidh a chéile,

Cor na réalt ag baint splancanna seaca
As urlár leathan na spéire os a gcionn,

Agus a fáinne féinig ag timpeallú na gealaí,
Ardáin feirme ar aon chéim léi faoin tsolas.

Taiscigh an uilíocht seo, agus taiscigh leis
Cuimhne na bainise a d'fháiltigh romhat isteach

Ina rince fada cheiliúrtha féin, nuair a casadh
Anseo thú bliain ó shoin don gcéad uair,

Agus cuimhne an ime á smearadh go Brídiúil,
Ráithiúil ar an lánúin óg ar feadh an ama.

Taiscigh seo agus taiscigh cantaireacht na manach
Tráthnóna, ag sútráil anam na marbh chun suaimhnis

Istigh, fad a rianaigh an *lama* óg roth na beatha
Ag bláthú ar fhallaí póirse na mainistreach amuigh.

A rianaigh, go háirithe, ifrinntí go gcuirimid
An gheal ina dubh orthu dár ndéanamh féin.

Taiscigh, a thaisce, gealadh gach lae faoi láthair
Ar an ndorchadas a chruthaís as do sholas féin istigh.

Taiscigh do ghile féinig ón lá seo go deireadh do ré,
Is rince na cruinne gan bhriseadh go deireadh an tsaoil.

THE LONG DANCE OF THULO SYBARU

Hoard this: the sheen of stars and moon over mountains,
As it was and as it will be, here, at the present time.

The name of the village also, hoard it, seeing that
The Long Dance is how it translates, and, look,

See the long stretch of mountains, step
After step linked in a snowy stateliness,

The reel of stars knocking frosty sparks
From the huge floor of the sky above,

And her own ring encircling the moon,
Farm terraces stepping it out under the light.

Hoard all of all of this, and hoard also
The memory of the wedding that welcomed you

Into its own long celebratory dance, when you chanced
By these parts for the first time last year,

And the memory of the young couple anointed
With butter, for prosperity, all through the day.

Hoard this, and hoard the monks chanting, this afternoon,
Sutras for the quiescence of the soul of the newly dead.

While, in the porch, the young lama traced for us
The wheel of life that flowered by the monastery door.

Traced, especially, those hells whose blacknesses,
In our own deceiving, we conjure from the light.

Hoard, my treasured one, the dawn of each present day
On the darkness you made of the light within yourself.

Hoard your own brightness for the rest of the days of your life,
And the long dance, unbroken, to the very borders of time.

Translated, from the Irish, by the author.

Paddy Bushe was born in Dublin in 1948, and now lives in Waterville, Co. Kerry. He writes in both Irish and English, and has published eight collections of poetry, most recently To Ring in Silence: New and Selected Poems *(Dedalus 2008), a bilingual volume.*

POEMS FROM INDIA

Sudeep Sen

CHOICE

drawing a breath between each
sentence, trailing closely every word.
– James Hoch

some things, I knew,
were beyond choosing:

didu – grandmother – wilting
under cancer's terminus care –

mama's mysterious disappearance –
ventilator vibrating, severed
silently, in the hospital's unkempt dark –

some friends' biting silence – unexplained –
promised loyalties melting for profit
abandoning long familial presences of trust –

devi's jealous heart misreading emails
hacked carefully under cover,
her fingernails ripping
unformed poems, bloodied, scarred –
my diary pages weeping wordlessly –
my children aborted, my poetry breathless forever.

these are acts that enact themselves, regardless –
helpless, as I am,
torn asunder permanently, drugged, numbed.

strange love, this is –
a salving: what medics and nurses do.

i live buddha-like, unblinking, a painted vacant smile –
one that stores pain and painlessness –
someone else's nirvana thrust upon me.

some things I once believed in
are *beyond* my *choosing* –
choosing is a choice unavailable to me.

THE WAILING WALL, REVISITED

Jerusalem, 2008

A human being
is not symmetrical.
– Srecko Kosovel

1.

I gently touch you now
not the way I did
eleven years ago –

not with that yearning
for faith and peace,
but with a private prayer

for inner calm, care,
  stillness; and
for forgiveness and love.

The gleaming hand-worn
  shine on Jerusalem stone,
where the public merges

with the private,
  where prayer and passion
collide and unite –

where a certain kind
  of kindness changes
to another kind –

where a certain kind
  of passion changes
to another kind

of desire. It is
  a blessing of time –
eleven years is a lifetime.

2.

As I tried once again
  to wedge in
a piece of coded-paper

into the cracks
  and joins of The Wall,
I discovered

another paper piece
  behind the new one
resisting my approach.

I tried to force it in –
  the more I tried
the more impossible it got.

Failing, I now tried to
  take out the old paper
that prevented my will,

take out that piece
  to resize
my own new prayers –

but the longing
  of past years resisted
to dislodge the old.

I prised out
  the old folded sheet –
it looked weathered

and yellow
  like the local stone's
sun-stained ochre.

I opened it –
  it was the same one
I had put in

eleven years ago.
  Time had preserved
memory,

preserved my wishes.
  Was I the same then
as I am now?

Was the feeling then
  more sincere
than now?

Passion for life
  never wanes for some.
New love

like old love
  balance
their inherent truths.

3.

Here, gun-slung soldiers,
  pilgrims, children,
and men in black garb –

move forwards
  and backwards –
their axis, their waist –

a symmetry
  that instills and heightens
their own faith –

a symmetry
  I cannot hope
to aspire to,

as I am –
  like Kosovel's man –
not symmetrical.

MATRIX

for PSC

Birds fly across the pale blue sky
cross-stitching a matrix in Pali –

a tongue now beautifully classical
like temple-toned Bharatanatyam.

Dialogues in *the other garden*
happen *not just* in *springtime. Yet*

you stare askance *talking poetry*
in silence, an angularity of stance

like a shot in a film-noir narrative
yet to be edited to form a whole.

What is a whole? Is it not a sum
of distilled parts, parts one chooses

to expose carefully like raw stock –
controlling patterns in the red light

of dark, a dark that eventually exposes.
There emerges at the end,

nests for imaginative flights to rest,
to weave our own stories braving

winds, currents, and the elements
of disguise. *Fireflies* in *the grove*

do not belong to numbered *generation* –
they only light up because line-breaks

like *varnam* keep purity alive –
enigmatic, disciplined, spontaneous.

Let the birds fly tracing angular paths,
let the dancer dance unbridled,

let the poet write unrestrained –
natural as breathing itself.

Matrix woven can be unwoven –
enjambments like invisible pauses

weave us back into algebraic patterns
that only heart and imagination can.

She walks porcupines – as you do –
and listens to the sound of the sea in a conch.

DREAMING OF CÉZANNE

> *Art is a harmony parallel to nature.*
> – Paul Cézanne

1. Jacket on a Chair

You carelessly tossed
the jacket on a chair.
The assembly of cloth

collapsed in slow motion
into a heap of cotton —
cotton freshly picked

from the fields —
like flesh
without a spine.

The chair's wooden
frame provided
a brief skeleton,

but it wasn't enough
to renew the coat's
shape, the body's

prior strength,
or the muscle
to hold its own.

When one peels off
one's outer skin,
it is difficult to hide

blood's liquid weave.
Wood, wool, stitches,
and joints — an epitaph

of a card player's shuffle,
and the history
of my dark faith.

(Based on Cézanne's Jacket on a Chair, *graphite and watercolour on paper, 1890-92.)*

2. The Skulls

The three gods
I worship

are dead.
They stare

from the backs
of their heads,

through
  the hollows

of their eyes –
  their vision

leaking from
  every fissure

and crack
  on the cranium.

The bone-skin
  of these skulls

shines like
  the silver sheen

of a new-born
  fish,

each plate
  like scales

restoring memory,
  genealogy –

secrets
  only fossils

keep alive.
  Skulls on wood,

on carpet,
  on drapery –

studies encrypted
like an unwrapped

pyramid of bones,
mummies waiting

to be embalmed
in oil and graphite –

as I sprinkle
water and colour

on the shrine
of my night gods.

(Based on Cézanne's series The Skulls, *oil on canvas/graphite and watercolour on paper, 1890-1906.*

3. The Card Players

The deal was done and stamped
on brown rough leather

of the parchment tabletop.
Crooked spindly legs

that propped up play
hardly held its own weight,

let alone the gravity
of smoke, spirit, connivance.

We held our fists
close to each other

clenching secrets,
as if in mistrust –

stiff cards in hand
  like little rectangular blades

to cut
  and bleed our lives away.

Future like the present
  was dark and unlit,

swirling unsteadily
  in tobacco stench

permanently embedded
  in the wood of the walls,

furniture, clothes,
  and our hearts.

But at least
  this was a gamble,

a zone of unsure light,
  an unpredictability

to hold onto amid all
  the grey, brown and blue –

cold,
  deep blue, and more blue.

(Based on Cézanne's The Card Players, *oil on canvas, 1893-96.)*

Sudeep Sen was born in New Delhi in 1964. He studied literature and film at the University of New Delhi and completed an MA at the Graduate School of Journalism at Colombia University. He is the author of 12 books of poems, most recently Blue Nude: New Selected Poems 1980-2010 *(forthcoming). He is the editorial director of Aark Arts, and Editor of the Indian literary journal,* Atlas. *He lives in New Delhi.*

POEM & TRANSLATION

Máire Mhac an tSaoi

In memoriam *Conor Cruise O'Brien*

(3 November 1917 – 18 December 2008)

NEC PATRIS LINQUENS DEXTRAM

Ar deire thiar dhein éan de –
Peata éin.
Chruinnigh éanlaith na coille ag an bhfuinneóig.
Ag faire air á bheathú –
Bhain grásta leis an uain sin,
Le radharc na spéire agus
Le humhlú na gcrann fé'n ngaoith –
Le mo sheanduine, le mo leanbh fir.

NOT LETTING GO THE FATHER'S RIGHT HAND

At the end he became a bird,
A pet bird.
The wild birds gathered at the window,
To watch him fed –
That was a time of grace,
With the wide sky and
The trees bowing in the wind –
My old love, my man-child.

Arna aistriú ó Ghearmáinis Rainer Maria Rilke.

AN SÉÚ MARBHNÚ

A chrainn fhige,
An fada ó shoin ó chuaidh i bhfeidhm orm
Go ndeineann tusa, nach mór,
Neamhshuim den mbláth;
Leaistigh den toradh, den meas mochdheimhnithe,
Taiscir, gan cur os ard, do ghlanrúndiamhair.
Mar uisce tré phíopaí na dtoibreacha,
Tiománann uillí sin do ghéag an sú
Le fánaig is in aghaidh an aird aníos.
Ar éigean ina ndúiseacht dóibh isea
Phreabaid ó shuan
Chun ratha is chun milseacht' an chonáigh …
Fair! Mar a théann an dia de léim san eala!

Maidir linne, moillímid;

Och! Tá ár nglóire sa bhláth!
Agus nuair 'shroiseam ar deireadh
Ródhéanach go croílár ár bhfómhair,
Feallann an chuaird sin orainn.
Tearc iad' aithníonn chomh híogair sin bagairt chun gníoʼrtha
Is go seasaid, faoi luisne chroífhlúirseach, an fód,
San am go n-oibríonn an flós a chluain-sean
Amhail leoithne mhánla na hoíche
Ar óige na mbeol
Is go gcimlíonn fabhraí na súl;
B'fhéidir gurb' amhlaidh don laoch
Agus dóibh siúd faoi chrann
Dulta sall uainn roimh am,
Nuair 'chuireann an garnóir báis
Malairt chlaonadh 'na gcuisleanna.

Pléascann siad so ar aghaidh,
Chun cinn ar a ngáire féinig,
Ar nós na gcuingreach gcapall maolghreanta,
Sna pictiúirí caoine sin Kharnac,
Chun cinn ar an mbuaiteoir ríoga.
Iontach é cóngar an laoich dosna marbháin óga.
Níl sé i gcúram an bhuanchais.
Is ann dó 'na thús;
Riamh agus choíche cuireann chun siúil,
Is céimníonn bealach baoil seasta
Trí chlaochló na reann.
Beag duine 'chuirfidh a rian ansúd.
Ach an chinniúint, tá modartha chughainne is balbh,
I dtobainne adhnann le hanam dó súd
Agus canann a shlí dhó
Go croílár shuaiteach dhoineanta an domhain aige.
Cantan é sin ná cloisim a chomhleithéid;
Pollann go haeibh mé, ar shruthlam an aeir,
An luinneog dhorcha.

Sa tráth san
Ná seachnóinn le fonn an tnúth?
Mo léan nach mise
An stócach 's é i mbéal na fáistine,
Suite ar a shocracht i mbaclainn an lae le teacht
Ag léamh dó faoi Shamsón,
Nár rug a mháthair
Aon faic go dtí gur shaolaigh an t-iomlán.

Freagair,
Nárbh' laoch é i mbroinn, a mháthar san
An chéad lá riamh?
Ionat, faoi d' choim nár thionscain an rogha thiarnúil?
Na mílte ag snáfairt sa tsrúill
Ar mhian leo a bheith ina n-eisean,
Féach mar a ghlac sé ar láimh iad 's mar lig sé chun siúil iad,
Mar roghnaigh agus mar tháinig.

Agus nuair leag sé colúin an phóirse ar lár,
Bhí faoi mar bhí
Nuair mhaidhm sé amach as domhanáras do choirp
I gcúngrach na beatha,
Mar ar lean sé ar rogha is ar chumas.
Sibhse, a mháithreacha na gcuradh,
Sibhse foinse na dtulcaí faoi ruathar!
Sibhse na failltreacha ar léim dá bhfaobhar 's iad ag scolfairt
Buíon maighdean,
Sa bhfáistine, íobartha 'on mhac.

Óir seo chughainn fuadar an laoich
Ná moillíonn i mbéal dhoras an cheana;
Ardaíonn gach buille dhe chroí fána thuairim chun siúil é,
Gach buille dá mbuailtear,
Agus a chúl in ár dtreo, seasaíonn sé ag clabhsúr an gháire –
Stroinséartha.

Nóta ón Údar: *Ba mhaith liom an saothar a thiomnadh le hómós, baochas agns cion don Dr Timothy Casey, iar-Ollamh le Gearmáinis in Ollscoil na hÉireann sa Ghaillimh. Grásta ar a anam uasal! Muna mbeadh an cúnamh flaithiúil agus an misneach a thug sé dom ní dócha go seolfainn go deo an obair chun criche. Ar ámhairí an tsaoil ní bheidh as so amach an chabhair sin ceilte orthu súd ar mhian leo aithne ó phréimh a chur ar an bhfile mór Eorpach arbh é Rilke é. D'fhág Tim ina dhiaidh seod de leabhar,* A Reader's Guide to Rilke's Sonnets to Orpheus, *ina bhfuil bailithe fómhar stileáilte a chaondúthrachta fada i mbun chultúr na Gearmáine.*

This is the sixth of Rilke's Duino Elegies. All 10 have been translated by Máire Mhac an tSaoi. Irish Pages *published the Tenth Duino Elegy in a previous issue ("The Media", Vol 4 No 1).*

One of the past century's most important Irish language writers, Máire Mhac an tSaoi was born in 1922 and educated at University College Dublin and the Sorbonne. Her first collection of poems, Margadh na Saoire *(Sáirséal & Dill) was published in 1956; her most recent,* Shoa agus Dánta Eile *(Sáirséal Ó Marcaigh), in 1999. Her acclaimed memoir,* The Same Age as the State *(O'Brien Press), appeared in 2003. She was married to Conor Cruise O'Brien (1917-2008) and lives in Howth, Co Dublin.*

ELEGIES

Gary Allen

MARY IN THE ROUND

Them were the days, the water frozen in the pump
the moon heavy as lead, cold in the ice-fogged window
sit closer, I don't see so well, one eye all but dead
traces of snow under the hedgerows, on the bare stone
and bog grass higher up, we brought in wood and sticks
looked to the chookies, milked the cow, before a breakfast
of stale bread and last night's tea, barefoot to school,
to the mills, the long walk back down mud lanes already
half-dark, a father cutting scrap iron in the yard, orange
sparks lepping in the air – sit closer to the fire, things
become vague, faces come and go, mixed up with time,
after the first death there is no other, I watched them all
getting carried out, and then you are old: the farmer
wanted the place down but I wouldn't go, not for love
of these old damp walls, holed roof, no plumbing –
so he puts rats in through the back door, scuttling everywhere,
they bit my legs and hands, but I'm still here, all he needed
to buy was a coffin – everything becomes confused, they want
me to go to a care home now, but it's not for me, all those fussy
people washing at you: once, I sneaked out at night, in the winter
time, the house quiet, everyone sleeping like the dead – why,
I don't know, but I went up to the bit of pine forest at the
Vanishing Lough, and sat shivering as I looked at the sliver
of bright moon on the water, one gleaming star, the air
so sharp it would cut the lungs from your body, and the world
seemed so big to a child back then – I don't know why
I remember this, why it's in my head at all, but there you are.

DOWN TO THE RIVER

In this field
cows stand passive –

hide-covered furniture:

think of iron into flesh
saw-teeth slicing bone

beetled skin
pounded hoof and horn –

nothing cannot be changed.

White mist covers the water,
stars sliding in the sky

are already dead,

We are alone, my father said,
in all the universe.

The dust of hoarfrost
making the tangled washing wires sing

grass break beneath our feet

the cows fade away from us
like ghosts

like stiffened shapes of work shirts
hanging from the lines:

I held my father's hand when he died
although I wasn't there

the fishing-rods we never owned
the fish we never caught
the universe we never sailed through –

I think it's time, he said,
to shine.

AD INFINITUM

He is below ground
asleep in a cardboard suitcase

tied down with knotted string.

I saw him go under
the meaningless words we scatter

to no one, in the name of nothing.

It will take many months
to pay out the funeral director

many years to settle –
earth, bones, confusion

as though something has come and gone:

it is morning
almost before anything will happen

so still, so still

the early sun a rim of silver reflection
rising and illuminating

the gorse, burns, boggy cover
on these low mountain tops

no footprints father
another place we will never walk
nothing to discuss

only the shadow of a plane
skimming across bare rock –

a crooked sideways cross.

Gary Allen was born in Ballymena, Co Antrim in 1959. He worked and travelled widely in continental Europe, settling for a period in Holland. He is the author of four collections of poetry, Languages *(Flambard, 2002),* Exile *(Black Mountain Press, 2004),* North of Nowhere *(Lagan Press, 2006) and* The Bone House *(Lagan Press, 2008). He continues to live in Ballymena, where he writes full-time.*

LÉACHT PHOIBLÍ *DUILLEOGA ÉIREANNACHA* 2008

Louis de Paor

"Cupáin, fochupáin agus tionlacan na n-óinseach."

(Editor's Note: *This address was delivered, with similtaneous English translation, as The Fourth Annual* Irish Pages *Lecture on 31 October, 2008 at The Linen Hall Library, Belfast. It is the author's wish not to include a translation or preface in English, since what is said is said fully in the essay itself.*)

Is cuimhin liom na chéad fhocail Ghaeilge gur cuimhin liom a léamh agus a chlos. Bhíodar ansan romham ar an gcéad leathanach den gcéad leabhar Gaeilge a tugadh dúinn i rang na naíonán sa bhunscoil.

Cupán.

Fochupán.

D'aithníos brí an chéad fhocail óna cholceathrar Béarla, é curtha as a riocht ag an síneadh fada a thug a fhuaim níos giorra do leagan Béarla eile a raibh cleachtadh maith againn air.

Cop on.

Bhí an tarna focal níos aite fós, is gan aon leide ina dheilbh a cheanglódh lenár saol laethúil Béarlúil é. Ba chuige sin na pictiúir, is dócha, cupán agus sásar os cionn na bhfocal a chomharthaigh iad. Tá a fhios agat fhéin na háraistí gorma agus bána sin a bhí coitianta fadó fadó in Éirinn a chuirfeadh laethanta fada samhraidh i dtigh aintín fén dtuath i gcuimhne dhuit níos faide anonn id shaol.

Is sa chéad leabhar Gaeilge is túisce a chonaic mé féin iad, áfach, is ní raibh aon dealramh acu leis na gréithre a bhí againn féin sa bhaile. Bhíodar chomh deoranta lem thaithí linbh is a bhí na focail nua.

Ní fhéadfainn a rá gur athraigh na focail nua mo thuiscint ná mo chiall don saol mar atá, nó mar a shamhlaímid le focail é, ach tá scóip fés na focail sin "cupán" agus "fochupán" i gcónaí im aigne, rud éigin fairsing, folláin, flaithiúil ná baineann lena macasamhail Bhéarla. Baineann "cups and saucers" níos mó le dea-bhéasa, le cuairteoirí, le heagla go ndoirtfear nó go mbrisfear rud éigin sara mbeidh deireadh déanta.

Ar na pictiúirí a chuirim an milleán faoi seo ar fad. Más é a bhí i gceist leo an Ghaeilge a cheangal leis an saol againn féin, ní ar an saol bruachbhailteach meánaicmeach a bhí á chaitheamh againne ar imeall thiar chathair Chorcaí a bhíothas ag cuimhneamh. Bhain na háraistí gorma agus bána le cistineacha tuaithe ná raibh aon chleachtadh againn orthu go fóill.

Tuigeadh dúinn ón gcéad uair a leagamar cois thar tairseach i gceann de na cistineacha san ar ball gur cuairteoirí ab ea sinn fhéin ó shaol toirtéiseach na "cups and saucers" dar leosan a bhí ag baile sa domhan cluthar leathchoimthíoch seo. Chuirfidis na múrtha fáilte romhainn i rith na laethanta saoire nó aon Domhnach i gcaitheamh na bliana ach ba léir nár linne an saol eile seo.

Le saol nár liom a shamhlaíos an Ghaeilge ar dtúis mar sin, saol fairsing, folláin, flaithiúil, a bhí fós á chaitheamh thar teorainn fisiciúil mo shaoil laethúil féin. Bhí sé chomh gairid dom go bhféadfainn dul amach ann ar mo rothar. Go deimhin, bhí colceathracha liom ina gcónaí ann is thagadh scata buachaillí uaidh chun na scoile ar an mbus gach maidin. Ba le saol sin na tuaithe a bhain na háraistí gorma agus bána cé ná raibh focal Gaeilge á labhairt ag éinne den dream a casadh orm ar mo chuid cuairteanna amach ann. Go deimhin, b'fhearr an Ghaeilge a bhí agam féin, de réir dhealraimh, ná ag éinne acusan cé gur ghiorra dá dtaithí siúd na focail nua ná dom thaithí féin.

Ba chuma san go fóill. Ba chuid dem shaol feasta an Ghaeilge, an teanga a labhair na múinteoirí eatarthu féin os ár gcomhair, is a bhaist gach duine againn as an nua nuair a léadh amach an leabhar rolla ar maidin.

Antóin de Búrca?
Anseo!
Antóin de Paor?
Anseo!

Má bhí an Ghaeilge as alt leis an saol a bhí á chaitheamh againn sa bhaile, sa tsráid, sna páirceanna timpeall orainn, i gclós na scoile féin, níor fhág san nár aimsigh sí a cúinne féin dár n-aigne is dár samhlaíocht linbh le cur fúithi ann. Bhain eachtraí Jimín Mháire Thaidhg le saol sin na samhlaíochta chomh mór is a bhain "My First Confession" le Frank O'Connor. Mhúscail na scéalta sin uaigneas anabaí i ndiaidh ár n-óige féin ionainn, cumha i ndiaidh saoil a aithníomar cé nach sinn fhéin a bhí á chaitheamh. Bhí na scéalta sa dá theanga ag freastal ar an gceantar mothála céanna ionainn, ceantar taibhrimh mar a thabharfadh Seán Ó Ríordáin air.

Le ceantar taibhrimh eile a bhain *Rotha Mór an tSaoil,* dúthaigh bhorb fhireann ar bhreá linn é a shiúl i dteannta Mhicí Mhic Gabhann nuair a bheimis fásta suas. Nuair a léamar scéal Jack London Chloich Chionnfhaola i rang a sé, bhí a chuid eachtraí chomh taitneamhach coimthíoch le scéalta na mbuachaillí bó nó na laochra cogaidh as Sasana agus Meiriceá sna *comics* a bhí á léamh againn faoi mbord nuair a fuaireamar deis agus droim an mhúinteora linn.

Faoiseamh ón saol agus éalú uainn féin ab ea na nithe sin ar fad, fairsingiú samhlaíochta a thug le fios go raibh an saol níos leithne ná Baile an Easpaig agus an duine níos mó ná sinn fhéin. Bhain an Ghaeilge leis an bhfairsingiú aigne san domsa ón tús; baineann i gcónaí.

Má éiríonn liom uaireanta a chur ina luí orm féin gur cuid dem scéal féin is ea litríocht na Gaeilge ó aimsir an éin bhig sin a lig fead de rinn goib ghlanbhuí os cionn Locha Liaigh ar aghaidh, ritheann sé liom chomh maith gurb é an bua is mó atá ag go leor den litríocht shinseartha ná go meabhraíonn sí saol agus aigne dom atá lasmuigh dem chleachtadh féin ach gur fairsingiú ar mo mhothú agus ar mo shamhlaíocht dul chomh gairid dóibh agus is féidir liom sa léitheoireacht.

Ar ndóigh, baineann sé seo leis an litríocht ar fad. Cuirimid sinn fhéin agus an saol mar atá ar ceal agus saothar litríochta a léamh againn le súil gur saibhre dá réir a bheidh ár dtuiscint orainn féin agus ar éagsúlacht mhíorúilteach an tsaoil nuair a fhillimid chugainn fhéin ar ball.

Nár chóir go mbeadh rud thairis sin ag baint le litríocht na Gaeilge dúinne, áfach? Má labhrann litríocht an domhain mhóir linn as an dtaithí atá i bpáirt ag an gcine daonna ar fad, bheifeá ag súil go labhródh litríocht na Gaeilge ar shlí speisialta linn ar ghnéithe dár dtaithí choitianta mar Éireannaigh a mhíníonn sinn dúinn fhéin ar shlí nach féidir le litríocht tíortha agus teangacha eile a dhéanamh.

Ba mhaith liom filleadh ar an gceist seo ar ball, ach is é atá á rá agam ag an bpointe seo ná gur mhair Deirdre agus Maedhbh agus Niamh Chinn Óir sa cheantar taibhrimh céanna le Snow White agus Sleeping Beauty, le Guinevere agus Joan of Arc, an uair sin im aigne, go mba chomarsana béal dorais im shamhlaíocht iad Cúchulainn agus Launcelot, David Copperfield agus David Balfour. Ní cuimhin liom go raibh aon éileamh speisialta ag laochra na Gaeilge orm seachas a ngaolta gearra Béarla; bhí slí dóibh go léir i measc na gcaisleán, míle míle ón saol mar a bhí, i ndomhan gan teorainn na samhlaíochta.

Fágaimis ceantar an taibhrimh agus na mbrionglóidí súiloscailte go fóill is fillimis ar an seomra ranga. Ba chuid dár saol laethúil an Ghaeilge ón gcéad lá sa bhunscoil. Bhain sí leis an seomra ranga, leis an nuacht gearr ar an raidió, le craobhacha mionúir na hÉireann, leis na leabhair ar sheilfeanna m'athar, is bhain sí linne chomh mór is a bhain an seomra ranga, an raidió, an All-Ireland, agus tigh m'athar.

Bhí cothú samhlaíochta agus oiliúint chultúrtha i gceist léi is níor bhraitheas riamh go mba throime an t-ualach í ná aon ní eile a múineadh dúinn. Bhí gach ábhar éigeantach is níor iarradh ár dtuairim i dtaobh na nithe a chaithfimis a fhoghlaim. Fuaireamar eolas nár iarramar ar Chúchulainn agus Aodh Rua Ó Néill, ar Florence Nightingale agus Grace Darling, ar Charles Dickins, Robert Service, Alfred Tennyson, agus Rudyard Kipling, ar Mháire Mhac an tSaoi, Sheán Ó Ríordáin, Raifteirí, agus An Seabhac.

Lasmuigh den seomra ranga, léamar Richmal Crompton, Éilís Dillon, agus Patricia Lynch ar dtúis, agus ina dhiaidh sin, John le Carré, P.G. Wodehouse, Louis L'Amour, Edgar Wallace, J.T. Edson, Zane Gray, agus Oliver Strange, an té a chruthaigh Sudden, an laocch is fearr dar iompair gunna obann agus luachanna fearúla riamh san Iarthar Fiáin, dar liom fhéin agus mo dheartháireacha.

Enid Blyton, Agatha Christie agus W.E. Johns a bhí ag labhairt as ceantar taibhrimh in íochtar a samhlaíochta le buachaillí eile is bhí oiread suime agam fhéin tráth i ngaiscí Douglas Bader agus na Dambusters is a bhí in eachtraí Oisín agus Fhinn Mhic Chumhaill. Bhí ainmneacha móra na ngaiscíoch Éireannach chomh coimhthíoch lenár dtaithí laethúil is a bhí ainmneacha na laochra impiriúla; mura raibh aon "Douglas" inár measc, ní raibh Caoilte ná Oscar ann ach oiread. Ba chuma san; má bhí bearna idir an Ghaeilge a d'fhoghlaimíomar ar scoil agus an chuid eile dár saol, bhí bearna éigin idir gach a múineadh dúinn ar scoil, agus an saol "fíor" a chaitheamar lasmuigh di.

Is é an chúis go luaim é seo ar fad ná go dtuigtear dom anois go raibh dhá idé-eolaíocht éagsúla ar a laghad laistiar de na téacsaí litríochta a roghnaíodh dúinn sa bhunscoil, agus sa bhaile, ceann amháin a bhain le athshealbhú an traidisiúin Ghaelaigh, ceann eile a thug ómós éigin do spiorad laochúil na seanimpireachta. Níor bhain na gnéithe Gallda ná na gnéithe Gaelacha dár gcuid léitheoireachta leis an saol bruachbhailteach a bhí á chaitheamh againne. Nílim ag gearán ina thaobhsan – bhí an saol sin rónua, in Éirinn ach go háirithe, adéarfainn, le go mbeadh aon rian de go fóill sa sna leabhair scoile, i mBéarla ná i nGaeilge.

Mar a tharlaíonn, is é an múinteoir céanna, Frank Murphy, a chuir Micí Mac Gabhann agus Jimín Mháire Thaidhg in aithne dúinn a scríobh an chéad leabhar do pháistí a bhí lonnaithe ar shlí shochreidte i gcathair Chorcaí. Bhí comhrá agus eachtraí na gcarachtar sa leabhar san *Lockie and Dadge* (1995) chomh taitneamhach coimthíoch dom leanaí féin nuair a léadar san Astráil é is a bhí scéalta William Brown agus Violet Elizabeth Botts dom féin fiche bliain roimhe sin, ach amháin gur thuigeadar, nó gur samhlaíodh dóibh, gur mhair a n-athair i saol eile an leabhair sin fadó fadó in Éirinn.

—

Ag féachaint siar dom anois air, is é is mó a chuireann iontas orm ná a laghad trácht a deineadh ar an nGaeltacht, agus an áit speisialta a bhí aici i scéal na teangan, nuair a bhíomair ar scoil. Ní foláir nó bhí a fhios againn go raibh a leithéid d'áit ann, i bhfad Éireann ón áit a raibh cónaí orainn féin, ach níor bhraitheas riamh go raibh aon éileamh speisialta ag an áit seo, a bhí glan lasmuigh dem thaithí féin, ormsa ná ar an teanga a bhí á léamh is á labhairt agam ó bhíos ceithre bliana d'aois. Ná níor tugadh le fios dúinn riamh, chomh fada lem chuimhne, go raibh teideal níos fearr ag éinne eile ar an nGaeilge ná mar a bhí againne. An té ab fhearr a d'fhoghlaim a chuid táblaí agus eile, ba é ab fhearr chun matamaitice; an té ab fhearr a thabharfadh leis matamamaitic na Gaeilge, ba é ab fhearr chuici. Is bhíos go maith chun na matamaitice áirithe sin.

San Ollscoil a cuireadh in iúl dom den gcéad uair nár liomsa dáiríre an Ghaeilge, gur ar iasacht nó le gadaíocht a bhí sí faighte againn ó mhuintir na Gaeltachta, ní hea, ach ó roinnt bheag seandaoine a raibh cuid bheag acu ina mbeathaidh fós i gCorca Dhuibhne, agus cuid eile ar shlí na fírinne. Ba é slí na fírinne slí an chirt ó thaobh na Gaeilge de agus ba é an bóthar siar ón Daingean an t-aon bhóthar a thabharfadh sinn chun na fírinne sin.

Bhí cleachtadh agam ar an dearcadh seo cheana. Nuair a bhíos sa bhunscoil, cuireadh go dtí *elocution lessons* sinn chun ár gcuid Béarla a cheartú agus blas Chorcaí a ghlanadh dár gcuid cainte, chun go labhróimis Béarla ceart, seachas an Béarla a bhí ag ár muintir romhainn. Tugadh cleachtaí teangan dúinn chun ár gcuid cainte a chur in oiriúint don gcanúint uasal Bhéarla a raibh údarás gach rí agus banríon Shasana, gach ollamh ollscoile in Oxbridge, gach léitheoir nuachta de chuid an BBC, ba dhóigh leat, laistiar dá cuid consan dícheannaithe, dá cuid siollaí martraithe inár mbéil thuata.

Fawthe's caw is a Jaguaw
And Paw drives rawthe fawst.

Cuireadh ar mo shúile anois dom go raibh mo chuid Gaeilge chomh mícheart le mo chuid Béarla; agus ar ndóigh, bhí, mura raibh sí níos measa go mór. Bhíos chomh mór ar strae ó shlí na fírinne a raibh *Received English* ar an gcomhartha bóthair os a cionn is a bhíos ón gceann a thabharfadh go dtí tobar fíorghlan na Gaeilge dúchais mé.

"Gaoluinn" a bhí á labhairt ag na cainteoirí údarásacha a gcaithfimis aithris a dhéanamh orthu, seachas "Gaeilge na leabhar" nó "School Irish". Nuair a thugas mo chéad turas ceart ar Chorca Dhuibhne, ní mór ná gur deineadh coinnealbhá orm nuair a dúrt an focal eiriciúil "freisin" is mé ag caint le fear an tí go rabhas ag fanúint ann.

> "Léan ort, a bhuachaill, nó cá bhfuairis an focal san? Leis, a gharsúin, leis adeirimidne."

Bhíos chomh cloíte an uair sin nár rith sé liom a rá leis nárbh an ionann an chiall a bhí aige féin don gcéad phearsa, uimhir iolra, den bhforainm pearsanta is a bhí agamsa. Fén dtráth san, bhíos tréis glacadh leis go raibh pribhléid ag cainteoirí dúchais Chorca Dhuibhne, fuaimeant agus údarás lena gcuid cainte ná beadh go deo agamsa is go gcaithfinn aithris chruinn a dhéanamh orthusan má theastaigh uaim Gaoluinn cheart a bheith agam. Istigh i mboth sa teanglann, is mé ag aithris chomh cruinn is a fhéadfainn ar chaint álainn shaibhir a fáisceadh as saol nár bhain liom, saol na gcupán is na bhfochupán gorma agus bána, bhíos dom chur féin ar ceal, ar fionraí.

Níorbh ionann é seo agus an cur ar ceal go rabhas ag trácht air níos túisce, an t-éalú uainn féin a bhaineann le léitheoireacht agus leis an ealaín i gcoitinne. Fén dtráth seo, bhíos tréis a áiteamh orm féin gur chuid dhílis dem mhodh maireachtana agus dem mhodh labhartha í an Ghaeilge, go raibh cearta áirithe agam anois ar dhá theanga a bhí ábalta ar mé a chur in iúl. A mhalairt glan a bhí á chur abhaile orm sna ranganna teangan, sna seomraí léachta, agus go háirithe sa teanglann. Dá fheabhas an aithris a bhí á dhéanamh agam ar na cainteoirí neamhchoitianta ar an dtéip, is ea is dlúithe a cheanglaíos aghaidh fidil Ghaoluinn na Gaeltachta díom féin, is ea is lú a bhíos dom chur féin in iúl mar dhuine a tógadh i mbruachbhaile nua meánaicmeach ar imeall na cathrach. Guthadóir boilg ab ea an seanchainteoir dúchais is ba mise an babliac ar a ghlúin.

Má bhíos míchinnte ar uairibh roimhe sin faoi ghramadach agus mheicníocht na teangan, bhí éiginnteacht de shaghas eile orm feasta. Bhíos chomh míshocair lem chuid Gaeilge anois is a bhíos lem chuid Béarla ina dhiaidh sin nuair a chuas don Astráil. An dá theanga a labhraíos as m'óige, bhíodar ait, as alt, dar le daoine a thuig agus a labhair na teangacha sin níos fearr agus níos cirte ná mé féin. Bhí údarás le caint daoine eile ná raibh sa chaint agamsa. Bhíos chomh míshocair sin, agus chomh mór sin faoi dhraíocht ag na cainteoirí iontacha a casadh orm idir an Buailtín agus Dún Chaoin, gur thosnaíos ag aithris orthu ar feadh tamaill, mar dhea is gur mac feirmeora nó iascaire as iarthar Chiarraí mé a saolaíodh roimis m'athair féin. "H'anam 'on diabhal, ambaiste!"

CHUGAT

ná fan rófhada liom
mura dtagaim sa samhradh bán
uaireanta meallann an fharraige mé

ar an mbóthar fada chugat
níl inti ach mo dheora féin

slánaigh do chroí
ná habair go dtréigeas tú
abair gur bádh mé

30 bliain geall leis ó léas an dán sin le Michael Davitt den gcéad uair, tá sé chomh glan, nua, dar liom, is dá scríobhfaí amáireach é. Nílim cinnte go dtuigim ar fad cad ina thaobh nach bhfuil na focail traochta tréis na mblianta fada ar an mbóthar ach braithim ar chuma éigin go bhfuil droim láimhe tabhartha acu, go fóill ach go háirithe, don sean agus gach a bhaineann leis. Ní bhaineann dán Davitt le stair ná le traidisiú, le háit speisialta ná le ham faoi leith. Nuair a léas ar dtúis é, bhraitheas go raibh an Ghaeilge ag cumadh saoil go bhféadfainnse bheith ag baile ann cé nach mise a chum.

Tá's agam gur próiseas cuardaigh agus tástála teanga is ea filíocht Mhichael ó thús deireadh, go raibh sé siar is aniar i gcónaí riamh idir an sean is an nua nó gur aimsigh sé raon teanga a bhí oiriúnach dá ghuthanna féin, meascán den dá rud a thug dánta chomh neamhchosúil le chéile dúinn is atá "Hiraeth", "Meirg agus Lios Luachra", "An Scáthán", "Urnaí Maidne", "Do Phound ó Dhia", "Lúnasa", "Dán Déanta as Glac Téarmaí ón gCoiste Téarmaíochta i g*Comhar*", agus mórán eile nach iad.

Ach is é an nuacht, mar mhalairt ar an sean, a bhain geit díom nuair a casadh an file agus a dhán orm den gcéad uair, loime agus easpa sinsearachta na teanga a raibh snaidhm uirthi im bhéal féin ag focail mhóra ar nós "dúchas", "traidisiún", "Gaoluinn", "Gaeltacht". Ualach agus laincis ab ea stair na teanga an uair sin ag teacht idir mé is na rudaí ba mhaith liom a rá i bhfocail ná raibh na mairbh ina gcónaí iontu. Nuair a d'osclaíos mo bhéal, nuair a chuireas peann le pár, bhraitheas iad ag éirí aníos as a gcuid uaigheanna compordacha chun an ruaig amach a chur ormsa agus mo leithéid.

Is é a theastaigh uaim ag an am ná filíocht a bhí folamh ó aon mhacalla a cheanglódh friotal an dáin le heolas pribhléidithe ná raibh agam toisc gur rugadh is gur tógadh mé in áit ná raibh stair, ná dúchas, ná traidisiún ann, de réir dhealraimh, seachas an méid a chumamar féin.

Má bhí easpa traidisiúin agus staire i mBaile an Easpaig, bhí saoirse dá réir ann, a mheasas. Má bhíomar scoite le cultúr Jimín Mháire Thaidhg agus Mhicí Mac Gabhann, bhíomar scoite chomh maith le Match of the Day, agus Top of the Pops agus fós bhí greim ag na nithe sin ar fad orainn. Is é a bhí sa chultúr againn ná meascán mearaí ná raibh aon ancaire stairiúil aige sa timpeallacht fhisiciúil inar mhaireamar. Ba í an eaglais Chaitliceach an ghné ba údarásaí uileghabhálaí den gcultúr sin is déarfainn gurb í ba mhó a chuir bonn socair seasmhach faoin tuiscint chultúrtha a bhí i bpáirt againn le chéile. Ar an meánscoil, fuaireamar blas speisialta ar Sheán Ó Ríordáin agus ar Gerard Manley Hopkins mar gur chuid dár n-oidhreacht choitianta an tuiscint chloíte a bhí acusan ar nádúr an pheaca is ar ísleacht an duine i láthair Dé. Ba chuma go raibh duine acu ag scríobh i nGaeilge agus an duine eile i mBéarla; bhí an aigne chéanna ag labhairt sa dá theanga ar nithe a thuigeamar mar go raibh cuid éigin den aigne choitianta sin i bpáirt againne leo.

Nuair a thosnaíos ag scríobh sa chéad bhliain dom ar an Ollscoil, is é a bhí uaim ná an teanga féin a shealbhú seachas domhan nó aigne na Gaeilge nár bhain liom pé scéal é. Ba é Davitt an t-eisiomláir mar gur ina chuid filíochta siúd is túisce a tháinig mé ar shaol den tsaghas a bhí á chaitheamh agam féin á chur in iúl go soiléir neamhleithscéalach as Gaeilge.

Agus fós, bhraitheas mí-oiriúnach ar an nGaoluinn, mar a bheadh easpa éigin ionam féin, peaca sinseartha nárbh fhéidir a mhaitheamh dom toisc nár saolaíodh mé in áit nó in am eile. Ba thúisce le daoine eile na focail bheannaithe ná liomsa; níorbh fhiú mé go dtiocfainn faoi dhíon ceanntuí na Gaeilge. Bhraitheas uaigneas agus cumha i ndiaidh saoil eile nár liom, saol an traidisiúin agus an dúchais, saol na Gaoluinne agus na Gaeltachta ar chaitheas oiread ama inti is a fhéadfainn chun feabhas a chur ar mo chaint mhíoiriúnach neamhdhúchasach féin.

Bhíos chomh maith sin ag foghlaim gur thosnaigh daoine dom mholadh arís ar a fheabhas a bhí an teanga agam. Ní aithneoidis go deo, adúradar, agus réalt mór óir á ghreamú acu do chóipleabhar mo chuid cainte, gur as cathair Chorcaí mé. Bhíos á rá le fear as Cúil Aodha le déanaí go stopaimis ag An Muileann i mBaile Bhúirne i gcónaí ar ár slí go Corca Dhuibhne. "Gach aon uair ar an mbóthar siar," ar seisean, "agus na haon uair ar an slí abhaile."

Bhíos im bhabliac chomh maith sin gur thosnaigh mo mháistir filíochta agus léinn Seán Ó Tuama ag tabhairt amach dom. "Ná bí ag déanamh cainteoir dúchais díot fhéin!" ar seisean. Is é a thuigeas uaidh sin, mar a thuigeas ó fhiliocht Davitt, go gcaithfeadh mo chuid Gaeilge, dá bhoichte í, a bheith dílis dom féin thar aon ní eile.

Is é an rud céanna a bhí á rá ar shlí eile, droim ar ais, is dóigh liom, ag fear ó Chois Fharraige a dúirt liom roinnt bhlianta ina dhiaidh sin: "ní maith linn daoine a bhíonns ag gaeilgeoireacht níos fearr ná muid fhéin". Is é sin, is linne is túisce an teanga seo is ní maith linn daoine a bhíonn á chur i gcéill go bhfuil na cearta céanna acu uirthi is atá againne. Bhí an ceart aige, ar ndóigh, ach cá bhfágann sé sin an chuid eile againn a dtéann an Ghaeilge siar chomh fada ionainn is a théann ár gcumas uimhríochta, ár n-eolas ar stair agus thíreolas, sa tslí gur cuid dínn féin í, dár ndeoin agus dár n-ainneoinn, agus fós nach linn í ar fad?

Sara bhféadfainn teacht ar mo ghuth féin sa Ghaeilge, chaitheas glacadh leis gur teanga leathliom ab ea í is nach bhféadfainn teanga lánliom a dhéanamh di go brách; níorbh fhéidir liom, ná níor cheart dom, cainteoir dúchais a dhéanamh díom féin. Masla dóibhsean go raibh an teanga acu ó dhúchas a bheadh sa chur i gcéill sin ach masla dom féin chomh maith go mbeadh mo dhúchas féin á cheilt agam, dúchas measctha a bhí ag tarrac as mórán foinsí contrártha i nGaeilge agus i mBéarla. Má labhair an Béarla níos airde, níos minicí, níos fearr ná a dheartháir óg, níor fhág san nárbh fhiú cluas a thabhairt don méid a bhí le rá ag trudaire cúthaileach na Gaeilge nuair a thoiligh sé labhairt.

Chaithfinn teacht ar shlí oiriúnach chun an dúchas neamhghlan sin a chur in iúl i bhfocail Ghaeilge a bheadh ag freastal go sásúil ar mo thaithí bhruachbhailteach mheánaicmeach féin, ar shaol a raibh séala an Bhéarla go láidir air. Ba é an dúshlán ná a fháil amach an raibh an Ghaeilge a fuaireas i seomraí ranga agus léachta, i leabhair agus ar théipeanna, i gCorca Dhuibhne agus i measc mo chairde féin i gCorcaigh ábalta chuige sin.

Nuair a léim saothar filí *Innti* anois, iadsan a bhfuil a n-ainmneacha in airde agus go leor eile a chuaigh tamall den mbóthar leo, braithim go bhfuil an dúshlán sin á fhreagairt ar shlí amháin nó ar shlí eile ag an gcuid is mó acu. Cé go bhfuil Gaeilge agus Gaoluinn álainn ar fud na háite agus ómós á thabhairt don nGaeltacht agus dá muintir go minic ar leathanaigh *Innti*, is é an rud is tábhachtaí, dar liom, sna heagráin is luaithe go speisialta, ná an tslí go scarann friotal na filíochta le teanga agus traidisiún na Gaeltachta mar mhaithe le canúintí nua Gaeilge nach bhfuil an t-údarás ná an saibhreas céanna stairiúil ag roinnt leo ach atá ag teacht níos fearr le taithí saoil agus taithí teangan na bhfilí nua.

Tá an Ghaeilge níos tanaí ar leathanaigh *Innti* go minic ná mar atá sa bhfilíocht a tháinig roimpi. Tá sí tuathalach, briste, earráideach, in áiteanna, agus mínádúrtha amach is amach in áiteanna eile sa mhéid is nár labhair aon phobal Gaeilge mar sin riamh. Má tá úsáid na teangan barántúil, ní hé go bhfuil sí ag teacht le "caint na ndaoine" mar a samhlaíodh roimhe seo í ach gur caint í atá oiriúnach don duine atá á scríobh is don domhan samhlaíochta atá á chruthú aige.

Ba ghá cur suas d'údarás an traidisiúin agus an dúchais, ar feadh tamaill ach go háirithe, le go mbeadh cead cainte as Gaeilge ag daoine nárbh fhéidir leo guth a thabhairt dá dtaithí agus dá samhlaíocht féin laistigh de Ghaoluinn na Gaeltachta. Fiú is gur bhain canúintí an údaráis sa chás seo le daoine nárbh fhéidir tiarnúlacht d'aon tsaghas eile a lua leo, ba í Gaeilge na Gaeltachta teanga phribhléidithe an cheannais agus luigh sí orthusan nár labhair agus nár scríobh i gceart í mar a luigh canúintí ceannais an Bhéarla ar Roddy Doyle agus James Kelman, ar James Joyce agus J.M. Synge.

Is é Seán Ó Ríordáin naomhphátrún na filíochta seo agus is aige atá an tuairisc is fearr ar an teannas idir traidisiún na Gaeilge agus riachtanas samhlaíochta an fhile aonair atá scoite leis an dtraidisiún sin.

> Ní ionam a bhí faic ach sa traidisiún. Is ann a bhí an uile ní. Bhíos múchta aige. Ansin, go hobann, chaitheas uaim é in ainm an diabhail agus fuaireas, láithreach, rud nach raibh aon tsúil agam leis, fuaireas cead cainte. Is gearr go dtáinig fonn orm éalú ón gcead cainte agus éalú uaim féin agus filleadh ar an traidisiún. Is mar sin a bhíonn an duine; anonn is anall ag leanúint a phearsantacht féin, scaitheamh, agus scaitheamh eile ag leanúint an traidisiúin. Pé ceann a leanann sé bíonn an ceann eile á thionlacan chomh maith. Sé tionlacan na n-óinseach é. (*Scriobh 2*,1975)

Ar ndóigh, baineann an teannas seo idir an scríbhneoir aonair is an traidisiún le gach aon teanga agus gach aon litríocht agus is teannas cruthaitheach de ghnáth é. D'fhéadfaí a áiteamh nach bhfuil ann ach go gcaitheann gach glúin scríbhneoirí na seanrialacha a bhriseadh agus teorainn an traidisiúin a shárú chun spás a aimsiú dóibh féin. Cad eile a bhí ar siúl, mar shampla, ag Dermot Bolger, Paul Mercier, agus Roddy Doyle i dtreo dheireadh an chéid seo caite nuair a éilíodar cead cainte do Bhéarla thuaisceart Bhaile Átha Cliath, canúint a bhí curtha ó dhoras roimhe sin ag traidisiún liteartha Bhéarla na hÉireann?

Is mór idir an Ghaeilge agus an Béarla sa chás seo áfach. Nuair a chuireann scríbhneoirí Béarla canúint "íseal" a bhí faoi thost roimhe sin chun cinn, bíonn pobal taobh thiar den gcanúint sin de ghnáth, pobal atá múchta, b'fhéidir, faoi cheilt nó faoi chois, ach go bhfuil saol áirithe á iompar mar sin féin ag a gcuid focal. Má tá Béarla pobail mar seo mícheart, de réir choinbhinsiúin na gcanúintí gradamúla, tá údarás an bhéil bheo ar a chúl. Glacann léitheoirí leis an gcanúint nua mar go mbraitheann siad go n-eascraíonn friotal an scríbhneora as gné éigin den saol mar atá is go bhfuil brí agus beatha dá réir sna focail.

Is í an fhadhb atá ag an scríbhneoir Gaeilge nach cainteoir dúchais é a fhéachann lena chuid féin a dhéanamh den teanga ná gur caint duine amháin a bhíonn aige go minic, a chuid cainte féin, nó, má bhíonn an t-ádh leis, caint roinnt bheag daoine a chuireann an Ghaeilge ag freastal chomh mór agus is féidir leo ar an gcuid áirithe sin den saol atá á chaitheamh acu i bpáirt le chéile as Gaeilge. Murab ionann le canúintí Béarla Roddy Doyle, nó James Kelman, nó James Joyce, a bhfuil saol pobail, agus údarás dá réir, laistiar dóibh, is canúint phearsanta a bhíonn ag an scríbhneoir Gaeilge a scarann le Gaeilge na Gaeltachta, canúint atá ag freastal go maith ar a riachtanas pearsanta, b'fhéidir, ach nach labhartar lasmuigh dá thigh féin nó dá láthair oibre, lasmuigh den nGaelscoil nó den gColáiste Samhraidh, de chlubanna an Chonartha agus na háiteanna fánacha a dtagann Gaeilgeoirí le chéile iontu lasmuigh den nGaeltacht.

"Ideolect", a tugtar ar a leithéid sa Bhéarla agus is é an leagan is barántúla di ná rámhaillí an "idiot", an duine buile atá chomh dílis sin do dhlí borb a aigne féin go dtéann a chuid cainte ó thuiscint ar dhaoine eile. Nuair a deirimid go bhfuil duine ag rámhaillí cainte, is é a bhíonn i gceist againn de ghnáth nach féidir linne a chuid cainte a thuiscint fiú amháin nuair is léir go bhfuil práinn leis an méid atá á rá aige is go bhfuil sé ar a mhíle dícheall ag iarraidh é féin a chur in iúl i bhfocail a bhfuil a mbrí ana-shoiléir dó féin.

Braithim ar uairibh gur mé fhéin amháin a thuigeann mo chuid dánta féin, ní toisc gur filíocht iad, ach toisc gur mise an t-aon chainteoir, agus dá bhrí sin, an t-aon léitheoir a thuigeann an chanúint áirithe atá á scríobh agam. Má bhím ag aithris dánta do dhaoine ar mo chuma féin a d'fhoghlaim an teanga, bíonn imní orm go bhfuil an chaint róchruaidh dóibh, nár shroiseadar fós an t-ardrang a bhfuil suíochán in áirithe i gcónaí dom féin sa tsraith chúil ann. Nuair a bhím ag léamh sa Ghaeltacht, braithim ar uairibh go bhfuil mo chuid dánta chomh hait, chomh doiléir le Béarla turasóra atá ag iarraidh comhrá a chur ar bun i dtigh tábhairne in iarthar na hÉireann agus leabhar póca de chuid Berlitz in íochtar a mhála aige. "How is the crack?" Nó c'ail an gabhar á róstadh 'nocht, a leaideanna?

Teanga phríobháideach, mar a thuig an Ríordánach an téarma sin, is ea teanga na filíochta agam más ea, teanga ait gur deacair ar uairibh í a aithint ó dhrochGhaeilge. Fiú amháin má bhíonn mo chuid Gaeilge glan ar aon bhotún, beidh sí ait cé go mbím ag iarraidh an t-aiteas a sheachaint chomh mór leis an drochGhaeilge. Is é atá á rá agam, is dócha, go bhfuil mo chuid Gaeilge féin, nuair is fearr atá sí ag freastal ormsa, mínádúrtha, tuathalach, as alt le caint na ndaoine arb í an chéad teanga acu í is nach bhfeictear dom go bhfuil aon leigheas air seo chomh fada is nach bhfuil saol agus urlabhra pobail laistiar dem chanúint phearsanta.

In agallamh raidió a craoladh ón Oireachtas i mBaile Átha Cliath in 1953, labhair Seán Ó Ríordáin ar an mbaol a bhí ar an dteangain agus ar a litríocht, dar leis, dá bhfanfadh Gaoluinn na Gaeltachta agus Gaeilge na cathrach scartha dá chéile.

> Bhuel bhíos ag éisteacht aréir leis na Gaeilgeoirí anso sa chathair agus do chonac gluaiseacht na Gaoluinne ana-shoiléir. Chonac Gaeilgeoirí na cathrach agus an fuadar san fúthu; lucht léitheoireachta agus lucht scríbhneoireachta is ea iad agus dul chun cinn iontu. Ansan chím muintir na Gaeltachta agus míle bliain den nGaoluinn laistiar de gach gach aon fhocal a thagann as a mbéal ach iad ina stad. Is mó de chainteoirí ná de scríbhneoirí iad. Ach tá an dá aicme seo deighilte amach ó chéile agus sin í an mháchail mhór dar liom atá ar an ngluaiseacht fé láthair – mar ná mairfidh aon taobh acu gan an taobh eile. Imeoidh an Ghaeltacht gan muintir na cathrach mar tá pairilis uirthi agus níl éinne eile ann chun í a chur isteach san uisce ach

> Gaeilgeoirí na cathrach. Ansan imeoidh Gaoluinn na cathrach mar smúit an bhalbháin bhéice gan saibhreas agus foirmeacha na Gaeltachta. Ní mór an scoilt seo a leigheas. Ní mór aigne agus Gaoluinn na Gaeltachta do chur ag rith trí aigne na Galltachta, dar liom. (RTÉ, 1953)

Cé gur éirigh leis an Ríordánach a theanga phríobháideach féin agus Gaoluinn na Gaeltachta a chur ag freastal ar a chéile ar feadh tamaill, d'fhéadfaí a rá gur mhúch a umhlaíocht do theanga neamhphollta Dhún Chaoin a ghuth Ríordánúil féin ar ball. Ní hamháin san, ach dá mhéid a shantaigh an Ríordánach bheith istigh i measc pobail neamhbhearnaithe a bhí teann as a gcultúr agus a dteanga dhúchais, dúirt a chara Joe Daly, duine a thuig aigne na Gaeltachta má thuig éinne riamh í, go raibh ardmheas ag muintir Dhún Chaoin ar an bhfile ach nár léadar a chuid dánta.

Bhí cúis mhaith leis sin, ar ndóigh. Is iad múnlaí bhéarsaíochta an traidisiúin bhéil atá in uachtar i gcónaí sa Ghaeltacht agus is beag an greim atá ag an nua-fhilíocht ar an bpobal fairsing bríomhár a thugann cluas ghéar do na healaíona traidisiúnta béil atá á saothrú go rábach ina measc. Ní dóigh liom go bhfuil aon fhile nua-aimseartha Gaeilge a bhfuil pobal aige nó aici mar atá ag na healaíona béil i gcónaí i measc mhuintir na Gaeltachta, pobal a thuigeann na luachanna aesteitice a théann leis an mbéalaithris is a bhíonn ag freagairt os ard don ealaíontóir nuair a chuireann sé a dhéantús i láthair ón ardán. Bheadh uaigneas ar an bhfile nua-aimseartha i ndiaidh pobail mar sin, pobal cáiréiseach a thuigeann ealaín a bhfuil feidhm shoiléir léi ina measc agus a éilíonn caighdeán ard dá réir sin ó ealaíontóirí atá ag plé le foirmeacha cumadóireachta gur cuid de chultúr coitianta na Gaeltachta le sinsearacht iad.

Is dócha gurb í Máire Mhac an tSaoi an file Gaeilge is mó a a d'fhéach lena guth féin a chur in oiriúint do thraidisiún dúchais na Gaeltachta, traidisiún sinseartha an phobail a fuair sí roimpi i nDún Chaoin lena hóige. In aiste chorraitheach a foilsíodh sa bhliain 1990, áfach, admhaíonn sí gur ceantar taibhrimh is ea Dún Chaoin a hóige feasta:

> Go dtí le fíordhéanaí ní rabhas i dtinneas aon phobail. Iadsan a chuir aithne in aois linbh ar an nGaeltacht mar bhí sí ins na fichidí tuigfidh siad mo mheon. Thaibhsigh an córas san don leanbh beagbheann ar imeacht na mblian, clasaiceach, réamhcheaptha, uileghabhálach, stóinsithe, i bhfad níos marthanaí agus níos iontaofa ná domhan an

Bhéarla. Chonac mo shaothar laistigh den gcóras san mar a bheadh cuid de thraidisiún an amhráin agus ní raibh aitheantas ná díolaíocht ag deanamh buartha dhom. Mhaireas os cionn leathchéad bliain ins an chluthaireacht san, á iompar timpeall liom im intinn go dtí gur dhúisíos ó chianaibhín agus go bhfuaireas mo chruinne ché leata ar an aer agus ceiliúrtha. Tá sé ródhéanach agam malairt timpeallachta a chuardach. Deirtí go mba phioróid é an cainteoir dúchais deireannach a mhair de chuid Bhreatain Chorn agus gur chónaigh sé i Ringsend. Mise an phioróid sin. Tá mo mheán eispreisiúna sásúil ar fad maidir liom féin ach an slán d'aon ráiteas ar an uaigneas gan cluas á éisteacht?

Cuireann sí i gcuimhne dhom radharc as scannán Astrálach Werner Herzog *Where the Green Ants Dream* (1984) ina dtugtar fear bundúchasach os comhair na cúirte chun fianaise a thabhairt. Cé ná stopann sé ach ag caint, mínítear don mbreitheamh gurb é "an balbhán" a leasainm, gurb é an cainteoir deireanach a labhrann a theanga dhúchais féin is ná tuigeann éinne a bhfuil á rá aige.

—

Mar adúrt ó chianaibh, is iad na gnéithe friththraidisiúnta cúl-le-dúchas, d'fhilíocht *Innti* is láidre a chuaigh i bhfeidhm orm nuair a thánag ar shaothar Mhichael Davitt is a chomhleacaithe ar dtúis. Bhí géarghá agam le heisiomláir a bhainfeadh srathar shibhialtacht na Gaeltachta agus aghaidh fidil an dúchais dem mheabhair. Ba ghá droim láimhe a thabhairt don dtraidisiún, bheith frithGhaeilge fiú, nó frithGhaelach pé scéal é, chun cead cainte a éileamh do shamhlaíocht agus do thaithí saoil a bhí as alt le dúchas stairiúil na teangan mar a thuigeas é sin ag an am.

Bhraitheas tréis tamaill, áfach, gur chúngú ar mo dhán agus orm féin ab ea é seo, is go gcaithfinn teacht ar shlí éigin chun spás a aimsiú im aigne agus im chuid filíochta do nithe a bhí curtha ó dhoras agam roimhe sin. Bhíos san Astráil nuair a tuigeadh dom nár cheart go mbeadh aon chuid de chultúr sinseartha na hÉireann, i nGaeilge ná i mBéarla, ná beadh ceart slí agus cead siúil agam tríd, fiú is gur le daoine eile teideal oidhreachtúil na talún ar a rabhas ag siúl.

Chuireas aithne éigin ar an bhfile Muimhneach Astrálach Vincent Buckley i Melbourne sna blianta sular cailleadh é, is bhíos ana-thógtha leis an méid a bhí le rá aige sa réamhrá a chuir sé lena leabhar ciotrúnta, suainseánach, eolgaiseach, *Memory Ireland* (1985). Eachtrannach is ea é féin in Éirinn, adeir sé, i dtosach na haiste sin: "a loving outsider: someone who … regards himself on one level as Irish but knows that on another level he is not"; "learning Ireland" is ábhar dá leabhar, "memory-work … for its hidden theme is Ireland's loss of its own memory".

Cuireann sé go láidir in aghaidh an *cliché* adeir go bhfuil muintir na hÉireann sáinnithe i dtromluí na staire is nach féidir leo dúiseacht.

> […] the real Irish joke is that the Irish are gullible, good natured, and inquisitive; and that, however hard they tried over the last hundred years to restore a memory which had been painfully and deliberately taken from them, they could not keep it up (poverty, migration, and economic dependence drove out the capacity for remembering before it had been fully settled); they have now abandoned the attempt. The visitor to Dublin sees gaps: the Irish memory is a structure of gaps. Gaps in the memory match those uncountable gaps in the line of a city wall, or in the contour of an estate boundary, or in the main street of a village. Nothing gets mended. When Irish country people speak of something's being "very old", it is likely they mean "from my grandparents' time". They do not like to approach time too closely or too directly, and they lack confidence in its permutations. […] One of the continuing tragedies of Ireland over centuries is that the conditions for sustaining corporate memory have been destroyed. […] Irish life loses its memory because it is both too rigidly confined and too casually dispersed.

Nuair a chuimhnímid ar chultúir an cheannais, ar shibhialtacht an Bhéarla, mar shampla, cuimhnímid ar fhoirgintí áirgiúla a bhfuil cuimhne na treibhe faoi chosaint iontu, ar leabharlanna agus áiléir ealaíne, ar mhúsaeim agus chartlanna, go mbeadh leisce ar na barbair is brúidiúla amuigh, ba dhóigh leat, iad a chreachadh. Ach is fothrach tréigthe mantach í cuimhne chorparáideach na hÉireann, de réir Buckley, rud briste pollta a bhfuil gaoth an ama ag séideadh tríd is gan éinne ag cuimhneamh ar na bearnaí a líonadh.

Nuair a léas *Memory Ireland*, bhraitheas gur fearr a thuig mo chompánach Gael-Astrálach mo chás ná mar a thuigeas féin é. Chomh fada le hÉirinn na Gaeilge agus na Gaeltachta de, is coimthíoch ceanúil mise agus mo leithéid atá ag iarraidh í a fhoghlaim. Ar ndóigh, má chaithimid Éire na Gaeilge a fhoghlaim, ní fearr áit chuige sin ná an seomra ranga. Cuid lárnach den bhfoghlaim chultúrtha sin is ea go gcaithfimid athghabháil a dhéanamh ar na coda sin dár gcuimhne choitianta atá dearmadta againn, curtha faoi cheilt, nó faoi chois, ag an stair. Má fhéachaimid ar an obair éachtach atá déanta ag scríbhneoirí Béarla na hÉireann i réimse an aistriúcháin ó aimsir na hathbheochana ar aghaidh, agus ag Thomas Kinsella, Seamus Heaney, agus Ciarán Carson lenár linn féin, d'fhéadfaí a áiteamh gur fearr a thuigeadarsan an méid sin ná mar a thuig filí na Gaeilge go minic. An fhaid a bhí na filí Béarla ag tochailt fúthu sa tseanlitríocht ag iarraidh a saothar féin a phréamhú níos doimhne sa traidisiún dúchais, bhí filí Gaeilge ag iarraidh marbhfháisc an traidisiúin chéanna a scaoileadh dóibh fhéin agus reilig an dúchais a sheachaint.

In aiste íogair ar thábhacht an dinnseanchais dó fhéin agus dá chomhfhilí Béarla, admhaíonn Seamus Heaney gur rud foghlamtha, seachas rud instinniúil nádúrtha, is ea an dáimh speisialta atá aige féin agus go leor dá chomhleacaithe lena gcuid áiteanna dúchais. Má tá scéal Chúchulainn agus Fhirdia i bhfolach faoi dhromchla an logainm Áth Fhirdia, ar seisean, is gá tamall a chaitheamh sa seomra ranga chun teacht air: "It now requires some small degree of learning to know this about Ardee". Sa tslí dhuit go gcaitheann filí Béarla na gnéithe sin den traidisiún atá chomh bunúsach is chomh láidir ina saothar go gceapfadh an léitheoir soineanta go rabhadar ginte ina gcnámha a fhoghlaim agus a shaothrú. Agus fós, braithim go mbíonn leisce ar scríbhneoirí agus léitheoirí Gaeilge a admháil nach le huacht ná le hoidhreacht a fuaireamar ná a gheobhaimid an nasc riachtanach sin idir sinn fhéin agus an traidisiún dúchais ach go gcaithimidne leis dul ag tochailt i measc na leabhar chun na hiarsmaí atá scaipthe ag an stair a chruinniú is a chur le chéile arís, más féidir.

An cumha i ndiaidh saol iomlán leanúnach neamhphollta a nascann an aimsir chaite is an aimsir láithreach le chéile, míníonn sí cuid mhaith an tóir atá againn ar an tuath, agus go háirithe ar an nGaeltacht, mar a bhfuil an t-am ag imeacht níos moille, dar linn, agus cuimhne na ndaoine níos faide ar an saol mar a bhí sular éag ár Róisín Dubh. Ar chúiseanna atá luaite agam cheana, níor bhraitheas riamh go bhféadfadh an tuath ná an Ghaeltacht fóirithint orm chun nasc beo a chruthú idir an sean agus an nua im chuid scríbhneoireachta féin. Agus fós, theastaigh uaim ancaire a chur síos óm dhánta féin chomh domhain is a fhéadfainn san am a caitheadh féachaint an bhfaigheadh sé greim in áit éigin sa chuimhne choitianta, sa traidisiún dúchais, a chuirfeadh bonn níos socra fúthu.

Is iad filí *Innti* a thug eolas na slí dom anso arís. Le tamall de bhlianta anois, tá iarracht leanúnach déanta ag Nuala Ní Dhomhnaill, Biddy Jenkinson, Liam Ó Muirthile agus Colm Breathnach go háirithe chun a nguthanna comhaimseartha féin a cheangal le guthanna múchta an traidisiúin, chun spás a thabhairt do throscán an dúchais i seomraí na samhlaíochta acu féin. Chuige sin, bhí "Gaeilge na leabhar" chomh tábhachtach céanna is a bhí "caint na ndaoine" mar fhoinse agus mar eisiomláir, agus is i dtreise atá tionchar na leabhar ag dul le himeacht aimsire.

Is sa seanlitríocht a fuair Biddy Jenkinson na banphearsana atá tréis aiséirí ó reilig na leabharlainne chun a gcosa a chur fúthu ina cuid dánta. Focaleolaí, téarmeolaí, agus aistritheoir gairmiúil is ea Colm Breathnach agus is é *Táin Bó Cuailgne* a thug dó an banlaoch Scáthach a labhrann go húdarásach agus go cráite linn sa leabhar is cumasaí dá chuid. Tá macalla á bhaint as liricí na Sean-Ghaeilge ag Liam Ó Muirthile i gcuid de na dánta is greanta atá scríofa aige le blianta beaga anuas agus is as láimhleabhar siúinéireachta a réitigh Donnchadh Ó Luasaigh do dhaltaí scoile a fuair sé an friotal teicniúil a chuir ar a chumas teangbháil a dhéanamh le taibhse a athar in *walking time agus dánta eile*. Fiú amháin Nuala Ní Dhomhnaill, an té is fearr agus is údarásaí atá tréis guth nua a thabhairt d'aigne an dúchais agus an *mentalité* Gaelach, is i measc na láimhscríbhinní i gcartlann Roinn an Bhéaloidis i gColáiste Ollscoile Bhaile Átha Cliath is mó a shaothraigh sí an nasc beo idir a riachtanas samhlaíochta féin agus iarsmaí an traidisiúin bhéaloidis. Sa tslí dhuit go bhfuil an focal scríofa agus an traidisiún liteartha gach pioc chomh tábhachtach le "caint na ndaoine" i saothrú na filíochta, is an leabharlann chomh riachtanach leis an nGaeltacht mar láthair cuardaigh agus oiliúna.

Sa léirmheas a dhein Liam Ó Muirthile ar *Bligeard Sráide* (1983) an dara leabhar filíochta le Michael Davitt, tá íomhá neamhcoitianta aige a bheireann ar an ngné threascartach de ghuth an fhile sa leabhar sin go speisialta: "agus é á leamh agam chuimhníos ó am go chéile ar an nglór a dhein fód féir ghlais á stoitheadh tráth, an stracadh stollta sin ón bpréimh". Nuair a léas é sin ar dtúis, bhraitheas gurb é a bhí i gceist ná go raibh gort an traidisiúin á réabadh ag Michael sna dánta ba nuálaí sa chnuasach nua aige. Is é a shamhlaím anois le samhail Liam ná go mba ghá fód uachtair an traidisiúin a réabadh sula bhféadfaí dul ag tochailt i gceart faoi dhromchla na talún a bhí á shiúl go héadrom ag filíocht na Gaeilge ar feadh tamaill roimis sin.

Tá an tochailt sin ar siúl le breis agus fiche bliain anois ag cuid de na filí is fearr dá bhfuil againn agus eolas níos doimhne dá réir againn ar an gcuimhne chorparáideach a bhfuil cuid mhaith mhór di fós faoi thalamh. Is sa traidisiún scríofa, agus an béaloideas san áireamh, a fuair filíocht chomhaimsire na

Gaeilge greim ar ais ar chuid d'iarsmaí na cuimhne coitianta sin atá scaipthe ag an stair, agus níl aimsithe go fóill ach na sraitheanna uachtair di. Ar nós a gcomhleacaithe Béarla, tuigeann na filí Gaeilge atá luaite agam gur rud saothraithe foghlamtha is ea an traidisiún liteartha atá á shealbhú acu seachas bua nádúrtha nó bronntanas ós na mairbh is gur gá filleadh ar an seomra ranga chun é a fhoghlaim.

Má chuir Pádraig Mac Piarais taibhse Chúchulainn ar garda in Ardoifig an Phoist, thug sé ar scoil é chomh maith, "an important if invisible member of the staff", de réir Desmond Ryan ina chuimhní cinn ar Sgoil Éanna. Nuair a thug an Piarsach cead siúil arís sa bhfilíocht don gCailleach Bhéarra agus do Chúchulainn, fuaireadar spás dóibh féin sa tsamhlaíocht choitianta le neadú ann nó go dtógfaí foirgneamh níos áirgiúla dóibh a bheadh ag teacht níos fearr lena sinsearacht agus lena ngradam. Foirgneamh bocht cúng ab ea tigh na filíochta in aimsir Mhic Phiarais ach tá seomraí breise curtha leis ag na glúnta filí a tháinig ina dhiaidh mar a bhfuil slí anois ag Meadhbh agus Mór is an Mhór-Ríon, ag Dubrois agus Scáthach, ag Deirdre agus Gráinne, agus go leor eile de na scáileanna beo a mhaireann i gcónaí sa bhfocal scríofa.

Ní clocha ar chairn na marbh, más ea, na tagairtí don seanlitríocht atá chomh fairsing sa bhfilíocht chomhaimisre ach iarsmaí athchóirithe ón dtraidisiún dúchais atá fuadaithe ó fhothraigh na díchuimhne, amhábhar samhlaíochta atá riachtanach chun áitreabh oiriúnach a sholáthar don gcuid sin den gcuimhne choitianta nach bhfuil caillte ar fad againn. Ní tigh ceann tuí, ná caisleán meánaoiseach, ná fothrach atógtha, a dhéanfaidh é sin, ach foirgneamh a mbeidh rian an traidisiúin go láidir air, a bheidh ag teacht mar sin féin leis an gcuid is fearr d'ailtireacht chultúrtha an lae inniu.

Pé crot a bheidh ar an bhfoirgneamh samhlaíochta seo, caithfidh sé bheith ag baile in Éirinn an lae inniu, agus fós a thabhairt le fios go raibh sé anso i gcónaí riamh.

Louis de Paor is one of the foremost poets and scholars in the Irish language. He was born in Cork in 1961 and educated at Coláiste an Spioraid Naoimh and University College Cork. In the early 1980s, he edited the Irish-langauge journal Innti, *and between 1987 and 1996 he lectured at the University of Sydney in Australia. His scholarly books include a study of narrative technique in the short fiction of Máirtín Ó Cadhain and an anthology of twentieth-century poetry in Irish co-edited with Seán Ó Tuama. He is currently working on a study of the writings of Flann O'Brien, and is Director of the Centre for Irish Studies at NUI Galway. He is the author of nine collections of poems, most recently* Ag Greadadh Bas sa Reilig *(*Clapping in the Cemetery, *Cló Iar-Chonnachta, 2006) and* Cúpla Siamach an Ama *(*The Siamese Twins of Time, *Coiscéim, 2006).*

LANGUAGE AS LIVED

Judith Hoad

Available words, available grammar.

Having two languages, English and Welsh, I was already used to having two windows in my head through which to view the world, when, about fifteen years ago, I encountered an idea wholly new to me. While reading F. David Peat's book, *Blackfoot Physics*, the idea emerged through his writing that European languages are object-based, while Native North American languages are process-based. Through experience and analysis, I hope to elucidate a relevance of language to worldview and how humanity lives.

Each of us has a worldview. We filter our concept of "the world" through the prism of experience. Our experiences we express through the language of our "world space". One language does not translate, word for word, into another language; idioms and metaphors are part of the stumbling block, but, it appears to me, the cultural-linguistic construction of any language is the major part of that stumbling block encountered in attempts to translate – even to interpret – another language.

> Although people are wonderfully diverse in skin colour and facial and other physical features the most significant differences between groups of human beings are not biological, but cultural and linguistic ... Culture and language have been our crucial attributes, enabling us to adapt to a wide range of surroundings and conditions. (Peat, *Blackfoot Physics,* 1994)

The "chicken-or-egg" situation is evident: is it language that influences culture and belief systems, or is it culture that conditions language? It is impossible for me to determine this, but there seems no doubt that the two are intertwined and that the revelations Peat makes can be extrapolated to show how the two (fundamental) cultures that result are probably largely uncomprehending of one another in some cultural aspects and that it is important to try to discover some chink to allow a degree of understanding to shine through. I intend to move into this territory. Without having any training in linguistics, I have arrived at the ideas I am attempting to share through observation and through reading. It seems to me that part of our incomprehension of one another as cultures on this planet results in our misuse of one another and much of that misuse, certainly in recent centuries, has been by Eurocentric societies who have misused non-Eurocentic societies through incomprehension and misunderstandings. If we could come to some greater understanding, maybe we could make up for some of that misuse and apply ourselves to trying to learn something about those other societies and how the way they function could help us to function better in our own society. It was that idea about language being object- or process-based that was to occupy me from when I first read Peat's book. If one's language was object-based – as English undoubtedly is – it seemed a natural extension that one's preoccupation would be with objects, their weights, size, colour and all forms of quantification and calibration, including hierarchy.

In attempting to clarify how the object base functions and using English as the sample, I got an image of the sentence as a suspension bridge. An anchor tower rises on each side of a canyon. Tower A is the subject of the sentence; Tower B is the object of the sentence; suspended between and joining the two towers is the bridge – the verb. There is a variety of "lanes" on the road suspended between the towers, but there is only "one-way traffic" – from A to B. For example, "Tommy is eating dinner": "Tommy" is Tower A, "dinner" is Tower B and "eating" is the (verb) lane leading across the bridge from the A to the B. Other lanes could carry adverbs.

The lanes suspended between the towers hang over the Canyon of Potentiality. The verb "eating" is a sort of shorthand; the Canyon of Potentiality contains the implications attached to "eating" – "seeing", "smelling", "salivating", "tasting", "enjoying", "swallowing", "digesting", "absorbing", "assimilating", "eliminating", "excreting", and many others. While we may colour the verb with adverbs, such as "fast", "slowly", "daintily", it remains the link that gets us from Tower A – the subject – to Tower B – the object. What becomes obvious with this analogy is that the verb – the lane that links – falls to the bottom of the Canyon if the towers are missing; it exists *only* as a link. That's what "object-based" means, to me. Without the objects, A and B in a sentence, communication becomes very limited by this technique.

Process-based language, I deduce, allows the communicator to explore the Canyon of Potentiality using verbs, which are all expressions of process in some guise or another, as ropes by which to descend, ascend and navigate around the floor of the canyon. There is no need to travel from A to B, because the whole edge, on both sides of the canyon, is open to access, but not as the most important part of the communication. The verb, expressing process, swilling around in the space of the canyon, is the fabric of all thoughts and conversation, by this technique. Mark Abley refers to a Harvard-trained law professor who is a Mi'kmaq-speaking Native American, Sa'ke'j Youngblood Henderson, and quotes him:

> "The use of verbs rather than nouny subjects and objects is important; it means that there are very few fixed and rigid objects in the Mi'kmaq world-view." The syntax of Mi'kmaq, that is to say, allows few objects to be easily labeled. Speakers of the language build up complex verb phrases by choosing from among hundreds of prefixes and suffixes. An intricately described action lies at the heart of a Mi'kmaq sentence – not, as in this sentence, a single brief verb buttressed by nouns. For Henderson, it's as if the rhythms and structures of the Mi'kmaq language open a door into the Mi'kmaq world. "To have to speak English," he has said, "is like having to put on a straitjacket." (Abley, *Spoken Here,* 2003)

Quoting the same man, Peat writes,

> One of the recurring themes of this book has been the role of chance, flux and process within Indigenous science. This worldview is perfectly reflected in many Native languages, in particular that of the Algonquin family (Cree, Ojibwaj, MicMac, Blackfoot, Cheyenne and several others).
>
> With its emphasis upon verbs it perfectly reflects a reality of transformation and change. Sa'ke'j Henderson has said that he can go a whole day without ever speaking a noun, just dealing in the rhythms and vibrations of process. Nouns do exist within the language, but, like the vortex that forms in a fast flowing river, the nouns are not primary in themselves, but are temporary aspects of an ever-flowing process.

Benjamin Lee Whorf, the linguist, who made an extensive study of Hopi culture and language – which he learned – writes:

> Hopi, with its preference for verbs, as contrasted to our own liking

for nouns, perpetually turns our propositions about things into propositions about events. (Benjamin Lee Whorf, *Language, Thought and Realtiy*, 1956)

By growing up in a culture dependent on object-based language, we could be described as "pedestrian", or, at best, vehicle-drivers. Process-based culture is about as accessible to our mindset as the ability to fly. Unaided, flying is a skill of which we are incapable. Process-based cultures fly all the time, only occasionally touching a foot to the ground; the speaker of process-based language is like the albatross – reputed to spend its entire life on the wing, unencumbered by belongings. We, the speakers of object-based language, tow trollies – drive pantechnicons, full of belongings and attachments – represented by all the nouns within all our sentences. And we make sure to identify these objects as "mine", or "his", or to qualify them as "brown", "valuable", "rotten", etc.

The difficulties of thinking as a process-based language speaker thinks, are analogous to stepping off the bridge over the canyon and going into dangerous freefall – the only way to fly is to attach the wings of learned language – to become a speaker of one of those process-based languages; which I am not, so I have to reach out to try to explain what I perceive within the context of English.

The validity of seeing cultures that use object-based language as concerned with material things, with calibration, quantification – and qualification – ownership, valuation and hierarchy, only stands up as related to the language when it is compared to the cultures that use process-based language, in whose societies relationship, harmony, balance and mutual responsibility (or "equivalency"), are found to exist. Such is demonstrable, but are the language and culture issues really related?

I feel they are. Millenia of using languages that are object-based has given rise to waves of ideas and lifestyles firmly rooted in the framework outlined in the previous paragraph. What's important, for me, is to recognize where this has brought our culture and to see if there are any adjustments that could usefully be made. Can those adjustments be found with the assistance of the other kind of culture, the one that has evolved in the matrix of process-based languages? Just accepting that possibility is to stretch our mind-set, like a bungee rope, suspending our minds over the Canyon of Potentiality.

Process-based language speakers represent indigenous, materially poor, industrially underdeveloped, "primitive" societies – while this may not be politically correct terminology, it is nonetheless the attitude inherent in the ways that the dominator societies of the speakers of object-based languages behave toward such societies. However, the people of Ecuador, a significant proportion of whom speak process-based Amerindian languages (in which relationship is vital), are the aspirational leaders of the world in having framed a new national constitution which includes a clause giving protection and rights to all ecosystems. Here lies evidence that we – people from the other culture – can learn from earth-based cultures that value relationships above possessions. And we need to give this fact recognition, to accompany our recognition that the globe's ecology is in danger from the excesses practised by our own, object-based culture.

Although, as liberal twenty-first century people, we give lip-service to our liberation from the concept that people with earth-based life-styles are "inferior", we still allow governments to act in our name using policies which contradict that liberation. For example, about ten years ago, the Australian government sent two school teachers, on secondment for two years, to spend that time establishing a primary education system for the people of Papua New Guinea. Papua New Guinea's population speaks over eight hundred distinct languages, not counting dialects. Of these, some are spoken only by a few hundred people and very few have any written form. Obviously, a unified education system run on Australian/Eurocentric lines, has to have a *lingua-franca* and it would be English. Just at a moment when the Australian authorities had begun to question their own, earlier policy of taking Australian aboriginal children from their families in order to educate them to forget their own languages and culture – so that they could be absorbed into Australian society (as menial workers) – they start up the same process in another region. Why does it seem important to replace the education that enables a child to grow to adulthood capable of continuing the culture into which he/she has been born, with an education based on the industrial and commercial paradigm? What threat is there in those societies that have little or no contact with industrialized culture?

There is great anguish expressed by an increasing number of experts on the destruction of biodiversity among non-human species – plants and animals of all sorts. I have heard or read very little mentioning the destruction of human cultural diversity. Eight hundred languages represents eight hundred ways of sensing and expressing those sensations; eight hundred ways of relating to other humans and all the neighbouring species. Where's the outcry against this depredation? Edward Sapir writes,

> No two languages are ever sufficiently similar to be considered as representing the same social reality. The words in which different cultures live are distinct worlds, not merely the same world with different labels attached. (*Collected Works*, 1989)

Why does the Australian government feel the need to dominate by education; what makes this policy valid? Why is no one seeking to learn from such ancient societies, instead of trying to change them?

The culture that underpins European culture is usually attributed to Aristotle and his successors in the "golden age" of Greek intellect in a period before the founding of Christianity, which became another major factor in the way in which we, the Europeans – and, by extension, our compatriots who went on to colonise other parts of the planet – live our lives.

To the east of the Mediterranean is the Tigris and Euphrates Valley, part of "The Fertile Crescent", the area in which our culture believes "civilisation" began. It was there that the earliest agriculture was developed – at least, on the Eurasian landmass. Who is to say that agriculture did not simultaneously (or even earlier?) develop on the twin landmasses of the Americas? (Jared Diamond, in his book *Guns, Germs and Steel*, enlarges on this theme). Families who settled in one place, grew crops and built permanent houses – if they were using object-based language – might find the notion of private ownership arising very early. A relevant statement was made by Terence Hay-Edie: "Commodification of Nature can be traced to the evolution of barter systems in early agricultural societies"(*Costing the Earth*, 2009).

While this statement can be recognized as correct in certain circumstances, it is not necessarily so in a culture that doesn't regard nature as a separate entity from humanity and its doings, as was the case in the Pre-Colombian Americas. Barter, or exchange, could occur in a culture dependent on equivalent relationship, rather than on hierarchy – and commodification of nature would *not* occur. In our own era, commercial colonialisation has arisen out of the commodification of nature, fed by the cult of consumerism which is promoted by world-dominating organisations, such as the International Monetary Fund and the World Trade Organisation.

It is estimated that the first farmers cultivated land in the Fertile Crescent about 10,000 years ago. Roughly 5,000 years later, by which time farming was well-established with many stages of agricultural and social development having arisen and died away, the idea of a single Sky God arose. This suppressed the earlier, Mother Earth-based beliefs and resulted, ultimately and in very broad terms, in the Eurocentric, technological, male-dominator society that caused Albert Einstein to comment:

> A human being is part of a whole, called by us the universe. A part limited in time and space. He experiences himself, his thoughts and his feelings, as something separate from the rest, a kind of optical delusion of his consciousness. This delusion is a kind of prison for us, restricting us to our personal desires and to affection for a few persons nearest to us. Our task must be to free ourselves from this prison by widening our circle of compassion to embrace all living creatures. (*Peace, a Dream Unfolding,* 1986)

Once again, I must emphasise, I am neither a linguist, nor a sociologist, just someone interested to observe what I can and to draw conclusions from those observations, which, as a great-grandmother, I have gleaned over a long time.

Paradoxically, the supra-eurocentic model has arisen at its strongest in the home of the process-based languages that preceded the arrival of Europeans, the continent of North America. Process-based language, as I have said, would appear to be more concerned with relationship than object-based language. When I first read Peat's book, I had not yet visited either North or South America, (subsequently, I have visited both), but from reading and from talking to people who had met Native North Americans, relationship seemed to be foremost in their cultures. They were conscious of a Great Spirit and also of other spirits. They thanked the animals they hunted for giving themselves up and they made sure to use every part of the creature and to give gifts to the Earth, even when they harvested plants. They had complex "relationship cultures", not overloaded with possessions, even when the culture was a settled one, rather than nomadic. Despite a capability for ferocious fighting, a federation of five great tribes, commonly referred to as The Iroquois Federation, was formed, making a sophisticated union very much concerned with relationship, (probably for mutual defence), out of whose philosophy, some of the altruism of the First Constitution of the United States was drawn (evidence for which is produced by James W. Loewen in his *Lies My Teacher Told Me*, 1995).

Societies organized on the basis of "relationship" I would refer to as concerned also with "equivalency", while object-based cultures, I would further argue, become concerned with hierarchy. William Ury simplifies these notions to "horizontally-organized societies" and "vertically-organized societies". In his writing on conflict he remarks:

> Prevention in vertically-organized societies generally entails suppression of conflict. In horizontally-organised societies, however, suppression is neither feasible nor desirable. Prevention means addressing the root causes of conflict and laying the foundations for the cooperative management of difficulties. (*Getting to Peace,* 1999)

– Mending relationships, in other words.

Implicit in this statement is the idea that the methods of preventing their conflict relate to self-containment within those respectively constructed societies. It's when these two forms of societal structure collide that anguish and mutual incomprehension seem to be virtually inevitable.

The expansionist Europeans of the last 500-700 years, initially and in general, had friendly exchanges with the societies they encountered in the North and Central Americas, and in Australia. However, their innate sense of superiority over peoples who didn't use the wheel and had no knowledge of explosives, or Christianity – in fact, people who appeared to be technologically "backward" – was such that they made little further attempt to understand their cultures. Instead, they made the unilateral decision to take what they wanted by way of land, artifacts, raw materials, goods, slaves, or concubines, by force, if necessary, and to impose their own religious observances. And this has continued to the present day. Referring to these traditional societies, Gro Larlem Brundtland, one-time Prime Minister of Norway, wrote in the report bearing her name,

> Their very survival has depended upon their ecological awareness and adaptation [...] These communities are the repositories of vast accumulations of traditional knowledge and experience that links humanity with its ancient origins. Their disappearance is a loss for the larger society, which could learn a great deal from their traditional skills in sustainably managing very complex ecological systems. It is a terrible irony that as formal development reaches more deeply into rainforests, deserts and other isolated environments, it tends to destroy the only cultures that have proved able to thrive in these environments. (*Our Common Future*, 1987)

Or, as in the view of a specific tribe described by Gerardo Reichel-Dolmatoff,

> There is no Master of Plants – in the culture of the Tukano Amazonian Tribe – but only a direct dependence on cosmic energy. On this abstract level, the "Tree People" ["Tree People" is how the Tukano refer to all plant-life, especially fruit-bearing trees of the forest] are not imagined as anthropomorphized, but as a category of animate beings, containing a variety of "heat energies" which are essential to life on earth. On the concrete level of everyday experience, they are incorporated into the kinship system ... (*The Forest Within*, 1996)

In another study, he writes:

> According to the Desana [the] inherent *stability* of the natural world is rooted in a vast web of reciprocal relationships that have always existed between all elements of nature. A reciprocity between the Earth, with its mountains and forests and rivers, and the first forms of life – animals, the plants, the Desana people – exists in harmony with all the rest of the universe. (*Amazonian Cosmos*, 1971)

Captain Cook thought the Aboriginal People of Australia extremely backward. Not alone did they appear to have no technology, they didn't wear clothes, even to the extent of the men leaving their genitals exposed. Not allowing himself, nor his underlings, time to learn any of the aboriginal language, he failed to discover how much more sophisticated much of the language was – and the attendant thought forms, law and beliefs that went with it – than is the English language. Not having invented writing, the Aboriginal people had to memorize the laws and complex beliefs they had evolved over countless millennia. This, in itself, required a large and complicated vocabulary, including detailed ways to express relationship and process.

Abley writes of the complexities of the pronoun systems in Aboriginal language. My emphasis here is to show how this relates to the Aboriginals' concern with relationship:

> Simplicity is not the reason for the language's success. Some of its complexities seem mind-numbing – unless you're willing to take the

> plunge and call them mind-expanding. In its pronoun system, where English slices the world into singular and plural, "*Murrinh-Patha*" (one of the languages of the Northern Territory of Australia) has four categories: singular, dual (with forms that vary for two males, two females and two siblings), paucal (meaning three to about fifteen people and again using different terms for males, females and siblings), and plural (more than fifteen people). Each of these categories, moreover, has separate words for the first person ("we two males", for example), the second person ("you two males"), and the third person ("these two males"). "How are you?" we say in English, no matter how many people we're addressing and who they happen to be. Murrinh-Patha is a lot more precise. For "you", it compels a choice among *nhinhi, nankunitha, nankungitha, nanku*, *nanjuneme, nankungime* and *nanki*.

More than ten years after first reading *Blackfoot Physics*, I went to work for two months in the Andes. I had encountered 50,000 Tibetans at an event in India in 1995; I had lived for a short, summery spell in Mongolia in 2002; I had taken part in a native Lakota sweat lodge in Canada in 1997. It was impossible not to believe the theory that Asian tribes had crossed a land-bridge where now are the Bering Straits. Did the indigenous languages of North and South America originate in central Asia? When I arrived in the Bolivian Andes, apart from their traditional garments, the indigenous people were indistinguishable from the thousands of Tibetans I had mingled with twelve years before and the Mongolians I had lived with in 2002.

At once, I started asking questions about the two most commonly used Andean languages: Quechua, the language of the Inca, who overran the Aymara-speaking people some five hundred years before the Spaniards arrived and overran them both. The answers came soon and in unexpected ways. Within less than a week, I had learned that the Quechua speak in plurals. For example, Evo Morales, Bolivia's President, then less than a year in office, was – unique among Latin American countries – an indigenous person. He was quoted as having said, several times, in Quechua, "Now we are President, my brothers and sisters" – and he wasn't using the "we" in the manner of the English Monarchy. Grimaldo Rengifo Vasquez elucidates the cultural context for this sort of statement:

> [...] to be richer and more powerful in a given situation must not be

> interpreted as synonymous with hierarchy and opposition in others; rather they are the attributes of the charismatic authority, of the person who assumes the responsibility (*cargo*) in a given moment and who possesses the greatest vigour and wealth needed to redistribute and to harmonise everyone in regenerating life. We are thus dealing with a world very different from the Western world which [...] has a different form [...] In this way of life, the presence of the "other" does not make its appearance as something distant and different from oneself. (*The Spirit of Regeneration,* 1998)

It was a couple of days after I heard Evo Morales quoted that I was presented with a copy of the essay by Vasquez that I quote above. The essay was a chapter in a collection of essays by a number of authors, all of whom were part of the first generation of Peruvian Andeans to receive all three levels of European education. They had all worked in "Development", which, despite varying the methodologies, they had found unworkable after twenty or thirty years of endeavour. Originally published in Spanish, *The Spirit of Regeneration* elucidates various aspects of the indigenous culture; and this particular essay by Vasquez, entitled "The Ayllu" (pronounced *aye-oo)*, answered some of my related questions in great detail.

The *ayllu* can be translated into English as "family", but what is meant by that, in English, is but a small part of the meaning of *ayllu*. Vasquez describes it in the first two paragraphs of his essay:

> This chapter discusses the community of relatives which is the *ayllu*. I shall not be concerned here simply with the structure and function of human kinship in the Andean peasant communities; rather the focus of this chapter will be to show the elasticity of this notion – the *ayllu* – which cannot be reduced to what is commonly known as social organization. At the same time, I shall argue that the Quechua word *runa* does not, nor does it have to, match the Western concept of man. Man in the West is not just another species; "man" is a category that radically separates that species from all others. These aspects are addressed in the first part of the chapter.
>
> The second part of the chapter discusses the way of being of all the components of the *ayllu*, and how their physiology is synchronized with the natural movements of expansion and contraction which happen in an "annual" cycle, or *wata*. In the *ayllu* the activity of its

> members is not modeled from the outside, it is not the product of a planning act that transcends it, but rather it is a result of the conversations that take place between the community of humans (*runas*), the community of *huacas* (deities), and the natural communities (*sallqa*), in a brotherly atmosphere of profound equivalency [...] An attribute of the *ayllu* is interpenetrability and an absence of exclusion among various forms of life.

Surely this is a culture of relationship. It is possible, therefore, to deduce that, if the languages of the relationship-conscious North American tribes are process-based, these Andean tribes, (whom, one might assume, were earlier migrators across the Bering Straits and who travelled further), whose sense of relationship is so highly and variously developed, also speak process-based languages.

So what about the lands from whence, many thousands of years ago, these people hailed? Could a Tibetan claim, as Vasquez does, "In the *ayllu* all share the same attributes; man is not the measure of things"?

The nearest I can come to discovering whether Tibetan is object-based, or process-based, is from the Introduction to the *Manual of Standard Tibetan*. Here the idea is expressed in a more complex way, but it would appear to bear out the idea that this central Asian language, at least, is *not* object-based:

> Tibetan contains a number of particular difficulties, mainly at the level of syntax and semantics. One of the fundamental features of Tibetan verbs is that they distinguish systematically between intentional and unintentional actions. Moreover, the ubiquity of agentive (or "ergative") constructions in which it is the agent, not the object, that is marked, sometimes creates the disconcerting impression that it is an entirely "passive" language. For example, the sentence "Lobsang drank the tea" would be translated into Tibetan as "lobsang-ki'chatung-song", which means literally, "By Lobsang drank tea". (Tournadre & Dorje, *Manual of Standard Tibetan,* 2003)

It could be said that Tibetan Buddhism, which has become the bedrock of Tibetan culture over the past twelve hundred years, is concerned with relationship, because the merit from any good deed of a Tibetan Buddhist is dedicated "for the benefit of all sentient beings". But does this argue interspecies dialogue and relationships of the same character as that of the *ayllu*? Not overtly so. However, Buddhism was a migrant force, arriving in Tibet from China and India, that became adapted to Tibetan ways. It is, after all, in Tibet, that the entire community respected all life forms so that animals and birds lived with less fear of humans – which is what made it so easy for them to be killed and conquered by the Chinese invaders of the middle of the twentieth century. Andeans and Amazonians, whose cultures bear many common features, lived thousands of years without such major influences, like those of China or India on Tibet. Furthermore, as in the instance of Mongolia, the influences of Buddhism sometimes came peaceably and as the result of philosophical enquiry; when the first major influence – the European – arrived in Central and South America, the alien ethos, lifestyle and belief-system was forcibly imposed on the indigenous people. Never in human history have hearts and minds been won by force, violence and cruelty – even if the George W. Bush administration thought it would work in Iraq in the twenty-first century.

For thirty years, Father Max Schiller (whom I met in Bolivia) has been the Roman Catholic Parish Priest in the village of Titicachi, ten tortuous hours' drive into the mountains north of La Paz. Despite all those years of living among the Andeans, learning Quechua and using it in his daily exchanges with his parishioners, he seemed to assume that all human cultures view relationship and social structure similarly; thus, in his Eurocentric way, he viewed his congregation as socially maladroit. In conversation with me, he voiced his irritation with them, because they do everything together; his voice rising with each statement, he told me, "They eat together, they sleep together, they do *everything* together!" Vasquez writes:

> Everyone is prepared to give their support to everything. There is no division of labour as in industry. There are no specialists; the Andeans are "generalists"; they do everything and because of that, they are ready to accompany anyone in any activity … For we Andeans, the Andes is a world of affectionate conversations because it is love for the world which allows life to flow. It is what makes the actions in life – such as eating, drinking, dancing, making *chakra,* raising potatoes and *ollucos* continue and multiply.

So far, I have not visited Australia, or Papua New Guinea, Malaysia, Indonesia or the Amazon, but it occurs to me that the Australian Aboriginal people, who were forcibly displaced and marginalized by the European interlopers, as well as the many tribes of Papua New Guinea, Malaysia, Indonesia and the Amazon, who remain fairly isolated from Eurasian influences, are all people who honour "Mother Earth" – as do indigenous Americans, North and South – feeling kindred with other species and not possesing any religion in the usual civilizational sense. Such religion compartmentalizes life, especially the Abrahamic faiths, which depend on hierarchy; at the top is the "All-seeing God(head)", made in the image of Man and with many of his attributes, such as Anger and Mercy and Revenge. These three religions depend on some intermediary between the ordinary man and his God, who can ensure these contacts take place at prescribed times and in prescribed places. They also tend to demand "blind faith". Mysticism, or spiritualism, are highly suspect and not to be encouraged, because they may result in personal experience of the Spirit, obviating the need for the intermediary and the control he can exert. Earth-honouring societies don't need such compartmentalized religion, because the entirety of life is imbued with spirituality as an integral part of every day.

Worship of a male sky deity is of recent origin in the history of humankind. A mere 5,000 to 7,000 years ago there arose in Eurasia the male-dominator societies that evolved into our own Eurocentric cultures. Ousted was the concept of the Earth as Mother, the Great Goddess, the Giver of Life, "whose worship was once the ideological core of a more peaceful and equalitarian society", as Riane Eisler expresses it in *The Chalice and The Blade* (1987).

Gone was that notion of "Mother Earth" with her inherent and constant nurturing of all forms of life, to be replaced by the hierarchical belief systems from which ours, the dominant culture of modernity, descends.

Blackfoot Physics is possibly unique, because it reports on encounters between the author, a quantum physicist and philosopher, and thinkers and philosophers among North American Native peoples, as they compared notes. Apart from anthropological studies, little time, space, or credence, is given to the thoughts and beliefs of indigenous peoples; even then, the approach is one of intellectual investigation, rather than of an equal and general acceptance of indigenous concepts – which amounts, I think, to a form of philosophical marginalization. Philosophical texts, statements about Modern Progress and political intention, are all posited from a Eurocentric, industrialized, vertically-organised society's viewpoint. "We", "the globe", "humanity", as they are invoked, are contstantly assuming "the world" is composed only of those people owing their societal structures, belief systems and religions to those thinkers and societies that first emerged around the Meditteranean, only to spread widely later. In such conceptual contexts too, non-colonising, unindustrialized, Earth-loving – and often indigenous – people are, yet again, marginalized.

I learned in my sojourn in the Andes in 2006-07 that the Roman Catholic Church is so disappointed with the ineffectiveness of its five hundred years of attempted conversion of the Native Andeans to Christianity – despite churches and priests and bishops *in situ* everywhere – that they are seriously considering re-evangelising the Andes. The Andeans, patently, have a belief system that suits them better than what they've seen of the Christian one. This is another instance of the collision of hierarchical societies (or institutions) with societies of equivalence: mutual incomprehension. When Spirit is an integral part of every minute of one's life, hierarchical religion is superfluous.

Does the absence of technology owe something to the sense of oneness with all other species – a condition I would call "ecokinship" – which in turn precludes certain forms of technological development, such as the explosive, centripetal energy that motivates almost all industrialized inventions? There's no want of intelligence, nor ingenuity, nor dexterous skill among people with lives embedded in ecokinship, but there often appears to be a want of inclination to industrialize. The absence of hierarchical aspects to their lives may also have a bearing – hierarchy and ecokinship being so incompatible – while hierarchy is endemic to the functions of manufacture and industrial commerce. Is the thought, prevalent among North American indigenous people, that one does nothing without first considering the effects on the subsequent seven generations, also replicated among these other cultures based on ecokinship, who speak process-based languages ?

I realize that more questions than answers arise out of such speculation. I also recognize that it would be easy to idealize cultures where ecokinship is the norm. I recognize that there are histories of violence and attempts, successful and otherwise, by some of the cultures we would usually refer to as "indigenous", or "underdeveloped", to dominate other cultures. Indigenous societies are just as vulnerable to human aberration as the peoples of dominant industrialized cultures. Yet "dominant" and "domination" seem to me to be strongest in those hierarchical societies, which speak the object-based languages. It is illustrative here to recall that the Inuit, living in harsh, Arctic conditions, almost on the cusp of the theoretical migratory pattern from Central Asia to the Americas, had no word that signifies "war", but many to describe snow. As Hugh, the School Master in Brian Friel's *Translations* tells Maire,

> I can provide you with the available words and the available grammar. But will that help you to interpret between privacies? I have no idea. But it's all we have. (1980)

In European languages, constructed on the object-based pattern, some topics are easier to discuss, or to explain in one language rather than another. That might also have something to do with the subtleties of European cultural mores and societal practices as well. I am, after all, generalizing, but I hope the generalizations highlight a truth about the basic differences between cultures whose manner of looking at life is substantially different.

Where are these ruminations going? I believe that the qualities of the emotional and creative lives of the indigenous peoples to whom I have referred, some of whom I have met and observed, are often better than those of industrialized peoples. It is known, for example, that depression is almost totally absent in non-industrialised societies. Given an absence of Eurocentric pressure, allowed to grow and develop with little or no outside influence, their lives have far more contentment and are proven to be sustainable, whereas ours are not. As "sustainable" is a word that now carries the additional meaning of "permitting life on Earth to continue", I imagine us de-constructing the prejudices arising from our Eurocenticism and taking lessons from those who live and practise ecokinship. If our collective obsession with technology and the maintenance of our profligate *status quo* could be set aside and we could learn to live with the abundance of sufficiency, could we become humble enough to learn from those societies and cultures that speak process-based languages and which have complex relationships with other life-forms? Could we abandon our millennia-old obsession with colonization – military, religious, or commercial – to listen to these human kin? I hope so.

A journalist, textile-artist and teacher, Judith Hoad was born in Bristol in 1937. She is the author of three non-fiction works, most recently This is Donegal Tweed *(Shoestring Publications, 1987) and* Need or Greed *(Gill and Macmillan, 1999). She was married to the Scots painter Jeremiah Hoad (1924-1999), with whom she moved in 1981 to Donegal, near Inver Bay, where she still lives.*

KADDISH

Gabriel Rosenstock

Espirit de corps – *and not just in Goldenbridge.*

The odd nightmare apart, Larry hadn't revisited boarding school. Strange, now, that he should agree, without thinking, to attend the reunion of past pupils of Carraig Pheadair, or Kerrickfeather, its official name.

Of the forty pupils who sat for the Leaving Certificate examination in 1979, he knew that two of them had gone on to receive their eternal reward; one of them had died in a crash, a professional rally driver, quite promising, too, by all accounts. The other died of a heart attack. There was some talk of suffocation during an act of auto-eroticism.

There would be a huge meal. Perhaps to compensate for the pig slurry dished out during six years of incarceration. Wine would be consumed. Fine wines. Not the thin altar-wine he had often purloined after serving Mass for a dotty old priest. They would spend the night in the same dormitory where they had slept as schoolboys. The current crop had gone home for the Christmas holidays. It used to be called Siberia. Larry expected the heating to be some degrees higher for past pupils.

The guy who slept next to him, Joxer, had a plastic statue of the Virgin Mary, full to the brim with "holy water". All you had to do was unscrew the head for a swig of pure vodka.

Of the thirty-eight souls still alive, seventeen appeared. The Angelus bell rang out across the tennis courts, out over the playing fields towards the cold boundary walls. Some of them were singing the silly old college song:

We're the boys, the boys of Kerrickfeather
We play hard – whatever the weather …

Larry never sang it. Because of this he was marked out as different, aloof.

The President, Fr Edwards, welcomed them. Larry had to shake his hand.

"Larry, isn't it? Good man! Welcome back!"

The priest had hardly changed, a little more baldy, perhaps? It was his fellow past-pupils that had aged. A few had changed beyond recognition. Old men.

Where's Jack Prendergast? Had he bothered to come at all? Would they recognise each other?

Grace Before Meals was said. The words came back to them, as though it were only yesterday, as though none of them had ever left. Some of them were still behaving like schoolboys.

Bottles of wine were opened. The first course was served. The windows began to steam up and soon he could no longer see the sun going down behind the wood. Larry felt trapped, hearing only snatches of the rowdy exchanges.

"Can't complain … you know… yeah, I own two garages now… how about yourself?"

"Two daughters and one son …"

"I live in Foxrock …"

"We sent the son to Belvedere …"

"Do you remember Harry?"

Spurts of laughter.

"Joxer's pissed already – look at the state of him!"

An hour went by.

Outside, in the open car park, frost had begun to glitter in the moonlight on the cars of the ex-pupils, a Jaguar here, a Volvo there, two Mercedes.

Larry couldn't concentrate on anything that was being said on either side of him, or opposite him; he failed to muster a laugh. The main course was served.

Ghosts, that's what they were. There's Jack Prendergast over there! He winked at Larry. Wouldn't you think – they hadn't seen each other until now – wouldn't you think after all they had been through so long ago … a wink? Wouldn't you imagine he'd get up from the table, walk over to Larry, shake his hand or place his hand on his shoulder. Were they not the best of friends? Hadn't they written to each other for five years – six years – after leaving Kerrickfeather? And then? Then what happened? Nothing. Not a Christmas card even. Wouldn't you think he'd say, "Shalom!"

A tightness in the throat. Larry looked at the roast potatoes, the lamb, the peas. The mint sauce. He felt queasy. "Pass the jug of water, please", he said to the person beside him.

"Would you not go for the wine? It's a grand Rioja …"

"Wat – water!" croaked Larry. The other fellow looked at him.

As he sipped the water they began to stare at him from the wall … the half-faded photographs of past Presidents of the college, a bishop or two, rugby heroes, a patriot and there, in the corner, Christ on his Cross, a gallery of greyness. Another era, another world.

Trophies and cups everywhere in the refectory, mostly for rugby. It's not that he hated it as a sport. It's just that he and Jack decided not to be part of the crowd, a decision that didn't make life easy for them.

You weren't liked – by other pupils or by teachers – if you were different. To have a mind of your own made you an object of suspicion. The word *Queer* was scrawled on Jack's locker and *Poof* on Larry's and this had nothing to do with their sexuality; it was because they were more interested in the few fringe elements on offer, debates, tennis, than in the official religion of the college, which was rugby. No attempt was made to discover who the graffitti-offenders might have been, something which led Jack and Larry to believe that the authorities were part of the conspiracy. Dessert was served.

Neither of them liked the brutal nature of rugby. They couldn't give two hoots about *esprit de corps,* a phrase that cropped up a little too often, they thought. And so they began to imagine that they were in a concentration camp and that instead of *Arbeit Macht Frei*, the words *Esprit de Corp*s stood over the gate. They pretended to be Jews and greeted each other surreptitiously with Shalom and the like. They stamped numbers on each other's wrist. Jack used to call Larry the Chief Rabbi. Whenever it was pork for dinner, they'd hand over their share to some hungry devil.

His stream of thought was interrupted by a bell. The President arose: "Coffee will be served presently. I would like to take this opportunity to congratulate you all. We are very proud of you, all of you. Clearly what you learned here and from our *esprit de corps* has not been wasted on you …" Twaddle!

He needed to stretch his legs. A few others needed some fresh air. He went out, stood next to his car and took out a packet of Silk Cut. Someone behind him was nattering into a mobile. More people were coming out now. He could see their breath in the air.

"Shalom!" came a voice behind him.

He turned around. It was Jack.

"Still smoking?" A toothy grin.

"Yeah … Jack." He offered him a cigarette. Jack refused with an air of disgust.

"Don't smoke any more."

Sounds of the night. Somebody was throwing up, cursing himself.

"How's the Chief Rabbi been all these years?" A suppressed titter.

Jack rolled up his sleeve a little and bared his wrist.

"Jaysus – you can't be serious!"

"I'm the same as I always was", said Larry. He turned from Jack and looked sourly at an amorphous cloud that was about to swallow the moon.

Translated, from the Irish, by the author.

A poet, short-story writer and translator, Gabriel Rosenstock was born in 1949 in Kilfinane, Co Limerick and is a graduate of University College Cork. One of the "Innti" poets that transformed Irish-language poetry in the 1970s, he writes primarily in Irish and is the author or translator of over 100 books. His most recent collection of poetry is Bliain an Bhandé (Year of the Goddess, *The Dedalus Press, 2007). He currently works for An Gúm, the publications branch of the North-South body that promotes the Irish language, Foras na Gaeilge.*

AT RISK OF INTERMENT: W.G. SEBALD IN BREENDONK AND TEREZÍN

Will Stone

There, in Flanders and the Czech lands,
the void unloosens time.

The supreme felicity of the thinker is to have explored the explorable
and to serenely venerate the inexplorable.
Goethe

I don't think you can focus on the horror of the Holocaust. It's like the head of the Medusa. You carry it with you in a sack, but if you looked at it, you'd be petrified.
W.G. Sebald

Introduction

My aim here is simply to discuss certain "creatively-enabled" melancholic gleanings made by W.G. Sebald from the morbidly endowed climate of two Holocaust-related locations which play a key role in his novel *Austerlitz* (2001), and to suggest how the historic realities harboured by such locations as well as their own unique post-atrocity atmospheres may have served to underscore the limits of the author's own sanity. The two locations in question, Terezín in the Czech Republic and Breendonk in Belgium, have a personal significance also in that I found my experience of visiting them at different periods of my life both before and after reading Sebald's works, appeared to curiously overlap with the tenor of those found in his texts, resulting in a kind of uncanny merging and subsequent blurring of events which defies explanation.

The circumstances of my encounter with Breendonk, for example, suggest that I was drawn to that location either by coincidence or fate shortly after the appearance of *Austerlitz* and the subsequent untimely death of its author, both of which were uppermost in my mind at the time. In the case of Breendonk, whilst traveling in Belgium on a research trip for a work of literary translation in January 2002, I happened to stumble completely by chance (literally driving past, in fact) on the entrance of the Breendonk fort which had made such an impression on me from Sebald's text but whose exact location I had barely absorbed. Without falling prey to over-dramatization, it did feel rather as if an unseen hand had directed me there at that particular moment. My visit came at a time when the memorial site was undergoing the ubiquitous visitor-friendly "make-over", the installation of giant displays and banners, recordings on TV monitors by white-haired survivors droning on in ill-lit cells to no one and the unremitting looped barkings of dogs ghosting the courtyards, attempts to educate the casual visitor and amplify the atmosphere, which were in many ways superfluous and proved an interference to the more unembellished encounter Sebald would have experienced years before. Thankfully, however, the architecture was still all too vividly disorientating and mentally imposing, the atmosphere still uniquely charged and heavily weighted with the significance of the past.

Breendonk

SS Fort Breendonk, situated some twenty miles south of Antwerp, was a mere dot in the vast Nazi camp system. Barbarity on an industrial scale was not its function, but between 1940 and 1944, as headquarters of the local Gestapo, it was set up as a brutal penal camp for Resistance members, communists and others deemed enemies of the Reich. Though it may lack the scale and global notoriety of an Auschwitz or Dachau, Breendonk's celebrity rests on being one of the best preserved sites of Nazi crimes, partly because of its unique situation in a moated fort which resists physical destruction. Virtually untouched since 1945, one can visit a building in which with only the feeblest of imaginations a visitor will sense the residue of inmates and their tormentors, whom (it seems) have only recently departed.

Sebald leads the reader into Breendonk through his preferred device of exposing human folly in overreaching architectural ambition. He employs this again at the close of the book when he makes a brief return to Breendonk, selecting another futile fort constructed at Kaunas in Lithuania. In the case of Breendonk, an absurdity worthy of the Maginot line is illustrated in the ambitious nineteenth-century construction of a defence line of forts which ultimately proves redundant as the galloping city of Antwerp catches up with it, forcing these leviathans further and further out into the countryside. So we learn of the circumstances around the location of Breendonk, a defiant leftover from this chain of forts, relatively innocuous until the Nazi occupation, when with their usual eye for the perfect existing building for committing evil deeds, the Nazi authorities took over the fort and established their prison.

The author or narrator arrives at Breendonk, we are told, in the year 1967, to symbolically face the fort upon the bridge which spans its moat. To the right he would have noted a watchtower of distinctive design and which appears in a clip from Alan Resnais' brief filmic response to the death camps, *Night and Fog*, in a sequence detailing the plethora of creative designs for the construction of the camps. It seems unlikely that Sebald would not be familiar with this unique film document and yet in characteristically reticent style he eschews mention of it, since it is perhaps too explicit a Holocaust reference and instead mentions later on in the book *Toute la Mémoire du Monde*, another short Resnais made about the mysterious inner workings of the Bibliothèque National in Paris. This determination to approach the Holocaust through some link that establishes our partial complicity as human beings with a communal history is why it seems to me Sebald chose the pre-Nazi era fort and Czech garrison town and what drew him to them – the historical human impetus in their initial construction and relative resignation from the modern world, suddenly skewed for eternity by the incomprehensible events that took place in them over those four years of German occupation. This would seem to have a deeper resonance than a row of functional wooden barracks by a pine forest, or the site of a purpose-built death factory whose facts we know about in tremendous detail but at whose cairns of stones and memorials, at whose torn rail-spurs inappropriately nestled in murmuring summer grasses, one simply stands shamed at one's failure to find any significant purchase, mentally asphyxiated by figures and images which, in deference to the mind's protection, cannot replicate accurately the true reality and within whose trailing weeds we become hopelessly enmeshed, or are left brimming over with an ever-increasing, endlessly sifted knowledge: a knowledge that one is obliged to lug around like a load of useless damp firewood, until it gradually forces us to our knees.

Approaching the dark muzzle-like portal of the fort, one leaves the bridge for ancient cobbles over which the police vehicles would have sped with their terrified captives. To left and right depressingly unrelieved windowless walls stretch away above an uncomfortably serene moat. In Sebald's own words: "what I saw now before me was a low-built concrete mass, rounded at its outer edges and giving the gruesome impression of something hunched and misshapen: the broad back of a monster, I thought, risen from this Flemish soil like a whale from the deep". Later, after failing to get a hold on the shape or design of the sprawling edifice and as he puts it "unable to connect it with anything shaped by human civilisation", he goes on to describe the walls as "covered in places by open ulcers with raw crushed stone erupting from them, encrusted by guano like droppings and calcareous streaks", the fort being "a monolithic monstrous incarnation of ugliness and blind violence" and "an anatomical blueprint of an alien crab-like creature". Two photos support this vision, the first showing fittingly a dead end where two walls join – one with the ulcer he describes, like the crude bite of a shark from the body of the whale, the other revealing stunted tower-like bastions with no sign of aperture or embrasure, and rising out of the pasture like some volcanic outcrop from the sea. There thus appears to be no opportunity anywhere for light to enter. Sunk in the earth this colossus of numbing concrete flaunts its ungainly claws and pincers, whilst seemingly endless exteriors of walls give an impression there is no interior behind them, as if they were only solid and utterly pointless, offering protection to nothing but their own inner core, the unrelieved whole resulting in a kind of force-field which induces a palpable darkening of the mood. This initial anxiety aroused from the demented crab-like form and aesthetically repellent decaying of the building materials, only serves to increase the inevitable sense of anxiety Sebald experiences on finally entering the fort and encountering evidence of the crippling punishment men endured there. He mentions, for example, the heavy primitive wheelbarrows and sees the unfortunate inmates "bracing themselves against the weight until their hearts burst". When he encounters the SS café and mess area still with its cheerful "bulging stove" and evidence of Germanic lettering on the beams and walls, Sebald quells his rage and merely reports. This uniquely preserved room, in its funereal stillness somehow mocking the existence of those rowdy Bavarian cellars devoured by Hitler's dark insistence, stands in triumphant indiscretion, only a stone's throw from the torture room.

Sebald includes a picture of one of the fort's electrically-lit cable-lined corridors with a cell door ajar. And here, as he descends symbolically again into the darkness, drawn into this echoing mine, this sepulchre, at imminent risk it would seem of interment, he responds: "... the darkness does not lift but becomes yet heavier as I think how little we can hold in mind, how everything is constantly lapsing into oblivion with every extinguished life, how the world is, as it were, draining itself ..." This corridor, with its numbing functionality, vertiginous perspective and suggestion of some unbearable subterranean pressure, recalls a passage bored deep into a cliff or a mine, or a more modern catacombs, like the briefly-calm corridor of a Victorian-era asylum or hospital. After encountering the torturer's cell within the casement, hook still visible in the ceiling, the nauseating scent of soft soap causes Sebald to swoon against a wall which "was gritty, covered with bluish spots and seemed to me to be perspiring with cold beads of sweat". Here it appears the very walls are alive but only in so far as they are rotting, the interior surface somehow gesturing to the "open ulcers", the gouged and pitted exterior which he had earlier explored. But crucially it is not the more obvious Jean Amèry-related trauma, the hook in the ceiling, that makes Sebald swoon, but the unwelcome scent of a particular soap which recalls some uncomfortable family memory.

Yet at this point, using his habitual bridging movement from one story to another, Sebald departs Breendonk, only returning at the close of the book. The night before he spends in a grotty hotel on the Astridplein in Antwerp, juxtaposed with an intriguing photo showing the view from his window over a depressing scene of grimy walls, ducts and pipes sealed with barbed wire. One would be mistaken for thinking that this was an image taken at Breendonk itself or indeed the roof of a gas chamber complete with vents. In fact, if you just flicked through casually, that might be your surmise. But this is a hotel, this is freedom, this is now – and here we are on the other side of the moat, Sebald seems to be saying, *and yet and yet* ...

But as Sebald leaves the hotel to return to Breendonk, he passes an unknown sick woman lying on a stretcher in the lobby. Such sightings occur throughout Sebald's works, for example "the disturbed individual waving his arms" Austerlitz encounters at Terezín who, Sebald suggests, "seems to have been swallowed up by the earth as they say, even as he was running off". Plausibly shadowing countless silent victims of the Holocaust, they are positioned to maximize feelings of dislocation and trauma, symbols of the individual's swift fall from perceived security. "I saw a pale faced woman of about forty with her eyes turned away lying on a high trolley down by the reception desk, where there was no one in evidence." It is both the last part "no one in evidence" and the line "with her eyes turned away" which properly fuel the haunting image. Sebald hurries past out into the world a free man, noting the woman but unable to assist, apart from exhuming her from oblivion in this random moment through memory, whilst she lies there "eyes turned away", awaiting a fate unknown to her or us. Totally vulnerable to the abrupt emergence of the void, her destiny suddenly rests in the hands of strangers, "the two ambulance men chatting outside".

Terezín

Languishing some thirty miles north of Prague with no defined role since the late 1880s, during the German occupation the garrison town of Terezín came to prominence in the mechanics of the final solution as a ghetto for deported Western European Jews. Terezín, or Theresienstadt as the occupiers renamed it, extends to about 1 km square, laid out to a symmetrical grid within fortified star-shaped walls, and designed for some two thousand residents. A quiet unremarkable place with its shops, bakeries, parks, bandstand and rather methodical tree-lined avenues, Sebald describes it as "a world made by reason, regulated in all conceivable respects". No wonder such a place was eagerly seized on by the German mind craving order and exactitude. Over two pages Sebald displays the numbingly precise yet disorientating German military map of the site, ushering in pictorially the mania for lists and records the Germans obsessed over, in order to support what lies beyond in the text. Close by the main town, but quite apart from it, was the "Kleine Festung", or Small Fortress. This was a prison within a prison and had always been so. Thus, as at Breedonk, the SS and local Gestapo found it was ideally situated and architecturally suited for the detainment, punishment and execution of special prisoners. For some reason, possibly because the Terezín fort seemed too close to that at Breendonk, Sebald chose not to clarify the separateness of the town of Terezín and the nearby prison, with the result that there is an important ambiguity in the text and photographs. A reader, then, would have no idea which location the image referred to. A clutch of initial photographs show the fortifications of the Small Fortress and how, like Breendonk, the fort seems organically subsumed in the landscape that encloses it. But unlike the bunker-like Breendonk, one observes pathologically undeviating flat walls of brick topped with stone, creating narrow terraces topped by weeds and creepers. Here nature has accepted the concrete and stone as a semi-permanent intruder and adapted to its contours. Ditches, dykes, glacis and embankments form labyrinthine layers of acute angles and confounding dead ends. Sickly turf, moss and high grasses adorn the roofs of the ugly drowned buildings, making nature seem somehow complicit in the fort's brutally unyielding presence.

As Austerlitz surveys the deserted townscape of Terezín town, we are granted a double-page spread of weary Terezín facades, their closed doors and windows seeming to resolutely deny access to the unsavory memories behind them, the peeling paint of the doors and walls showing not only the eagerly melancholic textures of decay but a human unwillingness to dabble here, to repair or maintain these mausoleums. A powerful image simply shows a row of metal dustbins, their numbers daubed in paint, before a wall clearly in the vanguard of dereliction. Like the photo of the hotel roof wreathed in barbed wire, the numbered dustbins seem here to be pointing us forward to the German fixation with lists, rolls calls and tallies, or as Sebald puts it, "their mania for order and purity, put into practice on a vast scale through measures partly improvised, partly devised with obsessive organizational zeal". On the following page, we find two more almost full-page vertical shots of grim doors sealed within walls of the crypt-like chambers and courtyards of the small fortress. These raw weathered walls seem to request demolition, yet in one case an impassable door absurdly overwhelmed with huge hinges and latches stands fast, as if sealed forever, somehow defying disintegration of the whole. The sense of abandonment and desolation these images cast is pervasive.

Austerlitz learns that into Terezín the Germans crammed some 60,000 Jewish men, women and children. Here many of the more well-off German Jews were brought, the cream of bourgeois and artistic Jewish society, artists, writers, professors, bankers, industrialists, but also shopkeepers, tradesmen and the like; so that this town now somehow resembled a microcosm of European Jewish society diabolically crammed into a sq km of space. And following meticulously formulated procedures, they were left to be whittled away by illness, exhaustion and despair in, as Sebald says, little more than 2 sq m of personal space, with only the chimneys of Auschwitz to break their unchanging horizon. But Terezín's most terrible secret and shame is (as Austerlitz soon discovers) the alarming juxtaposition of a skewed normality in the planned workings of this ghetto town, this civic dummy, with the coordinated extermination of its inhabitants, a fact which causes the mind to perpetually recoil, forever thrown back on itself, straining through the creepers of ever more bestial revelations and paralysing absurdities. It is the latter that Sebald seeks to convey. Note, then, how he laces the page with a form from the archives containing over fifty protracted German terms for offices and locations within the town, overblown compounds such as "Marketenderwarenerzeugung" that seem to haul their ludicrous linguistic vanity across the page and deposit them incongruously beside a less sophisticated entry such as the deceptively bovine "SS Garage".

Sebald focuses on the working conditions of Terezín, how the prisoners were compelled to work as slaves, their bank issuing a currency which had no value and with which nothing could be bought. He lists the wide variety of trades which prisoners toiled away at, even those flaunting their exotic specialism such as "the shearing of rabbit fur", "the bottling of ink dust" and, most memorably, "a silkworm breeding station run under the aegis of the SS". He describes the carefully tended vegetable plots and market gardens flourishing under the town's walls, the café, the theatre, even a lively cultural programme tolerated by the Germans. Sebald catalogues a dummy citadel forced to run itself, using customs from the outside world habitually ascribed to a process of life, but here for the convenience of their murderers merely fleshing out the procession to extinction. Already condemned, the inmates had become mannequins, ghosts acting out a tragic play at their masters' bequest. In line with their customary comedic abominations, the SS allowed a fleet of old decrepit hearses onto the Terezín streets for prisoners' use and these "oddly swaying conveyances", as he describes them, were hardly likely to be overlooked by Sebald. These pathetic vehicles, some with their ornate baroque roofs shorn off, were utilized for everything from delivering the bread ration to their original purpose – though not just one body in an ornate coffin, but teetering stacks of pine boxes – namely, to carry the hundred-plus who perished each day in Terezín. Jewish artists such as Leon Haas and Bedrich Fritta left memorable images showing them carrying new arrivals. The newcomers, intimately captured by Fritta, crestfallen, confused, slumped on their baggage, spending their first night in what they had been lead to believe by German propaganda was a luxurious "spa town", concern Sebald too. He includes the reproduction of a stamp with Terezín postmark, one from many postcards sent from newcomers to tell of a wonderful resort to which others too must make haste. As Sebald explains, the overcrowded conditions caused the extreme human attrition of elderly people especially, so rapidly reduced to infantilism and acute malnutrition. But everything, Sebald seems to suggest, however seemingly innocuous or fleeting, inane or tragic, is, through the SS logic of destruction, either a profitable or benign tributary that drains into the stronger current leading to extermination.

In the summer of 1944, the prisoners of Terezín were informed of the sudden plan to beautify the town for an proposed inspection by senior officials of the Red Cross. Recognizing a rare propaganda gift, the decision was taken to show the world a charitable haven of peace for Jews who clearly did not deserve such German benevolence. It was this, then – the pinnacle of Nazi deception and enforced victim-collusion, together with the survival of an accompanying film, *The Fuhrer Grants the Jews a Town,* that elevates Terezín from purely functional death camp anteroom to something even more disturbing (if such a thing is possible), a freakish hybrid poised over the abyss midway between ersatz normality and murderous depravity.

The Red Cross inspection team duly arrived on a fine July day and the ruse worked perfectly, largely due to the Germans' painstaking attention to detail and ruthless determination to erase any sign of the reality of life in Terezín. In advance of the visit, the whole town was scrubbed and revitalized. Berlin had decreed that anyone who did not look healthy enough or characteristically Jewish enough was to be immediately shipped East, a policy resulting in some seven thousand inmates and a whole TB ward being herded off. Sebald is at pains to communicate the grotesque deception and pregnant tragedy of this assiduous preparation, how Terezín reverses to a sham of its former state, a theatrical folly with its doomed players cast in their elected roles, the majority of whom were rewarded by being transported East soon after. He homes in on the relentless activity in the smithy, the pottery, the sewing and weaving workshops, the incessant "hammering, cutting, gluing and stitching ..." The prisoners are seized in a frenzy of progressive labour that mirrors the craftsmanship of the exterior world they have left, where something honestly made is for a useful purpose, whereas here there is no purpose since all is a facade. And in the false "Eldorado" of this new Terezín, they are forced to smile, to cheer and show those very emotions which are the antithesis of their appalling situation. Everything is thus turned on its head. Insanity prevails and any response fattened on a preceding history simply collapses in its tracks. Sebald also records the stringent refurbishments and new civic creations, "children's playgrounds, paddling pools, a coffee house with sun umbrellas, a cinema, shops stocked with provisions borrowed from the SS stores ..." Nothing was left to chance, no expense spared, every detail pored over. On the day of the inspection the pavements were scrubbed with soap, the bread ration was handed out by men in white drill gloves ... Sebald reports these incredible facts benignly, methodically, so that the sense of the plausible is intimately shadowed by the implausible. It was as if the SS were using the opportunity not only to fool the Red Cross and the world, but also revelling in this chance to further torture their victims, to tempt them with a world they would never see again. Not content with murdering them, they sought to humiliate them before death, the creation of the model town almost luring them onto ever greater psychopathic indulgences. In this passage Sebald culminates with the haunting image from the film of the residents, carefully choreographed, flocking to the ramparts at the end of a working day, or as he puts it, "to take the air, almost as if they were passengers enjoying an evening stroll on the deck of an ocean-going steamer ..."

In all this Sebald seems to be saying: not the embalmed rhetoric of "how can it have happened", but how can it have happened "in this particular way", and how can we return to our lives knowing this happened, how can we mirror such activities and not feel something of the resonance of those silent condemned individuals on the temporary Terezín stage within its grim fortified walls, enacting our future lives for us. This sense of sudden breaches in the dyke of linear continuation, a malign otherness, of something constantly jarring our consciousness, some "thing" recumbent, unaddressed, still languishing in the tidal outflow of atrocity, awaiting our true response, is exacerbated by the ingenious device of the tape of the Terezín film which Austerlitz views at a slower speed in an attempt to discern Agata's face in the crowd. Here a merry polka becomes "a funeral march dragging along at a grotesquely sluggish pace", the strenuous high-pitched German voiceover becomes "a menacing growl". The workers with their needles and thread are reduced in slow motion to dream-bound marionettes who "looked wearily up to the camera". Now the people are truly adrift, lacking all purchase on reality, moving, as Sebald suggests, "in a kind of subterranean world, through the most nightmarish depths, to which no human voice has ever descended". Would it not be too outlandish a presumption that these same depths are physically manifest in the descending casement of Breendonk where Sebald, at risk of interment, is overcome by nausea and "black striations across the eyes"? Are not these forts with their morbidly affluent architecture, their gratuitously symbolic moats and ramparts, their labyrinthine tunnels, stark cobbled courtyards, permanently chilled passages, dungeon-like cells and sepulchral casements, physical manifestations of a Piranesian descent into folly, nightmare and human extinction itself, yet also the warning beacon of a past which has learnt to secrete itself beneath the carapace of certain infected landscapes and edifices from which it will intermittently spring to assault a selective amnesia or that necessary rational "accommodation" of impossible realities which flatters the instinct for human prolongation? And is this amnesia or secret complacency, which blooms from that obscure selection of what is overlooked and what is compromised by saturation and interference via the current frantic exertions of the Holocaust marketplace, likely to be dented by the subtle soundings of Austerlitz?

The following lines, left by an unfortunate caught up in the hell of Terezín that somehow seem to look forward to and commend Sebald's lonely vigil, may help fill the space left by the absence of any answer. "The heaviest wheel rolls across our foreheads to bury itself somewhere deep inside our memories ..."

A poet, translator and essayist, Will Stone was born in 1966 and received an MA in Literary Translation from the University of East Anglia. His books of translation are Les Chimères *by Gerard de Nerval (Menard Press, 1999) and* To the Silenced: Selected Poems of Georg Trakl *(Arc Publications, 2005). His first collection of poems is* Glaciation *(Salt, 2007). He divides his time between England and the Continent.*

PHOTOGRAPHY, REPORTAGE & LITERATURE

Michael O'Sullivan

Walking the unwieldy line.

I

Work by the great German novelist W.G. Sebald, who died in 2001, continues to appear in English translation: *Unrecounted* (2004) is one of the latest such volumes. In this book, verse by Sebald accompanies etchings by Jan Peter Tripp. The etchings depict human faces, and are executed in such a hyper-realistic style that they might be mistaken for photographs. But Sebald, in an essay appended to the book, defends Tripp's art by contrasting it with photography. In the process, Sebald reveals something of his conception of art, and the arguments he presents may help us to understand his own haunting, enigmatic work.

Sebald's approach to photography derives in several key respects from that contained in Roland Barthes's short book *Camera Lucida*. Old photographs of those now dead do not restore them to life but embalm them. The more closely we examine photographs from the nineteenth century, the more alien their subjects come to seem; our capacity for empathy fails us. This explains the eerie feeling many of us experience on viewing very old photographs, a feeling which is in some ways the very opposite of our reaction to a great painting or literary work. We expect to respond intuitively to another human face, but the faces in old photographs have become mere objects, and our reaction is, accordingly, blank.

The photographer is an "undertaker", an "agent of death". Even photographs of the living make them seem dead: they too are reduced to pure image, pure object. The photographer's ruses of backdrops and naturalistic settings for their subjects are nothing but attempts to offset the inherent lifelessness of the photographed face. Further, Barthes writes, photographs *say* nothing about the people and scenes they depict, except that they were and were such. They have "no depth"; they tell us only that "that has been". As Sebald says, "the photographic image turns reality into a tautology".

It is in just these respects, for Sebald, that Tripp's art differs from photography. His etchings are based on photographs, and in fact differ from them only in the most subtle ways, but these traces of the artist's hand are enough to transform their meaning and purpose, and are what gives them their value. The difference between art and reportage may be as much a matter of form as of content; at any rate, the difference is crucial. Where superficially similar photographs present their subjects as though they were dead, Tripp's art is *about* death: "Life's closeness to death is its theme, not its addiction". By going beyond mere reportage, it expresses a little of what it means to be mortal.

II

Iris Murdoch, in her book *The Fire and the Sun: Why Plato Banished the Artists*, interprets Plato as believing that art is dangerous because it "undoes the work of philosophy". Where philosophy teaches us a proper scepticism about our ability to gain any real understanding of the world, art gives us an easy sense of insight into things. Through art we gain an illusion of intuitive understanding, which is just what philosophy combats. We cannot "see into the life of things", but art can fool us into thinking that we can.

This is similar, I think, to a line of thought pursued in *On the Natural History of Destruction,* another work by Sebald published in English since his death. Sebald faults postwar German culture for the lack of attention paid to the horrific effects of the Allied bombing of German cities during the Second World War. But he is also critical of those novelists who *have* dealt with the issue. They have been too quick, he argues, to resort to elaborate literary devices in order to represent their subject matter. They have tended to approach the destruction of German cities through metaphor, or to turn that destruction into metaphor. Another strategy has been to use grand metaphysical schemes to interpret events and give them some meaning.

In the face of the tremendous trauma with which these novelists are concerned, such strategies are, for Sebald, tasteless. Moreover, they are false to their subject matter. They have the effect of a pulled punch: the force of an inherently disturbing narrative is softened by the way in which it is presented. Conventional literary devices make sense of events for us, and thus make them palatable. Where first-hand experience would leave us speechless, confronted with a literary account we know just what to say.

Sebald recommends, instead, a matter-of-face tone, a bare retelling of events, reportage rather than art. This is the tone of those few authors who, he feels, have handled the issue well. It is also his own tone when, in the course of the book, he describes the bombings, and every reader will find these sections distressing.

III

We seem to be left with a choice between reportage and literature. On the one hand, reportage suffers from its own transparency. Old photographs have nothing to tell us beyond what is on their surface. Their subjects are nothing but dead. On the other hand, literature, in interpreting, falsifies, at least when it deals with events of the magnitude of the Second World War. Is there any way out of this quandary?

Sebald's own novels are characterised by sudden, often lengthy, incursions into history, memoir and biography. *The Rings of Saturn*, for example, is organised around an account of various walks along England's North Sea coast, but most of the text is taken up by narratives drawn from the history of China, the career of Roger Casement and any number of other fields. Some of these are put into the mouths of people whom the narrator meets on his walks, others relate to places and things he comes across, while some have only thematic connections to the rest of the novel.

One of the striking features of the novel is that the main narrative does not attempt to *explain* these sections. It provides a context for them, rather than a commentary. In consequence, the reader feels that the structure of the novel serves the numerous stories told within it, and not *vice versa*. The significance of these stories does not need to be advertised, nor their presence justified.

No reader will call Sebald's eloquent prose bald, or describe his elegiac tone as one of bare reportage. Still, the anecdotal passages to which I have referred are, in their way, transparent. It is the Taiping Rebellion itself that gives depth to the narrative of *The Rings of Saturn*, not the way in which Sebald writes about the Taiping Rebellion.

The Second World War, the Holocaust, the catastrophe of Central Europe in the twentieth century, are constant themes in Sebald's work. His task, one feels, has been to deal with such themes without patronising them, to walk the line between the deadening effects of photographic reportage and the distorting effects of literature. We may have in Sebald, at last, a Central European writer equal to the unwieldy legacy of his century.

An essayist and short-story writer, Michael O'Sullivan was born in Cork in 1979 and took a degree in philosophy at University College Cork. He is currently undertaking a PhD at King's College, University of London, and lives in Hackney.

From THE FINAL MOTHER-FUCK (PERHAPS)

Tom Mac Intyre

Fourteen times fourteen makes ...
three-score-and-ten.

CARE-HOME, HER BIRTHDAY

Avalon they call it, hard to blame
them, what are we to do when
the hand of the potter shakes? Room
here once a week to solace June,
pixillated beauty, gobbles my stories
of talkative blackberries in the August
vat; Nell, adipose, haze
about her, and transfixed, maladroit,
the smile; Emir, starved with the cold,
has me kiss and kiss her swollen thumb;
and here's the kid-sister, a grief untold.
"What age today" "Twenty-two."
Once I was shown her might have been;
sundown, a doorstep, before me a queen.

REFLECTIONS IN A RHEUMY EYE

"Holdin' your hand's like milkin' a cow."
"From where, tell us, the Rasputin smile?"
"Your love-sounds are tropical
birds." "Why, why so *bereaved* now?"
Old Lag, slack features a cage,
scratches his crotch from under the table,
defines, doleful, punani pilgrimage –
"Daddy-Long-Legs footless on marble",
listens, bothered ear, to Missy, The Maid,
who swears by the blue puss, blue fawn,
speaks, sings, of Time green in the blade,
pardons failure to greet The Unicorn,
adds, angel-eyed – "You're rough trade.
Pilgrimage means *a walk in the field*".

BUT AS MALES THEY DISLIKED

"Mere breath of your name," she phones,
"room's a slab of ice." "The heinous deed?"
"Guess, why don't ye?" Reflex thought is
where I slept last night, that broad
sloping meadow, serried flambeaux, green-
blue, of grown cabbage, a white butterfly proprietary above; down
my winter lane, a big Alsatian, Border
Guard, with spring to his tail, shouts – "Gimme
five!" And, first light, rap on the words
women have bestowed me, corblimey –
aibhleog, *rubato*, *désormais* –
how they love, loving are, the sylvan vowel –
"Still there?" "Suckin' diesel, Bella",
I reply.

ARTHURIAN MATTERS

Thigh-wound at three-score-and-ten
brackets you as halting *Fisher-King*,
prayer that it's idle misfortune
or, better, uterine, not worth a farthing.
My books, *my books*! Weeks with *Percival*
and *Gawain, Blanchfleur*, bleeding lance,
hags, hermits, questions – simplest of simple –
the hero will never ask, your lame dance
endures, *Forests of Heathendom* a mess
beyond navigation: you could be left
here for dead. Until, ex gratia, wet
Sabbath morning, lugging home the papers,
he meets me: ould goat, absorb'd wholly
in the breakfasting swans, nine-and-fifty,
beyond the mairn.

BIFTECK

On my plate – did I order un-
beknownst – badger steak, *bleu*, it
has no accompaniment, none
needed, raw clout sufficient, and – wait,
perpend – touching the bright cutlery,
I realise I *have* ordered it,
it's memorial, stage-lit,
thon badger, hoary stud, lately
seen crossing the spring morning garden,
dragging a spent body, back to the sett,
after a night of it; tristesse of that
slouch, driven skull, the combat zone:
the image resides – he sloped away –
badger grip. Your steak. *Mangez. Bleu.*

BLUEBEARD, PAST IT

You thought to find him zimmer-fram'd
bag o' bones in some Hospice for The Dying.
Really? Who's that, *Table Nine*, chatting
the young beauty, who listens, thrill'd,
as he prescribes, with panhandle
plawmas, *The Flaming Door* she
must abide if she's to meet the world,
two worlds, strokes her hand (shortly
the first pear-drop tear), he's telling
salt truth, that's why she listens, why
flushes, as the fondly tended ring-
lets fray, look, again, she's fit to cry ...
Is he fake? On his bed, she'll tell you,
a leopard's paw. Polish'd memento. So?

OTHER TOMS, OTHER MOORES

Once on the streets of the capital city
I met only honeyed young women,
now the collation's drystick old men.
X accosts me, just back from Italy,
would I admire his funereal tan?
Y, writer butty, lifts from the throng,
look, his hand's curious stiffening,
surgery scars, could be genetic, *Sam*
The Man had it. Enter *Z*, who text'd me
lately – "Trip Down Under off. Doctors
forbid". His walk soundless, queasy,
head aloft: lunch alone, with Dolours.
Home. Demoted fireguard by the armchair,
focus on the grate, your unhurried ember.

THE ASH

was no way shy yet from the word
Go, purdah our daylight, I gave her
the back of my hand, world my toaster,
Permanently Pensionable stepp'd
it out until, *They* don't forget, four-
o, thereabouts, she swoops, the car, I
was polishing the car, quick ear
to the ball-game (disaster), a mossy
cleft, hers, root zone, traps my eye;
scallops on offer, generous handful,
this pitted earth halts as I glare, giddy,
cramp, stew; scallops opening, bell
tolling, clits, cunts, muscles, torn
lawless juices, insisting they be known.

SPRING DAY

Meet him regular on my daily tramp,
he's the bit slow, never says much, today
he shows out of a pot-hole, touché
of apparition, head down, slow step;
he's approaching with barrow, call him beast
pushing barrow piled with daffodils:
turnips, spuds, daffodils, his resolute
step says, ordinaries of an April
showery day, he's do whatever he's
bid, I've overlooked a messenger
status – my careless eye – might be his:
on a tuppeny-h'apenny dray, Proser-
pina's blossoms, and I am still'd, yea,
quenched, *Timor mortis conturbat me.*

WHY VEINS SHOW

In the hall with this young woman
(only just met and we're about to part),
talking of the veins ferrying can after can
of sullied blood to the chambered heart.
"In the case of men", I suggest, "no veins
to be seen. With women quite the reverse."
"Changing Rooms", I add, rowdy confines,
where else, put me on to it first.
She takes me in. "And why should that be,
do you fancy?" "Haven't thought about it much."
Cartographer's dream and redolent sea
of unabashed filigree, she lifts the latch,
opens the door, *slán*, and, as she leaves,
what sundered music that fair hair retrieves.

CONCERNING SOPHIE

You should have known Eve, fine lassie
next door, big heart on her sleeve,
a green apple, a tear; toiled slave
to Helen's fancies, boudoir patchouli,
poetry talk, flight of those panties
a Greek vase soirée; sinner, braved
Sister Mary, born sinners to save,
pastoral smile, serial Assumptions,
flare-path Annunciations; roamed,
Chavalier, with Sophie, o, Eve with a passion,
Helen grown wise, Mary down from
the mountain, I sit lost by the phone,
Midnight, Noon, Blight & Cure, Amaze,
working pulse that flagrant virgin kiss.

THE MOLE

I'm the pits. No one will give Her
the time of day. Alert, She comes
to touch, firm, my thrawneen shoulder;
we meet – casual high drama – on the stairs,
She ascending (last brush, miracle
encounter, foot of the stairs, my letter
in her hand), now the house is canticle,
Canticle of Canticles, could she dwell here?
I stand beside her. She's simply clothed,
is my north, south, east and west,
and the no-delay/never-a-hurry kind;
a gentlest motion frees her left breast,
reveals the mole that proudly rears, says –
"Kiss, rest here, Man of Swithers & Swives".

THE FINAL MOTHER-FUCK (PERHAPS)

A good baker's dozen present, you
could say we made a meal of it,
musha, why not, this is The Big Split,
not the morning, China, the evening dew.
The guests sit in a circle, concerned to
miss nothing, we gild the transit
toward event cooly, content to target
their flea-market varieties of shoe.
Next, game on, we're coupling, audience
recede, with them least stim of voyeur
cosseting, we enter a shameless sense
of our story, no quarrel, not the colour
of it, no sweat, no flesh, no bone, ghosts
humping, the truth on its chosen salver.

THE 'FIFTIES

There were summers then, they passed us
by, our bibs wet, allegiance to the sour
tit total, how to gather, we'd ponder,
those uncontainable July evenings;
the *Pelican House* van, young nurses
in tow, aroused interest, *go for*
it; so to the neighbouring town, our
aspirant bodies washed, tilted towards
release, increase, surcease, end,
beginning, how we havered to the touch
of those *Nightingales*, this refined hand
of Venus, tourniquet, needle, rich
surrender of blood, a dark measure, stream-
ing, slowly, from some faery realm.

These poems are taken from a new and unpublished collection of one-hundred sonnets, entitled The Final Mother-Fuck (Perhaps).

A poet, dramatist and fiction-writer in both English and Irish, Tom Mac Intyre was born in Cavan in 1931. His most recent collections of poetry are Stories of the Wandering Moon *(The Lilliput Press, 2000) and* ABC *(New Island Books, 2006). His plays for the Abbey Theatre include* The Great Hunger *(1983),* Good Evening, Mr Collins *(1997), and his version of Brian Merriman's* Cúirt An Mhean Oiche/The Midnight Court *(1999). A collection of short fiction,* The Word for Yes: New and Selected Stories, *was published by The Gallery Press in 1991. He is a member of Aosdána, and lives in Co Cavan.*

AGAINST HISTORICAL FICTION

Toby Litt

A contract-in-bad-faith.

Historical fiction depends for its existence upon a pair of bad faiths – a reciprocal pair of bad faiths – the bad faith of the writer and the bad faith of the reader.

By "bad" I don't really mean "bad" – not in the sense of *malevolent*, *evil*. I'm using the term in something like the way Jean-Paul Sartre did; which means that although I may think historical fiction is deeply bogus, I don't think it's essentially reprehensible. To give historical fiction a serious kicking is a bit like berating cuddly old Stephen Fry for not having pursued an obscure and second-rate academic career writing on A. E. Housman. Historical fiction exists, gives pleasure to many, and will continue to do so whatever I say. It wouldn't be worth the effort, trying to persuade devotees to stop reading it. But I would like to spend some time examining how it is consumed and how it was produced.

It's not hard to demonstrate that historical fiction is written in bad faith. All you have to do is, for a moment, forget about bad faith and think about the purest good faith.

First, imagine an entirely naïve reader who picks up a novel by Philippa Gregory because they want to learn the truth about Anne Boleyn. Let's call this reader Alex. Alex completely trusts the writer not to mislead her (or him – Alex could be either) in any way about the past.

Philippa Gregory goes to a literary festival near where Alex lives and, because Alex feels s/he learnt so much about Anne Boleyn from Philippa Gregory's book, s/he goes along to say thank you. Alex stands in line with all the other Philippa Gregory fans – and when s/he gets to speak to her, and have his or her copy of *The Other Boleyn Girl* signed, Alex says something like this, "Dear Philippa, thank you for telling me the truth about the past. I believe Anne Boleyn was exactly as you described her. Having read your novel, I feel no need to read any other books about Anne Boleyn or her minx of a sister".

On hearing this, how does Philippa Gregory feel? What does she say? Does she feel, "Ah, I've done my job?" Or does she feel, "Look, here is my ideal reader?" And does she say, "You're quite right – there's no need to read any other books about Anne Boleyn – mine is the only true one because I am the only person who really understands the past?"

No, clearly she does not.

The relationship between the writer of historical fiction and the reader of it is much more complicated, much more implicated, than this. I'll come back to this later, and try to describe the relationship in detail.

But, if my first example of the innate bad faith of historical fiction didn't convince you, maybe my second will.

How would you feel if you knew that the history teacher teaching your child about the Tudor Period – call them Terry – how would you feel if Terry had read nothing about that period but historical fiction?

You would, I think, feel that Terry wasn't qualified to be a history teacher – because what Terry knew couldn't in any way be described as history. Yet if all Terry's reading material had, in fact, been written in good faith, why would you have any doubts about Terry's competence?

I'd go further – if I found out that my child's history teacher preferred reading historical novels to history books, I would instantly lose a great deal of trust in them. If, on the other hand, they confessed to reading – only the once, on holiday – a single Philippa Gregory novel (just to see what they were like), but with a constant queasy feeling of self-disgust, I would immediately trust them more *as a history teacher*.

So, I think, if you're honest, would you.

And the reason for this? The reason is that I believe most history books are written in good faith – which is to say, they are written in the honest hope of saying something useful and truthful about the past.

If this truth turns out to be less picturesque, dramatic, romantic or readable than the evidence previously suggested, or than the less reliable sources put forward, then the history book will still assert this dull truth. The same can't be said of historical fiction. In fact, it is inevitably drawn to the more speculative areas of the past – hidden love lives, disguised conspiracies.

A history textbook will not establish itself on the territory of pseudo-subjects – such as, to take one example, the secret sexual relationship between Queen Elizabeth the First and the Earl of Essex.

So, how does the contract between the historical fiction writer and the historical fiction reader work? And why am I describing it as being, at both ends, in bad faith?

Here, I'll have to try to define bad faith. As it takes Sartre about thirty dense pages of *Being and Nothingness* to do this, you'll understand that a certain amount of simplification will be required.

Here's part of the definition from the glossary at the back of the book, supplied by the translator. Bad faith is, "A lie to onseself within the unity of a single consciousness. Through bad faith a person seeks to escape the responsible freedom of Being-for-itself. *Bad faith rests on a vacillation between transcendence and facticity which refuses to recognize either one for what it really is or to synthesize them*" (Jean-Paul Sartre, *Being and Nothingness*, translated by Hazel Barnes, 2001: italics mine.)

Now, you'll see that I'm not talking about "the unity of a single consciousness" – I'm talking about a duality of two consciousnesses, writer and reader. But I think, in each case, the second part of the definition holds true.

This is clear even in the term "historical fiction". The first word is the element of facticity, the *what was* of the world; the second element is the transcendence, the *what might have been* of the world. To yoke the two words together is to create an oxymoron. (Historical fiction is neither historical nor fictional.)

Those who would defend historical fiction inevitably start to do as Sartre says, to "vacillate between transcendence and facticity".

Transcendence, in my argument, can be taken to mean anything that begins to rise above the available historical facts. So, when a defender of historical fiction says, "It's all just a bit of a romp – why can't you take it for what it is?" *that's* the transcendence. The romp, the energy of narrative arising out of a supposed historical basis, is a transcendent value.

Similarly, when a defender says, "There are imaginative leaps that the historical novelist can make which the plain historian wouldn't dare, but which may come closer to the truth than facts could ever tell" – *that's* the transcendence.

But the real proof of my argument comes when the defenders of historical fiction switch, or rather vacillate, from transcendence to facticity. At this point, they say something like, "A lot of historical novelists put a great deal of time and effort into making sure that they get the details of their historical period right". And *that's* the facticity. Or they say, "Even if you don't agree historical fiction is a reliable source of information about the past, you'll surely admit that a person who reads *The Other Boleyn Girl* knows more about Anne Boleyn after finishing the novel than they did before starting it". *That's* the facticity.

And I would answer, extremely austerely, by saying that No, I believe that the reader would *know* less about Anne Boleyn for having read the novel. Because they would have entirely corrupted their criteria of *knowing* anything about the past. In starting to read the novel, they would have accepted a woozy melding of fact with fiction – of accurate fripperies of dress and inaccurate motivations of the heart. And so they would have no basis for saying what they did or did not know to be true. What the reader will do is *feel* they know more about the past. They may even feel they know more about *how the past felt*, or *how the past felt itself to be as a passing present*. This kind of knowledge is as bogus as any writer saying, "This is what I think Queen Elizabeth felt she felt about the Earl of Essex".

These two sentences from Sartre's *Being and Nothingness* are, for me, the killer. They precisely anatomize the mental slippages required in order to produce and consume historical fiction.

For the writer, "Bad faith apprehends evidence but it is resigned in advance to not being fulfilled by this evidence, to not being persuaded and transformed into good faith. It makes itself humble and modest; it is not ignorant, it says, that faith is decision and that after each intuition, it much decide and *will what is*" (ibid).

For the reader, "... bad faith in its primitive project and in its coming into the world decides on the exact nature of its requirements. It stands forth in the firm resolution *not to demand too much*, to count itself satisfied when it is barely persuaded, to force itself in decisions to adhere to uncertain truths" (ibid).

To conclude, I'd like to try to state the terms of the contract-in-bad-faith between the writer and the reader of historical fiction. Remember, this isn't a contract that Alex, our naïve reader at the literary festival, would subscribe to. Alex is after the past in good faith. Neither is it a contract that any decent historian would go anywhere near. They, too, are after the past in good faith – even to the extent of spending most of their time questioning and analyzing the amount of bad faith this may involve.

The writer of historical fiction says to the reader: *It wasn't like this, but this is how I'm going to say it was.*

The reader of historical fiction says to the writer: *You say it wasn't like this, but we're going to read it as if it was.*

In other words, they mutually establish the ground upon which they are going to meet – a bracketed ground in which their pleasure will derive entirely from a vacillation between facticity and transcendence, between what may very well have been true and what can be proven to be bogus, between – in other words – the historical and the fictional.

This address was delivered on 27 February 2009 as part of The Irish Pages Debate, "On Historical Fiction," *one of the events in the Belfast Book Festival.*

Toby Litt was born in Bedford in 1968. He read English at Worcester College, Oxford and studied Creative Writing at the University of East Anglia. He is the author of two collections of short stories and eight novels, most recently I Played the Drums in a Band Called OK *(Penguin, 2008) and* Journey into Space *(Penguin, 2009). He lives in London.*

THE NINTH HANDSHAKE OF THOMAS D.

Hugo Hamilton

Like a sightless bird.

Out here on the bog, it must be the same as it ever was. It's the back of the earth that we're walking across, the big brown frame of Achill with the shoulders of Slievemore and Minaun set against the wind. We have left the houses behind. There are no cars out here. No people. No telephone lines. Only the bog and the sky, with the sun already gone down behind Achill Head and the clouds churning up the last pallet of grey, pink and amber. This has always been a place of colour, more for painters and poets. All around us a coat of rust and dark brown, the full range of L'Oréal hair dyes spreading out as far as the eye can see. Everywhere the black gashes left behind by turf-cutters, old scars and new scars. Shoe-polish black, ridges of turf still waiting to be cut. Little piles of sods left to dry, sods that will later be piled up in mounds outside houses like big slices of the famous Viennese chocolate cake, *Sacher Torte*.

Every now and again, we are forced back by the wind, brought to a standstill, walking on the spot until the gust eases off again and allows us to walk another few metres forward. At times we seem only to be miming progress along the stony track. We cannot speak. We cannot hear anything but the constant rush of wind in our ears. Whenever we try to say something, we are censored by the wind pushing the words back into our mouths. For the past three days, the gale has been targeting the house in Dugort, leaning against the walls, elbowing the windows, trying to lift the roof off and sending clouds of smoke down the chimney. "Is that what you call wind", they say over in Dooagh, where the full power of the gale comes straight in off the sea. During the week, a wooden gate went missing down there and they say it must be away up in Donegal by now.

The lights are on in Keel. There is a gauze of soft rain coming down off Slievemore which makes the houses look more like ships at anchor, bobbing up and down in the gathering mist as though they are about to drift away out to the sea, as though they have only been temporarily tied to the shore with ropes. We see the headlights of cars along the road, the bus to Westport floating across the edge of the bog like a giant biscuit tin. We can smell the turf smoke on the wind, and as we join back onto the road, we have to behave like sheep, hugging the grassy verge. At one point, we contemplate jumping across the bridge to avoid an oncoming van, but then we finally make it safely inside the Crossroads Bar, where the fire is blazing.

We are offered sandwiches which have been left over from a wedding breakfast earlier on that day. We had seen the signs along the road, saying *Congratulations Cormac and Tatiana*: a local man has got married to a girl from Romania and the biggest wedding reception of the year is going on over at the Achill Head Hotel. She's lovely, they all say. We eat the sandwiches and toast the couple in their absence.

Michael is sitting in his usual spot, drinking his pint of special, a mixture of Guinness and Smithwicks. He tells us how he used to fish lobster with his father off Keem Strand. He remembers how he and his father went to Scotland to dig potatoes. He knows every inch of Scotland and every inch of England. He lists off the towns and cities, pointing his finger directly into the palm of his hand, as if to show us on a map where the passenger ships docked, how the lorries were waiting to ferry them to the farms. I mind the time, he says, when a woman gave birth on the boat going over. I mind the time, he says, when a family was burned to death in their bothy over in Scotland. He remembers what they got paid, how much a loaf of bread cost, or a pint, or the fare on the boat in old money. He knows the names of cousins, uncles, every man from every family on the island that he met while working there. His uncle brought back the Scottish pipes to start the first pipe band in Achill, something which has now become a strong tradition here, with over eighty young members taking competitions back in Scotland every year. We begin to see how important the details are in Achill. It takes time to draw the exact sequence of a man's life, pointing again and again at the palm of his hand. He tells us where his uncle lived, and it takes time to describe the exact location of a house. There are no numbers here, no street names on the walls. Slowly and precisely, he tells us how to get there, going through all the features of the landscape that might help us to remember, even if we might never go. Here in Achill, there is still time to inherit this mental map, the map of the present as well as the map of the past.

Later on, when Michael is already gone home for the night and the bar begins to fill up, we get talking to two younger men who have their backs turned to the football match on TV. Manchester United is playing Lille, but nobody is really interested, even though there is a man named Fletcher playing, whose mother emigrated to Scotland from Achill.

"Manchester", one of them says. "I spent six months in jail there."

"What for?" we ask.

"Tax evasion."

The men introduce themselves. Jimmy tells us that he can't go back to England for another seven years, because he got caught a second time. But this time, he escaped while on bail and fled back to Ireland, getting on a trawler out of Norfolk and making it all the way round the coast of Scotland to Dun Laoghaire.

"It must have taken you a long time", the other man says. "Sure you might as well have done the six months again."

The men laugh at each other and we no longer know what to believe. Jimmy tells us that he had to swim ashore because he had no passport, that he is a descendent of the travellers, the original people of Ireland. He tells us that there is a river called Gallagher River nearby, named after his ancestors who settled near Dookinella. He and his younger cousin Tom worked on construction sites across Britain, on the nuclear power plants like Sizewell A and Sizewell B.

"Chester, Leicester and Manchester. All change at Crewe, platform two", Jimmy says into his pint.

The barman is pulling fresh pints. Jimmy continues his pub autobiography, saying he worked in America as well, in places like Cleveland, Boston, Manhattan, but that he got deported for stealing lead off the roofs.

"Manhattan?" I ask, trying to sieve the truth from the fiction. "You must have a great head for heights."

"Pay no attention to him", his cousin Thomas tells us.

And then comes the first handshake. They introduce themselves properly this time and the steel hand of Thomas D. confirms all the stories of building sites. He is aged around fifty but his hand is twice that. Every concrete block, every splinter of wood, every icy scaffold, every mistimed hammer blow is etched into this hand like a weathered glove. It's like the grip of a friendly lobster, an iron claw that makes you want to genuflect. But it's also full of warmth, a clasp of true companionship, practiced in bars and function halls with other construction workers from all over the globe. When he finally lets go and picks up his pint glass again, it looks like a thimble in his mighty fingers.

Thomas wants to know where we're from. Not only that but where our parents are from, father and mother, both sides, because without this knowledge he cannot fill in the map of identity.

"Germany", he says. "The best people in the world. They make you work hard, mind you, but they're fair."

By now he's already on his third handshake and my hand is numb with friendship. His older cousin Jimmy has his head bowed on the counter while we hear more accounts of construction sites in Berlin, German girlfriends, German cars, German beer. Of all the places he's worked in, he liked Berlin best and remembers drinking champagne with other Irish workers on a Sunday night in the Oscar Wilde Pub before they got on the train to Leipzig to start work on a Monday morning. Now there is plenty of work back in Ireland and they can stay home in Achill.

"Now it's the British and the Germans and the Polish people coming to work for us, tunnelling, digging, building roads and railways. Isn't that an extraordinary thing?" he says.

To make his point, he taps my upper arm with a big knuckle, as if he's knocking on a door. He tries to explain the phenomenon of Irish success and before we know it, we're into more handshakes, the fourth and fifth crunching grip of the evening to celebrate the meeting of minds.

Then we see a new Irish social invention in practice. The great smoker's exit line. Because of the ban, people who smoke have to leave the bar at certain moments, but the exit is timed with extraordinary skill to coincide with a punch-line, a joke, a philosophical or socio-political comment. Smoking has become a strategic prop. Before Thomas leaves, he takes out a cigarette, thinks deeply, then taps his cigarette on the packet before giving the exit line.

"The Irish will chance anything", he says. "That's the trick."

Before anyone in the bar can reply, he's gone. By the time he's back, it will be too late to contradict him, the conversation will have moved on. In the meantime, Jimmy orders another round of pints, then offers a bunch of dried black dillisk from his back pocket. He chews the dark seaweed and washes it down with Guinness.

"Chester, Leicester and Manchester. All change at Crewe, platform two", he says as though he's only half way through the rosary.

Some younger boys come in to play pool and the bar fills up with aftershave. We hear the barman telling one of them that the Crossroads Bar is in a shadow, that you can only make a call on a mobile phone by going outside and standing at the gable-end wall. By the time Thomas comes back in there are new pints standing on the counter. He's had time to think out there. As he steps back up to the bar, he carries the last puff of smoke inside and exhales a thin cloud of pure nostalgia towards the bottles of spirits behind the bar. He takes an almighty drink from the new pint, vacuums the froth from his upper lip and steps back to knock on my arm again.

"Will I tell you something about the Irish", he says, picking up from where he left off. Thomas tells us how he was working in London during the eighties, living in a place in North London called Wood Green. There were lots of Irish people up there drinking in the same bars together. Among them was a blind Irishman named Jack, or Blind Jack, who had managed to get a soft job in directory enquiries, giving out numbers all day and chatting to his friends. Jack needed no eyes in his head to lift a pint, it had to be said. By the end of the night, in fact, he could see about as much as the rest of the people in the pub with the amount of drink taken. Blind Jack was never unhappy, Thomas tells us. He lived a full life and drank as many pints as any other man in the bar. But on one particular night, he began to lament the fact that he could never in his life drive a car.

"I swear to God", Thomas says, "You could see the tears in his eyes. We consoled him with another pint and a small whiskey on top of that. But nothing could stop him groaning on about how he would never drive a car."

Then somebody asked why on earth he couldn't drive and Blind Jack turned around to say: "because I'm fuckin' blind, you know".

"I'm not joking you", Thomas says. "They started saying that driving was a human right, like freedom of speech, and it was disgraceful to deny a blind man those rights. And before we knew it, somebody handed Blind Jack the keys of his car, an old banger that was outside the pub because you'd be ashamed to park it in front of your own flat. Sure, there was moss growing on all the windows and cobwebs around the mirrors. It was old, yellow Toyota Corolla, and you could see the road through the floor."

Thomas tells us how they left the pub in Wood Green at closing time and Blind Jack got into the driver seat of the car. They explained to him how the gears functioned, where the accelerator and how to manoeuvre the clutch. Blind Jack had his hands on the steering wheel, revving up and imagining long trips across the English landscape, out to the cliffs of Dover, up to Whitby to see where Dracula came ashore.

"Somebody told Blind Jack to look in the mirror", Thomas tells us, and then he claps his hands. "The car suddenly lurched across the road. Smack. Straight into the side of a brand-new Rover."

"Nobody was hurt, do you follow me? I was in the back seat myself and I swear to God, there was a lot of glass. There was only one thing to do. The owner got the idea to say the car was stolen and took the keys out. So we all got out and ran away down the street. We had to hold Blind Jack on either side while we ran full pelt around the corner."

By now, Jimmy has sunk down under the weight of his laughing. Even the barman, who has tried to remain neutral up to now, has begun to chuckle. Thomas is back to shaking hands and I've counted eight by now. Already I can see the cigarette packet coming out and we know there is still a point to be made, a conclusion. He taps the cigarette on the packet and gets ready to make his point.

"We were half a mile away before we realized that Blind Jack had left his white stick behind, in the driving seat."

Then he's off. He waits long enough to listen to the moment of silence left around bar, before turning his back and striding out towards the door.

We are left thinking, imagining the scene for ourselves from that point on. We can only guess what the London policemen thought of this incident and how they might have put it down in their reports. Crashed car. Abandoned. Probably stolen. Blind man's stick found in driver's seat.

They would have puzzled about that one. Maybe they would have laughed and maybe they would have said there was something Irish about this. Or would they have narrowed their investigations down to all the blind Irish people of London.

And what is all this saying about the Irish? That we are driving into the future without any idea where we are going. That the Irish society has taken off like a sightless bird, without knowing where it will be possible to land again.

It seems like a good moment for us to leave, with an unfinished story in our heads. We step outside and see Thomas standing alone with his shoulder to the white wall of the Crossroads Bar, staring out towards Keel. He's thinking about Cormac and Tatiana, they must be dancing by now in the Achill Head. He turns and flicks the butt towards the road. There is a wisp of smoke escaping from his nostrils. He gives us another handshake, the last and final one, his ninth. And this time he will not let go. The ninth handshake of Thomas D. is one that goes on for three or four minutes, maybe even longer, indefinitely. It lasts long enough for me to feel every brick, every plank, every steel rod, the full, raw, cement-bitten biography of his palm. He wants to know why we're leaving so soon. It's a handshake that prevents us from leaving, pulling us back, imploring us not to let too much time go by before we come back to Achill again, a handshake that remains imprinted on my palm long after he's gone back inside and we're back out in the wind again.

The extract above was first published in German as a chapter of Die Redselige Insel *(Luchterhand Verlag, 2007), a travel book in which Hugo Hamilton retraced the Irish travels of Heinrich Boll, a half century after his renowned travelogue* Irisches Tagebuch (Irish Journal).

Hugo Hamilton was born in Dublin in 1953, of Irish-German parentage. He is the author one collection of short stories and six novels, most recently Disguise *(Fourth Estate, 2008). He has also published an acclaimed memoir of his Irish-German childhood,* The Speckled People *(Fourth Estate, 2003), and a sequel,* The Sailor in the Wardrobe *(Fourth Estate, 2006). He lives in Dublin.*

IN OTHER WORDS: IN THE SPANISH

Seamus Heaney & Pura López Colomé

HEANEY'S SONNETS IN SPANISH

Every language is part of Language, which is larger than any single language. Every individual literary work is part of Literature, which is larger than the literature of any single language ... Translation is the circulatory system of the world's literatures. Susan Sontag

The following 10 sonnets by Seamus Heaney are translated by one of México's foremost poets, Pura López Colomé. These translations, with facing originals, first appeared in *Sonetos* (DGE Equilibrista, Mexico City, 2008), which brings together all 61 of Heaney's sonnets in her magisterial versions. The book was launched in Dublin on 6 April 2009, but otherwise has not appeared, and is unavailable, in the Anglophone world. Clearly, in several senses, *Sonetos* is a signal and extraordinary publishing endeavour.

There is, firstly, the aforementioned distinction of the translations themselves: hard-won fruit born of a long-distance labour of love. Some 15 of the translations in *Sonetos* were done in the course of her previous translation of four Heaney collections, whilst the rest were completed for this volume. Each of the 61 sonnets is given two workings, one in poetic prose, and one in poetry *tout court*. The quite unique double result is a burnished mirroring of the actual linguistic process recognized by all translators of poetry, to some extent: the deconstruction of the original into unlineated and molten "literals", or "cribs", out of which emerges the rendered poem in a new tongue. To the high distinction of the actual translation, then, she adds something of the artisan fascination of how it evolves, how it is done, in the most adept hands.

If *Sonetos* is, indubitably, a long-term cultural gift not only to México, but to the whole of the Hispanic world in the Americas and Spain, it is also – obliquely – one to the English-speaking world.

In the case of *Shakespeare's Sonnets*, which cannot but spring to mind in this context, the dating of the work is opaque. In Heaney's case, his virtuosity in the form spans virtually his entire career, from his first collected sonnet in *Door into the Dark* ("The Forge") to the last in *District and Circle* ("Polish Sleepers"), with every intervening collection containing two or more examples, a number of which (such as "The Gaeltacht") are innovative recensions of this ancient template. Such are the multifarious supplenesses and subtleties and surprises in his handling of the form that the English-language reader begins wonder why no solo edition of Heaney's *Sonnets* has ever appeared in the Anglophone world; and thence to appreciate that this sudden inevitability, as it would seem, whenever it occurs, was nonetheless done first bilingually in México by *Sonetos*. To have, and to read, all of Heaney's sonnets between two covers – those of *Sonetos* – is, then, to glimpse his poetic genius in both perfect microcosm, and undimmed, unsurpassed, undaunted full-flight ... all the while beside its burnished Spanish *abrazo*. *The Editor*

from GLANMORE SONNETS *(I, II, X)*

for Ann Saddlemyer
"our heartiest welcomer"

I

Vowels ploughed into other: opened ground.
The mildest February for twenty years
Is mist bands over furrows, a deep no sound
Vulnerable to distant gargling tractors.
Our road is steaming, the turned-up acres breathe.
Now the good life could be to cross a field
And art a paradigm of earth new from the lathe
Of ploughs. My lea is deeply tilled.
Old plough-socks gorge the subsoil of each sense
And I am quickened with a redolence
Of farmland as a dark unblown rose.
Wait then... Breasting the mist, in sowers' aprons,
My ghosts come striding into their spring stations.
The dream grain whirls like freakish Easter snows.

SONETOS DE GLANMORE

Para Ann Saddlemyer
"por su calurosa bienvenida"

I

Las vocales araron unas en otras: terreno abierto. El febrero más benigno de los últimos veinte años es tiras de bruma sobre un profundo sinsonido, vulnerable a las lejanas gárgaras de los tractores. Nuestro camino vaporiza, los surcos revueltos respiran. Ahora, la buena vida podría ser cruzar un campo, y el arte un paradigma de la tierra nueva desde el torno de los arados. Mi dehesa labrada a fondo. Viejas rejas de arado engullen el subsuelo de cada sentido: me anima la fragancia de los campos de cultivo, como una rosa oscura sin abrir. Espera entonces ... Abriéndose paso entre la bruma, con mandil de sembrador, mis fantasmas llegan a zancadas hasta su agrimensura. La semilla del sueño gira, como las caprichosas nieves pascuales.

Vocales: surco arado y abierto.
En veinte años, el más leve febrero.
Bruma en tiras, un sinsonido hondo,
vulnerable a los tractores remotos.

Camino: inhala el terreno revuelto.
Buena vida, cruzar a campo abierto;
y el arte un paradigma, tierra, torno,
arar. Mi campo labrado a fondo.

El viejo arado el subsuelo degusta
del sentido: el aroma regional,
cultivo, como rosas sin rosal.

Espera ... Se abren paso entre la bruma:
agrimensura, tan primaveral.
Grano del sueño entre nieve pascual.

II

Sensings, mountings from the hiding places,
Words entering almost the sense of touch,
Ferreting themselves out of their dark hutch–
"These things are not secrets but mysteries",
Oisin Kelly told me years ago
In Belfast, hankering after stone
That connived with the chisel, as if the grain
Remembered what the mallet tapped to know.
Then I landed in the hedge-school of Glanmore
And from the backs of ditches hoped to raise
A voice caught back off slug-horn and slow chanter
That might continue, hold, dispel, appease:
Vowels ploughed into other, opened ground,
Each verse returning like the plough turned round.

II

Sentires, remontares desde los escondites, palabras que casi penetran el sentido del tacto, husmeando desde su oscura madriguera. "Estas cosas no son secretos sino misterios", me dijo Oisin Kelly hace años en Belfast, ansiando la piedra en connivencia con el cincel, como si el grano recordara lo que el mazo golpeteaba por saber. Aterricé entonces en la escuela rural de Glanmore, y desde el fondo de las zanjas esperaba alzar una voz atrapada entre corno y lento canto, que pudiera continuar, detenerse, desvanecerse, apaciguarse: vocales aradas en un terreno distinto, abierto, cada verso de regreso, como el revés de un arado.

Sentires, remontares encubiertos;
husmeando allá en su oscura madriguera,
palabras en el sentido del tacto.
Como Oisin Kelly me dijo hace años:

"Todo esto es un misterio, no un secreto",
en Belfast, ansiando cincel, piedra
en connivencia, como si el grano
recordara lo que deseaba el mazo.

Llego a la escuela rural de Glanmore
y desde el fondo de zanjas espero;
una voz entre corno y canto lento

se desvanecería sin temor.
Vocales: surco arado y abierto,
cual revés de un arado cada verso.

X

I dreamt we slept in a moss in Donegal
On turf banks under blankets, with our faces
Exposed all night in a wetting drizzle,
Pallid as the dripping sapling birches.
Lorenzo and Jessica in a cold climate.
Diarmuid and Grainne waiting to be found.
Darkly asperged and censed, we were laid out
Like breathing effigies on a raised ground.
And in that dream I dreamt – how like you this? –
Our first night years ago in that hotel
When you came with your deliberate kiss
To raise us towards the lovely and painful
Covenants of flesh; our separateness;
The respite in our dewy dreaming faces.

X

Soñé que dormíamos sobre musgo en Donegal, en terraplenes de turba, cobijados, a la intemperie, de cara a una llovizna intensa toda la noche, pálidos como los jóvenes, goteantes abedules. Lorenzo y Jessica en un clima frío. Diarmuid y Grainne esperando a sus captores. Oscuramente empapados e incensados, yacíamos cual efigies respirando sobre terreno alzado. Y en ese sueño -¿qué te parece?- vi nuestra primera noche hace años en aquel hotel, cuando llegaste con tu beso intencional a elevarnos a los hermosos y dolorosos pactos de la carne. Nuestro cada quien por su lado, el sosiego en nuestros rostros soñadores, bañados de rocío.

Dormidos nos soñé a la intemperie:
Donegal, sobre musgo y terraplenes,
siempre de cara a una llovizna intensa,
pálidos abedules que gotean.

Lorenzo y Jessica en clima inclemente.
Diarmuid y Grainne. Muy oscuramente
mojados e incensados, a la espera,
efigies respirando en tierra abierta.

¿Cómo ves?, en el sueño vi de pronto
nuestra primera noche de hotel, años
ha, y tu beso que llegó a elevarnos

al pacto de la carne, doloroso.
Y nuestros seres, los dos por su lado,
jóvenes rostros, rocío perlado.

from CLEARANCES *(III,V)*

In memoriam M.K.H., 1911-1984

III

When all the others were away at Mass
I was all hers as we peeled potatoes.
They broke the silence, let fall one by one
Like solder weeping off the soldering iron:
Cold comforts set between us, things to share
Gleaming in a bucket of clean water.
And again let fall. Little pleasant splashes
From each other's work would bring us to our senses.

So while the parish priest at her bedside
Went hammer and tongs at the prayers for the dying
And some were responding and some crying
I remembered her head bent towards my head,
Her breath in mine, our fluent dipping knives–
Never closer the whole rest of our lives.

ESPACIOS LIBRES

In memoriam M.K.H., 1911-1984

III

Cuando todos los demás se iban a misa, yo era todo suyo mientras pelábamos papas. Rompían el silencio al ir cayendo una por una, como briznas de soldadura escurriendo del cautín: frías comodidades dispuestas entre nosotros, cosas que compratir, cintilando en una cubeta de agua limpia. Y, de nuevo, la caída. Los placenteros chapaleos de la labor de cada quien nos hacían volver a los cabales. Así que mientras el párroco, junto a su cama, seguía dale que dale con las fúnebres plegarias, y había quien respondía y quien lloraba, yo recordaba su cabeza inclinada frente a la mía, su aliento en el mío, cómo se hundían nuestros cuchillos suavemente, nunca más cerca uno del otro por el resto de nuestras vidas.

En tanto los demás iban a misa,
yo era todo suyo al pelar papas.
Una por una el sielncio quebraban,
cautín en chorros, soldadura en briznas:

brillando en la cubeta de agua limpia,
algo que compartir –alivio entre ambas
manos- seguía cayendo. Salpicadas
notas con las que alzábamos la vista.

Mientras el párroco, junto a su cama,
exequia tras exequia ahí rezaba
y otros entre responsos le lloraban,

yo recordaba su frente en la mía,
nuestros eran el vaho y las cuchillas,
nunca más cerca en todas nuestras vidas.

V

The cool that came off sheets just off the line
Made me think the damp must still be in them
But when I took my corners of the linen
And pulled against her, first straight down the hem
And then diagonally, then flapped and shook
The fabric like a sail in a cross-wind,
They made a dried-out undulating thwack.
So we'd stretch and fold and end up hand to hand
For a split second as if nothing had happened
For nothing had that had not always happened
Beforehand, day by day, just touch and go,
Coming close again by holding back
In moves where I was X and she was O
Inscribed in sheets she'd sewn from ripped-out flour sacks.

V

La frescura que provenía de las sábanas recién bajadas del tendedero me hacía pensar en la humedad aún en ellas; pero cuando tomaba las esquinas que me tocaba doblar, y jalaba en sentido contrario a ella, enderezando primero el dobladillo y luego en diagonal, para después sacudir y agitar la tela como una vela de barco ante vientos cruzados, su respuesta era un golpe sonoro, seco y ondulante. Así estirábamos y doblábamos y juntábamos los cabos, mano contra mano durante una fracción de segundo como si nada hubiera pasado, pues nada había pasado que no hubiera pasado siempre con anterioridad, día tras día, pendiendo de un hilo, de nuevo logrando la cercanía al detenernos en pasos donde a mí me tocaba la *x* y a ella la *o*, letras inscritas en sábanas que había cosido a partir de costales de harina rasgados.

Las frescas sábanas del tendedero
remitían a su humedad, acaso;
pero al tomar la esquina de mi lado,
justo al jalar al contrario, primero

en diagonal ajustando y luego
con la tela cual vela de un barco
ante vientos cruzados, su ondulado
golpe se oía. Doblar cabos sueltos

como si nada hubiera pasado:
pues todo parecía haber pasado,
sólo de un hilo al pender, cercanía,

día tras día hubiera logrado,
x en mí, en ella *o*, los trazos,
sábanas sobre costales de harina.

IN MEMORIAM: ROBERT FITZGERALD

The socket of each axehead like the squared
Doorway to a megalithic tomb
With its slabbed passage that keeps opening forward
To face another corbelled stone-faced door
That opens on a third. There is no last door,
Just threshold stone, stone jambs, stone crossbeam
Repeating *enter, enter, enter*.
Lintel and upright fly past in the dark.

After the bowstring sang a swallow's note,
The arrow whose migration is its mark
Leaves a whispered breath in every socket.
The great test over, while the gut's still humming,
This time it travels out of all knowing
Perfectly aimed towards the vacant centre.

IN MEMORIAM ROBERT FITZGERALD

La órbita de toda cabeza de hacha es el vano cuadrado de la entrada a una tumba megalítica, con su túnel de losas abriéndose hacia adelante, de cara a otra puerta voladiza de piedra, que da a una tercera. No hay última puerta, sólo piedra de umbral, quicial de piedra, viga de piedra, que repiten *entra, entra, entra*. Dintel y montante pasan volando en la oscuridad. La cuerda del arco canta la nota de una golondrina y, después, la flecha cuya migración marca su huella deja un susurrado aliento en toda órbita. Una vez pasada la gran prueba, mientras la cuerda de tripa tararea, viaja lejos de todo lo consabido, perfectamente dirigida hacia el centro vacío.

Órbita y testa del hacha es el vano
de esta tumba dolménica, cuadrado
túnel de losas abriéndose al claro
hacia otra puerta, como plano

a la tercera. No hay última puerta,
sí hay umbral, quicial, viga de piedra
repitiendo *entra, entra, entra*.
Quicio y dintel, oscura noche alerta.

Nota de golondrina, arco en cuerda;
migración de la flecha marca un hito,
deja un aliento de órbita en sigilo.

Y mientras esa cuerda tararea,
viaja lejos de todo lo sabido,
bien dirigida hacia el centro vacío.

from GLANMORE REVISITED *(5,6)*

5. LUSTRAL SONNET

Breaking and entering: from early on,
Words that thrilled me far more than they scared me –
And still did, when I came into my own
Masquerade as a man of property.
Even then, my first impulse was never
To double-bar a door or lock a gate;
And fitted blinds and curtains drawn over
Seemed far too self-protective and uptight.

But I scared myself when I re-entered here,
My own first breaker-in, with an instruction
To saw up the old bed-frame, since the stair
Was much too narrow for it. A bad action,
So Greek with consequence, so dangerous,
Only pure words and deeds secure the house.

REGRESO A GLANMORE

5. LUSTRAL

Romper y rasgar: desde muy joven, las palabras, más que asustarme, me fascinaban... y seguían haciéndolo cuando me enfrenté a mi propia mascarada como propietario. Incluso entonces, mi primer impulso no fue nunca poner doble tranca o candado a una reja; y las persianas cerradas o las cortinas corridas me parecían demasiado protectoras y autocontenidas. Pero sí que me asusté cuando volví a entrar aquí, mi propio abrirme paso, con instrucciones de rebajar un viejo armazón de cama, ya que la escalera era demasiado angosta. Mala acción, tan griega en cuanto a sus consecuencias, tan peligrosa: sólo palabras y obras puras afianzan la casa.

Rompe y rasga: tan joven, las palabras
más que asustarme, sí que me encantaban;
rasgar el velo fue ahí el sumario
de mi mascarada de propietario.

Pero nunca el primer impulso a puerta
fue poner tranca, o candado en la reja;
justas persianas, cortinas corridas
autocontenidas me parecían.

Mas ahí me asusté al rasgar el velo,
mi primer rompe y entra, la advertencia:
el armazón de la cama con sierra

rebajé: no cabía en la escalera.
Mala acción, riesgo, griega consecuencia:
verbo, obra pura: casa sin desvelo.

6. BEDSIDE READING

The whole place airier. Big summer trees
Stirring at eye level when we waken
And little shoots of ivy creeping in
Unless they've been trained out – like memories
You've trained so long now they can show their face
And keep their distance. White-mouthed depression
Swims out from its shadow like a dolphin
With wet, unreadable, unfurtive eyes.

I swim in Homer. In Book Twenty-three.
At last Odysseus and Penelope
Waken together. One bedpost of the bed
Is the living trunk of an old olive tree
And is their secret. As ours could have been ivy,
Evergreen, atremble and unsaid.

6. LIBRO DE CABECERA

Todo mucho más ventilado. Enormes árboles veraniegos agitándose a la altura de la vista al despertar, y pequeños brotes de hiedra arrastrándose, a menos que se les pusieran guías de salida, como recuerdos tan impuestos a las guías que ya pueden mostrar su rostro y mantener su distancia. La depresión espumea por la boca, escapa de su sombra nadando como un delfín de ojos húmedos, ilegibles, sin disimulo. Yo nado en Homero. En el Libro Veintitrés. Por fin Odiseo y Penélope despiertan juntos. Un poste de la cama es el tronco vivo de un viejo olivo, y también su secreto. Como el nuestro podía haber sido la hiedra, siempreviva temblorosa e inefable.

Viento, árboles que empiezan a temblar
a la altura de la vista al despertar;
invaden brotes de hiedra rastreros
si les faltan guías afuera, recuerdos

tan sometidos a guías que apenas
se asoman. La depresión espumea,
sale nadando de su sombra, delfín
de ojos incautos, ilegibles en fin.

Libro Veintitrés: yo nado en Homero.
Por fin despiertan juntos Odiseo
y Penélope. Un poste de su lecho,

un tronco fresco de un olivo viejo:
su secreto. Y el nuestro ser podría
la trémula, inefable siempreviva.

THE WALK

Glamoured the road, the day, and him and her
And everywhere they took me. When we stepped out
Cobbles were riverbed, the Sunday air
A high stream-roof that moved in silence over
Rhododendrons in full bloom, foxgloves
And hemlock, robin-run-the-hedge, the hedge
With its deckled ivy and thick shadows –
Until the riverbed itself appeared,
Gravelly, shallowly, summery with pools,
And made a world rim that was not for crossing.
Love brought me that far by the hand, without
The slightest doubt or irony, dry-eyed
And knowledgeable, contrary as be damned;
Then just kept standing there, not letting go.

EL SENDERO

Galanura en el camino, el día, él y ella, y donde sea que me llevaran. Poner pie fuera significaba empedrados que eran lecho de río, aire dominguero, techo del arroyo que fluía en silencio sobre rododendros en flor, dedaleras y cicuta acuática, setos vivos, el seto con sus hierbas barbudas y sombras gruesas... Hasta que el lecho mismo del río parecía de grava, poco profundo, veraniego, con sus pozas, sus márgenes del mundo que impedían el cruce. De la mano me llevó el amor tan lejos, sin la menor duda o ironía, los ojos secos, ávidos de sabiduría, llevando la contraria hasta que ya. Y en adelante me mantuvo en pie, sin soltar nunca.

Es galanura el camino, él y ella
y adonde fuéramos. Pie fuera, lecho
de río, empedrados que eso eran,
dominguero aire, arroyo muy quieto,

los rododendros en flor, dedaleras,
cicuta acuática, los vivos setos,
hierbas barbudas con sombras muy gruesas ...
Hasta que iba emergiendo el mismo lecho

de grava y veraniego, no profundo:
sus pozas eran márgenes del mundo.
De mano del amor llegué tan lejos,

sin duda o ironía, ojos secos,
llevando la contraria, ávidos, punto.
Desde ahí en pie sin soltar me sostuvo.

THE GAELTACHT

I wish, *mon vieux*, that you and Barlo and I
Were back in Rosguill, on the Atlantic Drive,
And that it was again nineteen-sixty
And Barlo was alive

And Paddy Joe and Chips Rafferty and Dicky
Were there talking Irish, for I believe
In that case Aoibheann Marren and Margaret Conway
And M. and M. and Deirdre Morton and Niamh

Would be there as well. And it would be great too
If we could see ourselves, if the people we are now
Could hear what we were saying, and if this sonnet

In imitation of Dante's, where he's set free
In a boat with Lapo and Guido, with their girlfriends in it,
Could be the wildtrack of our gabble above the sea.

EL *GAELTACHT*

Cómo me gustaría, *viejo*, que tú y Barlo y yo volviéramos a Rosguill, en la costa del Atlántico, y que fuera de nuevo mil novecientos sesenta, y Barlo estuviera vivo, y Paddy Joe, Chips Rafferty y Dicky estuvieran ahí hablando en irlandés, pues de ser así, creo, estarían ahí también Aoibheann Marren, Margaret Conway, M., M., Dierdre Morton y Niamh. Y sería fabuloso también que pudiéramos vernos a nosotros mismos, que los que somos hoy pudieran escuchar lo que estábamos diciendo, y que este soneto en imitación al de Dante, donde se le pone en libertad en un barco junto con Lapo y Guido, con todo y sus novias, fuera tras las salvajes huellas de nuestro cotorreo sobre el mar.

Me gustaría ir contigo y Barlo,
mi viejo, a Rosguill, en el Atlántico,
de nuevo en años sesenta y tánticos,
y Barlo ahí mismo, vivito y coleando,

con Paddy y Chips Rafferty y Dicky hablando
irlandés, pues de ser así, sin pánico,
se encontrarían, de modo epifánico,
Aoibheann, Margaret, M y M al lado,

Dierdre Morton y Niamh. Qué fabuloso
voltear atrás, que los que hoy somos
aquello oyeran, y este soneto

que pretende seguirle a Dante el modo,
con Lapo y Guido y sus novias a bordo,
al mar se hiciera tras el cotorreo.

TRANSLATOR'S NOTE

Pura López Colomé

A burnished, reflecting surface: a reverberation.

It is in this sense that I have undertaken the honorable task of translating Mr Seamus Heaney's work. As one of his tutelary spirits, William Shakespeare, expressed it, founder and dweller of the English language kingdom in which our author belongs, true poets wish to give "that airy nothing/a local habitation and a name". With his regional English word, his *locus amoenus*, his Irish English and his English Irish, Heaney has given back to me the confidence I thought I'd lost in my own *locus amoenus*: my Mexican Spanish or Spanish Mexican tongue.

Ever since I put on paper the first fistful of words which I dared to name a poem, I understood, "without/The slightest doubt or irony, dry-eyed/And knowledgeable, contrary as be damned" (*The Spirit Level*, "The Walk"), that this linguistic territory was really mine, and that I could not feel anything, conceive of anything, use my five senses in any place that would not be there.

I believe more in the tongue than in language, that is, more in Spanish or English as Almighty God, than in poetry itself, which in order to be uttered needs the sonority of a word like *euphoria*, with its five unrepeated vowels; needs the glittering semantic plurality of a word like *unfathomable*. Loving their tongue, "the bastion of sensation", poets must obey the dictum: "Do not waver/Into language. Do not waver in it" (*Seeing Things*, "Clearances", II).

"The fifth attempt cannot fail", according to a popular saying in Mexico. *Sonnets* is the fifth book by Heaney I have tried to render into my mother tongue, after *Station Island*, *Seeing Things*, *The Spirit Level*, and *The Light of the Leaves*. I say this not with the slightest arrogance, but with pride, because whether it contain flaws or finds, linguistic failings or strengths – this already a sublime pretension – readers will see them in full color, complete with smell, taste, sound and touch, sincerely projected as a simple act of worship.

We have cherished this project for many years, and I speak in plural to include the author of the images that accompany the poems [Alberto Darszon: see *Portfolio* on the facing page]. He is not only the love of my life, but an unprofessed artist who thinks of himself as a disciplined student of nature, a scientist who sees himself with the utmost objectivity. It is with this same objectivity that tonight I'd like to salute the subjectivity of his

Continued after Portfolio

PORTFOLIO

Alberto Darszon

Harmony of the Ineffable

Alberto Darszon was born in México, D.F., in 1950. He received his undergraduate degree in Organic Chemistry from the Universidad Iberoamericana in 1972. He undertook a PhD in Biochemistry at the Instituto Politécnico Nacional in Mexico City (working with rhodopsin, the membrane protein that allows us to see), followed by postdoctoral training at the University of California in San Diego. He is currently the Head of the Department of Developmental Genetics and Physiology, Universidad Nacional Autónoma de México, Cuernavaca, where the main subject of his research is sperm physiology, with a particular focus on fertilization. For the past 40 years, he has also had major interest in photography, occasionally publishing his work in magazines and participating in exhibitions. Some of the fifteen untitled photographs in these pages were first published as an aesthetic collaboration in Sonetos, *a book bringing together all Seamus Heaney's sonnets, translated into Spanish by Pura López Colomé, his wife* *(see pp. 123-146)*

Of his work, Luis Roberto Vera has written: "Isn't it strange that he only exceptionally records his everyday surroundings? It is because his necessity for order, discipline, reflection, and affection is solved in a day-by-day basis. This is why his photographs are the pages of a traveler's diary, the notches of an itinerary: the disperse, fragmentary and ephemeral being portrayed in them is our own condition, a way of encapsulating a privileged portion of the contemplated space, mere samples for a future or an immediate examination, like those transported in a test tube, being at the same time the channel, the means as well as the message through which the predisposition to a permanent and constant insight is expressed, shaped and rebuilt. The world seems to have emerged after catastrophe. There is an absence of human beings, except for their prints, their marks: this is the harmony of an ineffable scar."

The following photographs are all untouched, unaltered and untitled images of "the real world".

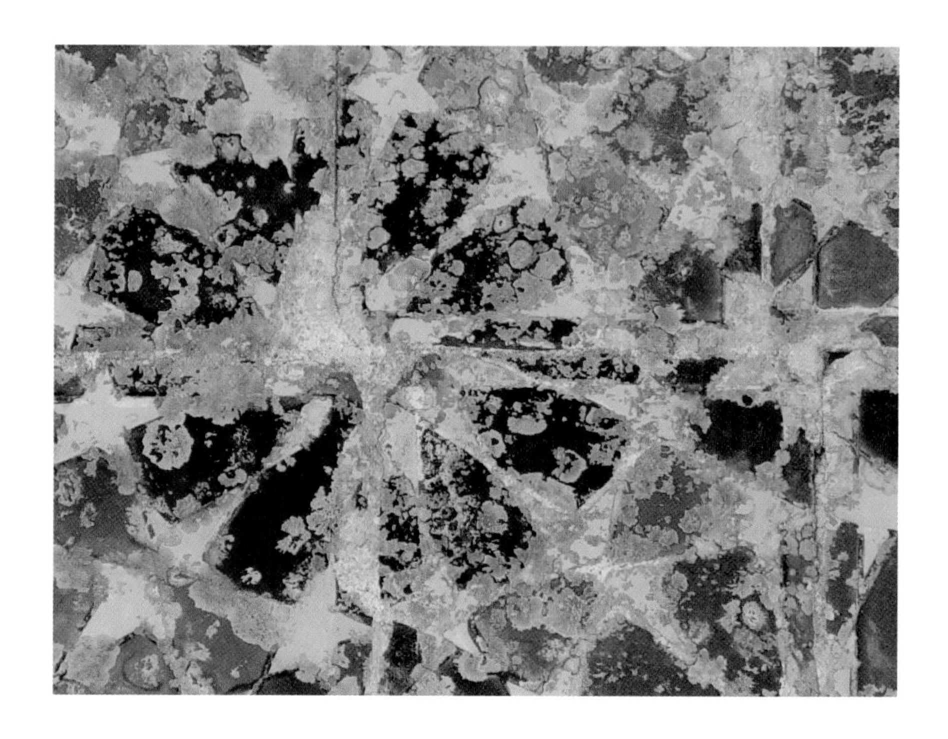

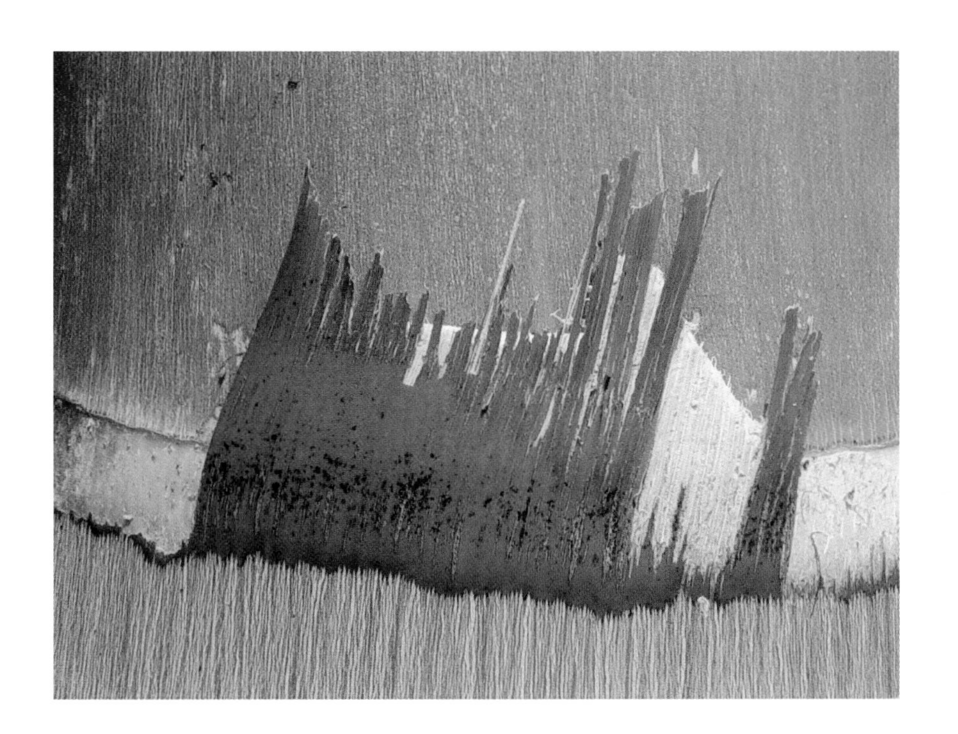

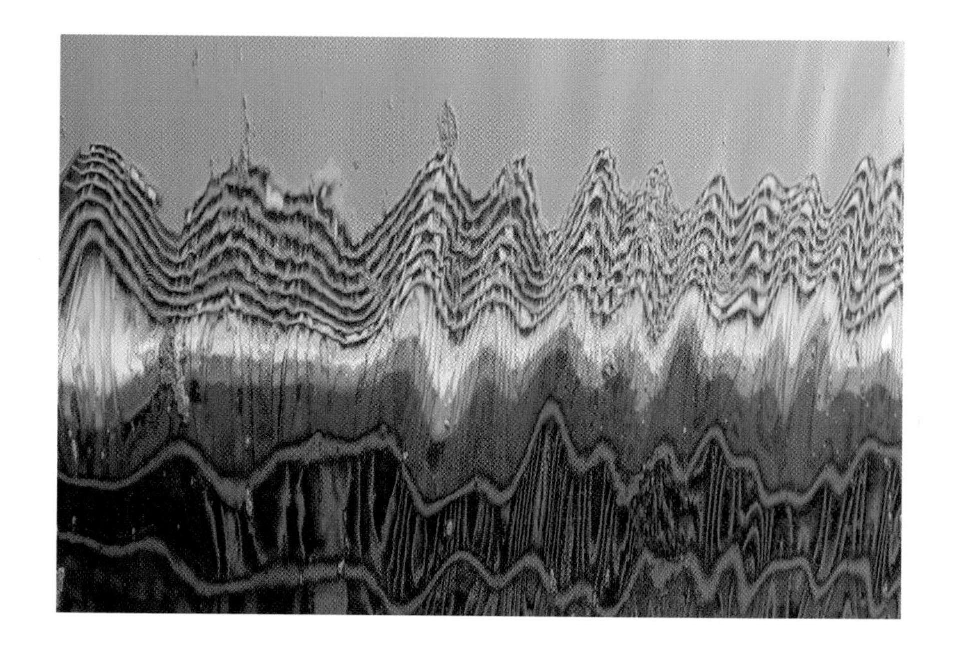

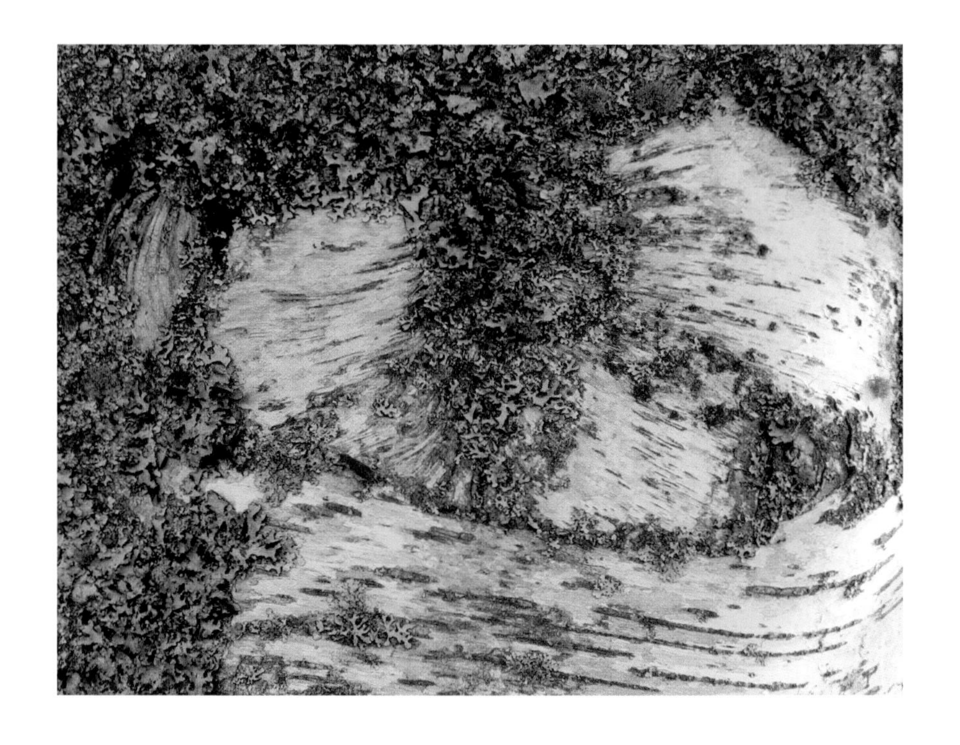

PORTFOLIO

is generously supported by Nicholson & Bass Ltd, Belfast.

photographic art. The artist Barrie Cooke has called my attention to the fact that all great abstract art is also figurative: parallel to this, I would say that all subjectivity can result in objectivity.

In his Nobel Lecture, Seamus Heaney insists upon the necessary union of form and content within the poem: "Poetic form is both the ship and the anchor. It is at once a buoyancy and a holding, allowing for the simultaneous gratification of whatever is centrifugal and centripetal in mind and body. [...] The form of the poem, in other words, is crucial to poetry's power to [...] persuade that vulnerable part of our consciousness of its rightness in spite of the evidence of wrongness all around it" (*Crediting Poetry*, 1995). Preserving both form and content as inseparable parts of this expressive journey, I have launched with full sail a ship that is guided by my own compass, perhaps too bold: magnetic needle of the universe carried by the winds of my mother tongue. Not those that bear the sounds of the European North, but the slightly sibilant sounds of the Latin American South. Thus do the gods Boreas and Auster come together, bilingually, in one creative breath for a moment in time: now.

AUTHOR'S NOTE

Seamus Heaney

Pura López Colomé is a woman of style and stamina, a poet of imaginative sweep and staying power, a brilliant creature, as Yeats might have called her. Distinguished and honoured for her original poetry in the Spanish language, awarded Mexico's highest literary honour a couple of years ago – she is equally distinguished as a translator and I have benefited to the point of being blessed by having her as the one who cared for my work and carried it over to a Mexican audience. Ever since she took it into her head some years ago to translate *Station Island*, she has worked at the task with all the intensity of her distinguished scientist husband at his microscope. Once Pura focuses and fixes on a purpose or a poem, she becomes a finder and a keeper. She fires up, flares, and follows through. Her literary intelligence is swift and subtle, her ear full of echoes from poetry in many languages, but particularly sensitive to the literary acoustic of English. She is erudite and intuitive, she is Keats's chameleon poet, full of negative capability, ready as a translator to take on the identity of other poets. I am lucky to have come to her attention and held it this far.

The preceding 10 sonnets in English are published courtesy of the author and Faber & Faber.

One of Mexico's most distinguished poets and translators, Pura López Colomé was born in Mexico City in 1952, but also spent part of her childhood and youth in Mérida, capital of the state of Yucatan. When she was 12, following her mother's death, she was sent to a Catholic boarding school run by the Benedictine Sisters, in South Dakota. Of this American period, she has written: "The Sister who taught English was Irish: I owe her my early enthusiasm and later devotion to poetry in general, as well as to Irish poetry in particular. It was there I wrote my first poems, and translated, perhaps a bit too boldly, some poetry by W.B. Yeats and Patrick Kavanagh." On her return to Mexico after high-school graduation, she took a degree in Spanish and Latin American Literature at the Universidad Nacional Autónoma de México, subsequently abandoning postgraduate studies for a full-time devotion to poetry, critical essays and translation. She is the author of nine books of poems, most recently Santo y seña *(*Watchword*, 2008), and* Reliquia *(*Relic*, 2009), and selections of her poetry have been translated into English by the American poet Forrest Gander (*No Shelter*, Graywolf Press, 2002) and the Irish poet Lorna Shaughnessy (*Mother Tongue*, Salmon, 2007).*

BROKEN NEWS

Belinda McKeon

Its own way of happening.

Chances are you can guess which line of poetry I'm going to begin with today. This is, after all, a talk about poetry and the world, poetry and actuality. About the truth of poetry and the reality of what happens.

> *Poetry makes nothing happen.*

So Auden said. So Auden has been quoted, over and over again, in endless attempted underminings of the power, and the place, and the point – if there could be such a thing – of poetry. But of course, that's not all Auden said about poetry and about what happens. Not by half.

I've long loved that line, from Auden's elegy for W.B. Yeats. It has long read, for me, as being so ruthless, so brittle, so blunt, in its dismissal of all the desperate hopes and yearnings it seems possible, yet somehow foolhardy, to invest in poetry. It has seemed so sweeping in its refutation of everything we might hope a poem can be or a poem can do.

But that line alone is not Auden. That line alone is not poetry. That line alone is the province, rather, of news, of a newsroom, I mean – of a sound byte, of a headline, of the search for a phrase to fit in the right number of column inches, to sum up the right handful of raced-through notions and squeezed-in voices, to catch the eye and lure the reader in. And well the words can be imagined as a headline, or as part of one:

> *Poetry Makes Nothing Happen, Obama Tells Congress.*
> *Poetry Makes Nothing Happen, Poll Reveals.*
> *Poetry Makes Nothing Happen: Massive Funding Cuts Proposed.*

The truth is, I barely know how to read this line, how to say it aloud. I can only chance it. Where does the emphasis go? Which word bears all the burden? *Poetry* makes nothing happen. Poetry *makes* nothing happen. Poetry makes *nothing* happen. Poetry makes nothing *happen*.

Certainly, the Cliff Notes are out there, but they won't help us with this uncertainty. They won't clear up this mystery – and thank goodness for that.

I'm sure I'm not alone in wanting to wonder, always, about this line, in wanting to swim to one end of its suggestion and find myself tugged immediately into another stream. And anyway, the stream goes on, and the line goes on, as Auden mourns for his master, disappeared in the dead of winter:

> ... Mad Ireland hurt you into poetry.
> Now Ireland has her madness and her weather still,
> For poetry makes nothing happen: it survives
> In the valley of its making where executives
> Would never want to tamper, flows on south
> From ranches of isolation and the busy griefs,
> Raw towns that we believe and die in; it survives,
> A way of happening, a mouth.

Now, granted, there is desolation in this poem. There is bleakness, and not just because Yeats is gone. This poem was written following Yeats's death in 1939 – written, that is, on the threshold of the Second World War, a threshold on which, as Auden goes on, "All the dogs of Europe bark/And the living nations wait/Each sequestered in its hate". But still, Auden is not saying, in this elegy, that poetry is somehow useless, faced with those dogs, sequestered in that hatred. Auden is not giving us a release, an excuse. He is not providing us with a defeatist turning from the task of the writer, or that of the reader. Poetry is not *behind* what happens, he is saying; poetry will not be the *reason* for what happens; poetry is, rather, the *means* by which something happens. Poetry is the means by which a happening thing reaches us as a thing more lasting, more vital; as a thing whole, and full, and graspable by each one of us in a different way.

So then, the happening thing, if poetry is understood in this sense, will not be a war or a death or a hurt inflicted by a mad nation. What happens will not be understandable if we insist on seeing it as an event, as a fact or a rumour, as a story we might read about in the news. What happens, I am suggesting, in the "happening" that is poetry, is a way, a possibility, of making sense of such things. Of making them mean something – through language, through rhythm, through metre, through metaphor, through line. Poetry, Auden is telling us, does not make things arise. It makes things *ours*. It does not cause things to come to pass. It causes them to come to light, and to come to meaning. It is broken news, broken out of headlines and broken into fuller being.

Those final months of the 1930s claimed another figure in whom it was a tragedy to see, as Auden wrote of Yeats, the squares of his mind emptied, the current of his feeling failed: the German thinker Edmund Husserl, the founder of the philosophical school known as phenomenology.

Now, why drop the phenomenology bomb in a lecture about poetry and actuality? Because phenomenology is, I think, the stuff of which Auden's vision of poetry is comprised. This formulation – my formulation – is lazy, clouded by colloquialism and imprecision; it would stand up neither for Auden nor for Husserl. But phenomenology gives us the key, I believe, to understanding Auden's complex, provocative vision of how things are comprised, how things happen in and through poetry. And phenomenology, Husserl's phenomenology, which is fundamentally the study of how we have in our experience those things we experience, gives us what I think is one of the most penetrating and beautiful formulations by which to understand what a poem can do, as against what a sound byte or a headline or a news story can do. By which, that is, to understand the particular power of poetry, by which to understand how and why poetry, when it comes to what happens, is not a why or a wherefore, but a how, and a way.

That phenomenological formulation is that of the difference between what Husserl called an empty and a full intention of an object. What kind of object, firstly? Anything, from a table, to a feeling, to a sound. Or a war, or a death, or the damage done by Mad Ireland, or Mad Germany, for that matter. An object, that is, as any of the many experiences involved in being human. And what is it, within the terms of phenomenology, to intend an object, whether in an empty or a full way? Phenomenology's recruitment of the term "intention" has nothing to do with the usual sense of meaning or resolving to do something, but delves, rather, into the Latin roots of the word *intendere* – a stretching out, a straining or extending towards. And so for me to intend an object is for my consciousness to stretch out towards that object, for my consciousness, at that moment, to be *about* that object.

Sometimes that aboutness is full. Sometimes it is not; sometimes it is only half-full, half-hearted. Sometimes my consciousness does not strain fully enough towards the object for me to truly "have" it; I merely skim it, I merely glance. In fact, Husserl believed, most of the time I do this, since empty intendings comprise the majority of our conscious acts. Indeed, it was a source of constant wonderment to Husserl how humans could truly be said to be conscious beings at all, given how they wandered around only half-seeing the world before their eyes, only half-experiencing the things which made up their lives.

The classic example of an act of empty intention? The way our eyes hover over the headlines of a newspaper. The way we scan the events of a day, or a week, or a year, registering some of it, reacting to even less. Robert Pinsky's poem "Newspaper" gets to the empty heart of this kind of intention with its observation, of the stuff of daily news, that "they make the paper with an invisible grain/so you can tear straight down a vertical column". We tear straight through it, without even seeing it – and yet it's with, Pinsky says, "the craving for some redemption" that we open the morning paper, "fresh, fallible, plausible … the skin of days". Pinsky's poem enacts this failing, this ultimate emptiness of the encounter with the headline, but it also presents its opposite, its redemption, the act of intending that is fulfilled, successful, whole. Pinsky's poem is in itself that "way of happening", of stretching towards experience, whether public or private, and illuminating it into meaning.

Or take this description of what happens when a poem stretches towards an event. The event, in this poem by Tomas Venclova (translated by Constantine Rusanov), is not named. It is dated, however, and it is placed, and it is attached to a person: "Landscape, Summer 2001", the title of the poem reads, subtitled "For Susan Sontag". The landscape is that of a ruined city, over which an archangel's trumpet roars, over which dust wafts, in which "unremitting chance wipes out completely/a star's reflection in the quivering waters". Venclova's landscape is chilling and surreal; that force of "unremitting chance" shares a stanza with something as innocent as a butterfly, though that it is an "unseen butterfly" only adds to the uneasy, dream-like strangeness of the vista. And though chance may rule in one stanza, God rules in another: "God, upon waking, reduces the square to a pinch of love and ashes".

And the poet? To the poet, I think, Venclova – possibly with Sontag in mind – gives the last word, gives the authority to turn "unremitting chance" into something less destructive. In the final stanza,

> The sun comes up above the ruined city
> Light gropes for the desk and quickly finds it,
> and empty time is severed by a sentence
> which contradicts the night that has just ended.

Light comes through, and it comes through in the form of the poet, for it is the poet who gropes for the desk, groping towards words, towards a way of happening for whatever meaning this ruined city can acquire. And fullness comes, too, as an answer to "empty time": the answer to that emptiness is the word, the line, the sentence which has the power to refute, or at least to transform, the overwhelming darkness of histories recent and otherwise, to "contradict the night that has just ended".

This is poetry as a form of prayer; poetry as transformation.

But it is a battle. The poet, at a difficult time or in the face of difficult realities in the world, will feel the pressure of those events, of that news. They will force their way into the poem. The poet, indeed, has responsibilities towards them, but the poet has responsibilities also to the poem. Harry Clifton's title poem in his collection *Secular Eden* points straight to this responsibility; his title seems to epitomise that which poetry, with its transformative powers, can be: a secular miracle, a secular route towards redemption. He writes from this secular Eden, this place where:

> No-one will ever fall from grace
> Where the bells are electric, and the chimes
> Of a French municipal hall
> Preserve us in time.

Later, he writes of how "the flight-paths/Write their Celestial Word/On the sky above us". But the light here is artificial, coming from "cash-dispensers/ From the all-night banks" which come on "as if by a hidden hand". In such a place, Clifton writes, there can be "No guilt now, only vertigo/To the end of time, if anyone stops to think".

But there is the rub: someone must stop to think. This someone, as the rest of Clifton's collection makes clear in its thoughtfulness, and its care, and its investment in language, must be the poet. That is the poet's responsibility; to stretch towards what happens, to meet it and make language of it. Like phenomenology as envisioned by Husserl, poetry then becomes an ethical task.

Just as the word "intention" is best understood through its etymological root, so is the word "responsibility", and it's useful here to look to the formulation of our keynote speaker, Robert Pinsky, who thinks about "responsibility" in terms of its roots in the notion of response, in terms of the duty to answer to something. Seamus Heaney takes comfort from this idea, he has said; the idea that, as long as you feel the need to answer, you, as poet, are being responsible, because it is in the ground of one's answering being that the responsibility of the poet is lodged.

> Follow poet, follow right
> To the bottom of the night,
> With your unconstraining voice
> Still persuade us to rejoice;
> With the farming of a verse
> Make a vineyard of the curse.

Thus does Auden speak at the end of elegy for Yeats. He is speaking to Yeats, but he is surely speaking, also, to the poets who endure now that Yeats has disappeared from the world. Here is what Yeats did, here is what poetry must try, in his wake, to do still: to make a vineyard of the curse.

In the wake of September 11, 2001, it was a poem by Auden which circulated through countless e-mail inboxes in the United States and beyond. To this poem, Auden's "September 1, 1939", Americans, in particular, turned for something – solace, meaning, nourishment of the heart and the mind. And in this poem they found a striking, almost uncanny prescience. The poem's intention – by which I mean its "aboutness" in the phenomenological sense – was Hitler's invasion of Poland. But those readers whom the poem found in 2001 saw in it language which seemed fitted just as well to the 9/11 hijackers as to Hitler, and to the riven new Manhattan, with that "unmentionable odour of death" which Auden posited as offending the September night. "May I ... Beleaguered by the same/Negation and despair/Show an affirming flame", the poem closed; a flickering of hope upon which its desperate new readers seized, pressing "send" and "send all" in their tens of thousands that week, that month.

Auden himself, then, was recruited in the weary, frightened task of making a vineyard from a curse. Cruel reality needed a poem, and a poem was found. But when the poems truly of that September began to come, began to happen, they were striking in their lack of comfort. Venclova's "Anno Domino 2002" opens under the light of a "homeless star", in a city where "the towers/shiver" and "[t]he white statue has lost her/place". The subject of the poem sits at the site of Auden's poem, on 52nd Street, "uncertain, afraid/... while an occasional dirty snowflake/marks the era like a cross ..." and somewhere, elsewhere

a young man dreams of glory games, airplanes –
fire. We alone have created him. For him there is only
this destiny. Now it is time to pay.

No comfort. Even the snowflakes are dirty. No comfort, either, in the British poet Ian Duhig's "9/11 offering", as the Guardian newspaper referred to his poem "Midnight on the Water". This poem tries, like those many e-mailers, to draw meaning from an earlier poem, Lorca's "Poet in New York", with its line about being "Assassinated by the Sky"; but Duhig's vision of hope is an uncertain one, as from the window of his long-delayed train home, he "sees out the night/ And the stars on the windows/Extinguished with light". Which is more hopeful, the stars or the daylight? Little is certain. The poem knows not where, exactly, to seek out its source of light; knows not from whence to draw its sense of its own responsibility, its purpose.

A vineyard from a curse? Here is how Frank Bidart's 9/11 poem opens:

May breath for a dead moment cease as jerking your

head upward you hear as if in slow motion floor

collapse evenly upon floor as one hundred and ten

floors descend upon you.

May what you have made descend upon you.
May the listening ears of your victims   their   eyes   their

breath

enter you, and eat like acid
the bubble of rectitude that allowed you breath.

May their breath now, in eternity, be your breath.

That is "Curse", from Bidart's 2005 collection *Star Dust*. The curse that Bidart has wrought in this poem is a deliberate and painstakingly crafted one; the notion of curse is not working as a metaphor, but as a stark, frank presence, a way of farming terrible reality into verse. This is a poem about the tearing down of the Twin Towers. The "you" addressed, Bidart informs us in a note to the poem, is the "you" who tore those towers down. The poem is a curse on that "you", calling down a punishment in direct relation and proportion to the nature of the atrocity. Here are the final two lines of this short, bruising creation:

> Out of the great secret of morals, *the imagination to enter*
> *the skin of another*, what I have made is a curse.

Is this Auden's vineyard, farmed from the curse? Yes, but the grapes are bitter, almost poison. They have to be. Here, the responsibility of the poet is felt, and expresses itself, as a necessary anger. Empathy or fellow-feeling, the well out of which a poem such as this – a poem, that is, in response to the communal nightmare that was September 11, 2001 – is made, is twisted by Bidart into the most vicious of punishments. That "great secret of morals" to which he refers in the closing lines is, he tells us in the note, Shelley's notion of how to act morally: to be able to identify with another, to feel your way into the skin of another, to imagine what is experienced by another as a result of your action. This very empathy, this very identification, becomes in Bidart's hands a way of imagining the very worst for a fellow human, or for the ghost of a fellow human: "May what you have made descend upon you./May the listening ears of your victims their eyes their/breath/enter you and eat like acid ..."

—

Bidart's breakneck twist is to show that empathy, that well of fellow-feeling from which a poem like this would seem to spring, is complicated, both as form and as content. It can be used for ill as much as for good. It can become a dangerous failure. Because a world in which every individual intended their objects of experience in wildly diverse ways – in which everyone gave to every single object a vastly private, different meaning – would be a world of chaos, of fracture, and of course ultimately of endless war, it should come as no surprise to learn that empathy – in the German *Einfuhlung*, or feeling-into – was the cornerstone of Husserl's phenomenology as well as the bane of its existence. Why? Because of the very complexity which Bidart's poem throws into unforgiving illumination. Husserl considered his phenomenology to be an ethical task – the shared task of renewing and transforming culture to yield unity through differing perspectives on experience, rather than allowing a pre-existing unity or meaning to be imposed upon experience. To such a shared task, the possibility of empathy was of course vital. But empathy turned out to be the object of experience which eluded Husserl all through his career. The question of how we understand even those who are starkly different to us proved more than even his thousands and thousands of handwritten manuscripts could fully articulate. And I think that a poem like Bidart's "Curse" shows why, and shows how difficult is the ethical task facing both the phenomenologist and the poet. How to fulfill responsibility, to the world of experience and the world of the poem? Through consolation, comfort, through the nurture of soothing ideas? No, says Bidart; through the blunt weapon of honesty, even if it is unpalatable. If there is catharsis for the reader to be found in "Curse", then I would argue that that catharsis is only the poem's secondary concern. Its priority is make room for rage. This poet does, as Auden directs, "follow right to the bottom of the night", but if his "unconstraining voice" persuades us to rejoice in anything, it is in poetry itself, in how the dealt lines of these two stanzas can beat down polite speech and cut to the furious quick. Poetry makes this much happen. The news – that which happened out there – through these lines, becomes now even clearer, now that much more appalling in its truth.

Something like this happens, too, in two poems by Paddy Bushe, both carrying their year in their title, both written in the first days of the Iraq war in 2003. The first poem, "Full Moon, 18 March 2003", trembles, like the moon of its title, "Over the dark horizon/like an unshed tear". The second poem, "15 April, 2003", almost a month later in its dating, sees the moon whittled down to a crescent, in a sky that has "disintegrated", in which "the stars are clustered like bombs", towards which "words of mass destruction/howl". The poem itself, charged with language much more visceral, with a pace much brusquer than that of the first poem, is in fact the enactment of that howling, a twenty-first-century sermon, each four line stanza beginning with the word "Now", in a laying down of what has occurred, of how far gone we now find ourselves to be. "Now the sky has disintegrated ... Now truth's an unspoken whisper ... Now history's a looted city ... Now evil has developed an axis ... Now government meets in the market."

Bushe, driven to malediction by the actions of his namesake (sorry, Paddy ...), gifts us with the dilemma of the poet in this plugged-in age, when headlines are unavoidable, when war wavers somehow blandly before us, in real time, on the television screen; that dilemma being between the need to speak now, and the need to draw breath, take stock and tell of this later. But there is, perhaps, little time in which to wait and see; the next headline slams in before breath can be taken. And if the poem does not happen in that moment, has the poet missed something, shirked something, shrugged in the face of some responsibility?

And then, who is to say what is and is not news? What is and is not an event, a happening vital or enormous or significant enough that it should make poetry happen? In that same final verse of his elegy, Auden instructed the poet to "sing of human unsuccess/In a rapture of distress". And the poems in Carol Ann Duffy's *Rapture*, a paean to a love found and then foundered, are a reminder that what happens within a life, behind closed doors, within one heart or two, can be all the human unsuccess, all the stark actuality, that a poem or, indeed, a whole book of poems, requires out of which to emerge. Duffy's "Over", like Bidart's "Curse", is a poem of human reeling in the wake of catastrophe. Like Venclova's "Landscape", it is a poem about a ruined world:

> I wake to a dark hour out of time, go to the window.
> No stars in the black sky, no moon to speak of, no name
> or number to the hour, no skelf of light. I let in air.
> The garden's sudden scent's an open grave.
> What do I have
> to help me, without spell or prayer
> endure this hour, endless, heartless, anonymous,
> the death of love?

The act itself of making a poem out of "a dark hour" is here dramatized; the elements out of which such a poem longs towards shape are quickly set down, pinioned in their absence: the naming, numbering, figuring, shaping that make it possible "to speak", that can function, in a terrible way, almost like a "spell or prayer", that, to return to Auden's elegy and to Bidart's searing twist on its vision, can make a vineyard out of a curse. Unable to name, unable to number, the poet flails and struggles; the poem seems unlikely to "endure". There needs be no war, no terrorist atrocity, no genocide to hurt poetry into being; "the death of love" is enough, "the death of love" is the lead item on the newsreel of this poem's world. The release, when it comes – the chance of redemption – comes from that act of naming of which, at first, the poem seemed to believe itself incapable. "I say your name/again", the last stanza announces, although there has been no prior naming, at least not to the eye of the reader:

> It is a key, unlocking all the dark
> so death swings open on its hinge.
> I hear a bird being its song
> piercing the hour, to bring first light this Christmas dawn
> a gift, the blush of memory.

The poem becomes its own act of healing, its own way of happening; against the reality of overwhelming darkness, only the act of making the poem – the naming, the numbering, the painful bearing of private witness – makes possible the gift that the poem can be. As in Venclova's "Landscape", the structure of the poem is its own groping or stretching towards light, towards the letting in of air, towards that night which has just ended. What's striking in both these poems is the way that condensed, purposefully tightened form allows for this straining, through the stanzas, towards final, merciful illumination. In each case, there is so much else to say, but the shape of the poem can only admit these straitened human inchings.

—

Auden put a date on his September poem. Those who co-opted the poem sixty-two years later overlooked the precision of that date; does this matter? Perhaps not. Tomas Venclova's poem "In Memoriam, Henkus Hapensus" takes its name and its subject from the artificial gravestone in the window of a Lithuanian funeral parlour, for a dead person with a name non-existent in Lithuanian, with nonsense birth and death dates. The shopkeepers had not wanted to offend any living person with a possible coincidence or connection. And yet, from this fake life, from within this fake bracket of dates, Venclova creates a subject utterly affecting, moving, as memorable as any lost, living soul could be, and all the more so for his identity as "a true nobody", "a fate that never existed". Dates are ours to play with, the poem suggests.

Play is of course too flippant a description here; look at what Ellen Hinsey does with dates, how she can make a poem with a title far before her time, before our time, sing for all time: "March 26, 1827, Beethoven on his deathbed". The worry that with him, music would somehow die; that "the last of the sound would be carted off", because this man "had only ever been borrowed" and was now being "carted back". At the poem's close, it is sound itself that weeps for the lost composer – "knowing the future's empty/shape, seeing events and figures in the angled glass", knowing that "dark times" will "henceforth call it back". Thus, the date, March 26, 1827, becomes about not just that date, but about all dates that follow it, and about all dates that will continue to do so: those dark times that have come since then, those dark times that will come to us yet.

Of course, it works both ways. I can't help but see a common thread in the epigraph chosen by Ellen Hinsey for the 1996 collection from which this poem comes, *Cities of Memory*, and that chosen by Colette Bryce for her very recent collection, *Self-Portrait in the Dark*. Hinsey quotes Goethe's Faust: "once more, dim wavering figures from the past/You come, who once rose to my troubled eyes/Shall I attempt this time to hold you fast?" Bryce chooses Louis MacNeice, from *Selva Oscura*: "A house can be haunted by those who were never there".

The ghosts of the past will find their way into the poetry of the present, invited or not. They will transform the meaning of that poetry. Bryce's "Belfast Waking, 6 a.m." is crowded with ghosts, without ever referring to them, without ever admitting their presence to the poem's careful frame. This is a poem of post-Troubles Belfast – a poem with a frame that, as we have learned in recent weeks, is never invulnerable, is never safe from the ghosts of what has happened and what, horribly, might happen again.

Bryce gives us a portrait of Belfast city waking to an ordinary dawn. A maintenance man attends to the phone booths, "the city's empty confessionals". Again emptiness comes to signify disconnection from the hard stuff of reality. "Sites of anonymous threat/or sanctuary, they are out of place/in the cool new century", Bryce writes. A refuse truck backs out of an avenue, and casts its "amber, interrupted beam". A car door makes this sound: "a muffled whump" as it shuts. No acknowledged ghosts, but are they not everywhere? That whump, that searching beam of headlight, even that unnerving slink of a feline or a fox; in this landscape, such simple things bear heavy meanings. The city's confessionals are not empty, not really; they are loaded.

And yet, fixed dates are sacred. A date, so often, is a poem's title, because no other word or set of words can do. In "The Anniversary", against a backdrop of the spectacle of repetitive gazing at the TV screens on which

Sept 11 blazed, making us sick not just of what we watched, but "of the very systems of our watching", Pinsky marvels at how

> The date became a word, an anniversary
> That we inscribed with meanings – who keep so few,
>
> More likely to name an airport for an actor
> Or athlete than "First of May" or "Fourth of July".

Sujata Bhatt's poem "3 November 1984" dramatises Bhatt's reaction, as a poet, to the 1984 anti-Sikh massacres in India, viewed from the safety of her vantage point in the United States. It is fascinating as a poem of reaction to what has happened, to the news; it is a poem which practises an act of empty intention as a deliberate strategy for survival. "I won't buy/ *The New York Times* today", it opens. "I can't. I'm sorry." But in the bookstore, the poet "can't help reading the front page", can't help staring "at the photographs/ of dead men and women I know I've seen alive".

She does not want to think about what has happened. She resolves that her writing, that even the very ink in which she does that writing, will deny and turn from what has happened: "I've made up my mind," she writes, "today I'll write in peacock-greenish-sea-green ink I'll write/poems about everything else. /I'll think of the five Americans/ who made it to Annapurna without Sherpa help. /I won't think of hemorrhaging trains", she writes. And yet, "instead of completing this poem", she finds herself thinking, over and over, about one of the friends in India for whom she is so desperately worried. "Now instead of completing this poem," the last line reads, "I'm thinking of Amrit."

What is happening here? Much. The poem is made in spite of the refusal to write a poem. And also, the poem is made by dramatizing that refusal, that struggle; by looking at it from a poetic vantage point. It is a refusal to write a poem with a specific "aboutness", and yet that "aboutness" forces its way into every line, and is of course permitted to force its way into every line. A double consciousness is at work: one in denial, one drawing on the drama of that denial. In the act of refusing the machinations of poem-writing, this poem exposes those machinations.

And the date? The date as title? No other words would do; that is part of the subject's denial. No worst, there is none – Hopkins's line seems to toll, like a bell, over the broken world of Bhatt's poem. In one sense, the act of naming a poem with a date sees the poet shoulder an almost impossible weight of responsibility – a given date will, of course, mean something different to everyone, no matter how painful it might be for one person or one country – but the act of giving a date to a poem as title ignores that diversity somewhat; it is an act of pinning down, of definition, of saying, this is what happened then, this is how I saw it, but also, this is what it meant. In another sense, it is a recognition of that very loneliness of meaning – a loneliness so much like that of the desk, that of the study, that of the blank page; an attempt towards unified meaning that knows its own limits, knows that it can only ever, truly, be an account of one person's day.

—

Is this enough? Is this, after all, that full intention, that full experience of the meaning of the thing, of that which has happened? Or is it just another version, just another stretching towards life, ultimately flawed, ultimately only partial in its grasp? I'll end today with a poem which suggests that yes, this is so. But also that, no, this doesn't matter so much, at the end of all. Because what has been written along the way matters a great deal more. Whether of one person's date, or, as in the case of Tomas Venclova's poem "For R.K.", one person's century.

"I only know that is is now over (or nearly) – /this black century", begins Venclova's poem. This was a century in which nothingness, the abyss was "touted as hope/I'd say, not without success". What did we do in this century? Not a lot, and yet a lot:

> ...Yet we accepted
> truth's bitter gift – we didn't extol death,
> watched angels above rails and concrete,
> fell in love, turned lights on in the library,
> called good and evil by their names, seeing
> how hard it is to tell them apart. This we
> take into the dark. This is probably enough.

Well, isn't it?

This address was delivered at the Dun Laoghaire-Rathdown Poetry Now International Poetry Festival, at the Pavilion Theatre, Dun Laoghaire, on March 26, 2009.

A journalist and playwright, Belinda McKeon was born in Longford in 1979 and is a graduate of Trinity College Dublin. She is the author of three short plays – Word of Mouth *(2005),* Drapes *(2006) and* Two Houses *(2008) – and is currently working on a full-length pay and a novel. She writes regularly on the arts for* The Irish Times *and other publications. In 2007, she was appointed as Curator of the Poetry Now Festival in Dun Laoghaire, Co Dublin. She currently lives in Brooklyn, New York.*

AT THE CENTRE OF THE CIRCLE

Seamus Heaney

Celebrating Heaney's 70th.

(Editor's Note: *These remarks followed "At Centre of the Circle", a gala reading by 17 Irish and international poets in celebration of Seamus Heaney's 70th birthday, at the Poetry Now International Festival of Poetry, Dun Laoghaire, 28 March 2009.*)

This festival began with a wonderfully perceptive and intellectually forceful lecture by Belinda McKeon on poetry, a lecture that took as its text Auden's sound bite line that "poetry makes nothing happen". Belinda contemplated the line, contextualized it, contested it, and quickly and surely established poetry's claim to be the art which gives us the full feel and meaning of what happens, the art that *tends* to the world, and thereby intends to know the world and helps us to attend better to it through that poetic knowledge. Her address was an altogether serious and stimulating meditation, totally in keeping with what this festival has come to stand for, namely, poetry for its own sake, poetry – in the words of Czeslaw Milosz – as "a dividend from what we are".

So, even though in these days of economic downturn and depression and disgrace, the word "dividend" may associate poetry with less creditable human concerns, poetry itself is still to be credited. And Robert Pinsky's keynote address further articulated the reasons *why* it is to be credited and proved it on the pulses, as it were, by reading aloud poems from the canon and poems which he himself had written and translated.

It was a fortifying experience to listen to these speakers, feel the force of their conviction, and be reminded by them of the seriousness and sweetness of poetry's endeavour. And it is fortifying also to hear and have the company of our guest poets, some younger yet already distinguished, others long distinguished yet still young at heart and in their art.

The generosity of the tribute they have paid to me, however, has been more than fortifying. It has been a unique honour and an unforgettable one. At the same time, I have to admit that when I woke this morning and thought of this afternoon's event, what I felt was more like anxiety than honour. Anxiety because while I can always credit poetry, I cannot always credit myself. And different lines of my own came into my head, ones that

I gave to Mad Sweeney, where he says:

> And there I was, incredible to myself
> Among people far too eager to believe me
> And my story, even if it happened to be true.

But other lines came into my head as well, including one from a poem called "Mint" that goes "My last things will be the first things slipping from me". I realized, in other words, that from now on this afternoon's readings by these brothers and sisters in the art are going to be among the first and last things of importance in my life. So I would like to quote another poet, not present at the festival, Geoffrey Hill, who once wrote "This is plenty. This is more than enough": and to quote also a poet and a friend who is present, Frank Bidart. Frank gave expression to a yearning that we all feel when he wrote,

> The love I've known is the love of
> two people staring
> not at each other, but in the same direction.

Ultimately, the joy of this occasion has not been the experience of being stared at as the birthday boy, but rather the experience of being – to quote yet again – "true brother of a company" that sing to sweeten and strengthen – and are still singing.

Seamus Heaney was awarded the Nobel Prize for Literature in 1995.

ON ACHILL ISLAND: TWO POEMS

John F. Deane

EYE OF THE HARE

There! amongst lean-to grasses and trailing vetch
catch her? – vagrant, free-range and alert;

I saw the eager watch-tower of the ears, I knew
the power of legs that would fling her into flight;

concentrate, he said, and focus: you must love
the soft-flesh shoulder-muscles where the bullet bites,

caress – and do not jerk – the trigger: be all-embracing, be
delicate. I had no difficulty with the saucepan lid

down at the end of the meadow, lifted, for practice,
against the rhododendron hedge, I could sight

its smug self-satisfaction and shoot a hole
pea-perfect and clean through. Attention to the hare

left me perplexed for I, too, relish the vision
I imaged in its round dark eye, of a green world

easy under sunlight, of sweet sorrel and sacred herbs –
and I turned away, embarrassed, and absolved.

THE HEINRICH BÖLL COTTAGE ON ACHILL ISLAND

Against the white-washed walls of the house
scarlet blinds across which sunlight
plays its shiftless games of shadows;

here the writer sat, watching through the window
the white war-horses out on Blacksod Bay, remembering
body-crushing tanks and the meres of blood;

down the road to the small harbour
the evening chills under the gouged slope of a mountain
looming beneath grey clouds; fishermen, smoking,

slice crumbs off the flesh of mackerel
to be bait for a hoped-for ray; the writer,
patient too, nods and turns, back to the desk and the strained

rifle-shot quickness of the typewriter.
Here, where nothing happens, where a ram
blunders in through a hedge and a pregnant cat

comes pleading to the back door, he is laying to rest the ghosts
that have followed him everywhere, here
where now only the scented heathers watch

through the breath-fogged window. The writer
sits at his table, smoking, knowing the human heart remains
uneasy in its faithfulness; he has found innocence

on an island in the far west, a place
constrained by weathers and the asking
of a rigorous God; this, only, this always, and always

it is too much. Later he will stand
bemused by family, beret
comically perched and braces taut, will watch his children rush

laughing against the waves, as if they
could hold the lifting waters back, as if they, innocent,
might shoulder as he does the whole world's burdens.

John F. Deane was born in 1943 on Achill Island, Co Mayo. He is the author of two novels and nine collections of poetry, most recently The Instruments of Art *(2005) and* A Little Book of Hours *(2008), both from Carcanet Press. In 1979, he founded Poetry Ireland, the national poetry organization, and* Poetry Ireland Review. *He lives in Dublin.*

TWO POEMS

Moya Cannon

ORCHIDS

Today the hospital is filling up with orchids.
Beyond the pink terraced house and the January trees
the clouds break apart
to illuminate curtain after curtain of grey hail,
battering in fast across the bay,
and tall orchids have arrived in the cancer wards,
magnificent as crinolined beauties
at the ball
before a battle.

ELIZA MURPHY

What will survive of us is love.
Philip Larkin

Seventeen-month-old Eliza Murphy died
in eighteen twenty-seven
and was buried in April,
in a field south of a garden.

Perhaps spring gales prevented them
from rowing her body
across the short stretch of water
to blessed ground in Killeenaran.

We do not know what brought on her death –
fever, famine or whooping cough.
We do not know whether her hair was black,
or whether her eyes were brown.

We do not know who raised
the carved stone to her memory –
perhaps an older sister or brother, who, later,
sent money from America,

or whether, at low spring tide, she had ever
been carried across the sandbar to the mainland,
past regiments of squirting razor-fish
and sponges like staring moon-cabbages.

Neither can we be sure that she lived
in the row of cottages beyond the garden
or that she was born in one of the rooms
now brimming with sycamores.

We cannot be certain that she had learned
to balance on her feet before illness came
or was able to toddle about on the cobbles.
We cannot know her small store of words.

We know only that she sleeps
where the otter and the fox pad through the long grass
and that she died in April,
dearly beloved.

Moya Cannon was born in Dunfanaghy, Co Donegal, and now lives in Galway. Her third collection of poems, Carrying the Songs: New and Selected Poems, *was published by Carcanet Press in the autumn of 2007.*

LATE ARRIVAL IN ATHENS

Manus Charleton

Awareness.

He stepped back from the doorway and looked up: the hotel sign *was* there and it was lit. *Delphi*: the name was right. And the address – it was there in front of him on a brass plate. His eyes went up the façade over closed windows that were dark and some shuttered: calling out would be pointless.

He stepped up to the door and peered again through the small square of glass. Inside was nothing more than a passageway, dimly lit, with a tiled floor, bare walls and, at the far end, a closed door. It was hard to believe the building was a hotel. It did not even seem occupied. The bell was either broken or disconnected, but he pressed it again, the lack of tension in the spring unnerving him. Then once more he rapped hard on the door with his knuckles, changing to blows from the side of his fist, but the sound was unlikely to carry beyond the passageway.

He looked up and down the street, a street in a city into which he suddenly felt thrust, a city of people immersed in the immediacy of their directions, then back at the hotel, but there was no sign he was going to be able to get in. He looked again at his watch, knowing already it was late, past midnight. He had been here more than half an hour.

He took up the suitcase and went looking for another hotel. Shuttered shops and cafés ... grimy offices and apartments. He turned right and went down a long street, searching ahead for a hotel sign. He walked fast, the suitcase knocking off his legs. At the end, an intersection, and he stood glancing down streets none of which looked promising. Unsurely, he went down one and, after a short distance, turning to go back, saw the hostel, its outer door open. Inside, a porch, dimly-lit. On the wall a notice, in Greek first, then English, to use the intercom to ask for service. He pressed it on, and it connected with a scratchy noise; from the other end a curt, interrogative voice in Greek. He bent his head towards a grille, "Have ... you ... a ... room. I'm ... looking ... for ... a ... room". In broken English a reply that the hostel was full. "Do ... you ... know ... of ... any ..." – the intercom was cut. He pressed again, but as soon as he started to speak the intercom went dead. Outside, he tried to get the attention of a passerby, but the man gestured incomprehension and kept walking. Across the street a fight – nightclub doormen and a group of youths. Cautiously, he went farther, but at the rising noise of a fast-approaching siren he turned and went back towards the hotel. A hotel he had booked over the Internet. Bizarrely for a hotel, for a small one at that, its website boasted a library that included Greek classics in translation. He had been taken by it, wryly seeing it as propitious, his Odyssean fair wind. An inflated sense of his own knowingness had got the better of him.

The hotel was still shut and without a sign of life. He had either to stay or give up on it and go. Stay in the hope that a guest who had a key would return. At this stage just to get inside would be a relief. An armchair in the lounge would do for the night. Or go searching more extensively for a hotel with a vacant room in a city he didn't know. Search with the help of a taxi if his luck turned and he found one. But lucky was precisely what he had not been. And if his luck did not turn, then neither possibility would happen. No guest would return and he would find no accommodation. He might not even find an all-night café, and could have to wait out the night on a park bench or in a subway. "Here – we – go – again", he uttered the phrase, emphasizing the words with barely controlled rage. Not for the first time had this kind of thing happened to him. He looked up again at the windows, but there was still no sign of anyone inside. About to turn to try the door once more, he stopped, the last window holding his look. It was as if he was up there, up there in that room on the top floor looking down on this person trying to get in.

Stay or go? The question roused him. The longer he stayed the less likely he would find accommodation; yet if he went perhaps he would miss a returning guest. Stay or go? What could he do without an answer except shift anxiously between the options? And he began moving in and out of the doorway, thumping the door and looking up and down the street.

He caught sight of a man, white-haired, stocky, and watched him approach. Something about him suggested he knew the street, and might be of help. And then, his steps slowing, the man was looking at him with interest. "Are you the Irish person who booked for three nights?"

"I am. Ultan is my name."

The man extended his hand, "Nikos Haviaras. Welcome to my hotel".

He unclipped a bunch of keys from his belt and unlocked the door. "I had been expecting you earlier. I didn't think you'd come this late."

"There was a delay at Belfast airport."

"A security alert?"

"A technical fault, we were told." As they went down the passageway he explained the cancelled flight, the delay transferring to another airline, and to another one again in London. Then he was listening as Nikos recounted the trouble he had been caused by a delayed flight. And he couldn't help thinking he had told his story often before, each time in the same aggrieved tone, with the same emphasis on certain words, for it sounded as though in a groove.

"Your first visit?"

"Yes."

Nikos started telling him about Athens, but to be alert to the danger of pickpockets. "Much has changed in recent years ... the immigrants ... the buildings ... and the traffic ... but in the Agora and at the Parthenon there's still a sense of old Athens, even though they're besieged by all that's going on around them." He brought him to "Reception", his office on the first floor, where the hotel entrance was on a monitor. All the time he had been out there he was being filmed by a security camera. The thought that he was now caught on tape in some desperation trying to get in did not appeal to him; it was not how he wanted to be seen. Had not the ancient Greeks taught the power of holding yourself together and acting from reflective calm? Old advice more honoured in the breach ... Their emphasis on it suggested they knew all too well how volatile we can be when blocked, how liable we are to react with excess and make matters worse.

He was given a key to his room and another for the entrance door. "I keep the entrance door locked except for during the day when I'm here in the office. You can't be too careful." Then, "Belfast, did you say you flew out of Belfast?"

He hesitated before saying, "Yes", for he anticipated what would come next, a question to explain the violence. It was what people abroad wanted to know. Invariably they asked about it as soon as they learnt he came from Ireland. But since there was no one simple explanation he preferred not to go into it.

"Can you tell me what all the violence was about?"

"It has its roots in history, but it's hard to understand why it still happened."

His standard reply, which was usually enough to see the subject dropped.

Nikos carried his suitcase for him to the lift, still giving him information and advice.

A lift with sides of metal bars in an open shaft of cables and pulley-wheels. Around the shaft, a spiral of stairs. In his room he began to unpack, thinking of Nikos. In trying to be helpful perhaps he felt obliged to make up for not having been at the hotel. But his tone spoke more of his own concerns. As for the conflict in the North, during those decades when it had seemed without end he sometimes wondered how it might have appeared to citizens of such cities as Paris and Amsterdam. He had pictured them in cafés watching reports of bombs having gone off in streets and pubs and of sectarian shootings. For they belonged to a café culture, spending time in those congenial meeting-places for people of all creeds and races, a café culture at once an everyday occurrence and an emblem of a liberal European civilization based on respect and tolerance. A culture that owes its origin to Athens. And yet here for a number of years in the sixties and seventies there had been a military dictatorship – the infamous antithesis of the city's legacy.

The legacy of history only part of the North's conflict. There was more to it than taking up a position, of co-opting views of events to a current agenda. If it was only a matter of history, reflection on that "taking up" might have been all that was needed to separate "a position" from the whole truth and allow for accommodation. Any explanation had to be more deep-rooted. But to see it as a reversion by some to acting from a tribal instinct of aggression and defense when they felt their people's interests sufficiently threatened did not seem adequate. After all, it had become evident we share the planet. People had walked on the moon. We had seen from space the pictures of our home. "A jewel", it had been called, and that's how it looked. Yes, there were immediate emotional issues powerfully at work: the feeling of suffering injustice, the fear of losing out, the fear of being dominated and, once it began, the anger and revenge that fed the cycle of violence. But into the causal mix he would put the need to found personal identity in a belief. When intensified in "a cause", personal identity in belief can become highly charged. Through it is also a means to try to satisfy a desire for power. The need for identity in some belief goes deep. For Pascal it comes from the "eternal silence of these infinite spaces". A silence that terrified him when he faced it as all that is ultimately the case. His need to be shielded from it led him to wager on God's existence. As Lichtenberg acutely perceived, rather than from truth, belief comes from need: "Before you believe you have to believe".

He switched on the bedside lamp and switched off the overhead light and sat on the bed and slowly began to take off his shoes, but felt too wound up for sleep. The anxiety out there in the street – it had not yet passed. In that anxiety was there not something else? "To stay or go", the question had framed his indecision, rebounding it off the two options. What is indecision? A recurring moment no longer subsumed in an orientation. A recurring moment that made transparent the proximity of orientation without there being any one orientation that had to be taken. Lack of conviction about an orientation – that was what he had been faced with. And, in essence, that was the reason, was it not, for his visit? To find some orientation he could live with. Find it here where wonder about such matters had arisen for philosophers, dramatists and poets at the dawn of Western civilization, and where they had been open to experience in all its strangeness.

The guide book lay on the bed where he had thrown it. There would be a lot to see. But it wasn't for a lot to see that he had come. Nor for information. Of that a surfeit. He saw himself wandering among the remnants of ancient Athens, or gazing upon an azure, glinting sea as he took a ferry to the islands, clichéd though such images may be. That was what he had come to do. To be in places where the ancient Greeks had been, and look around where they would have looked, not quite knowing what he would see, but on the off-chance that something would emerge. "Orientation": the word that came to mind for what he hoped might become clear, some direction for a way to be.

Out there on the street, when the window had held his look as though he was looking down on himself, he had become almost indifferent for a few moments. An indifference that came from realizing the kind of thing that was happening to him had happened before. It was nothing new. Havana last year. After the assault and robbery there was no way out of the country until he could prove his identity. All he could do then was ask for directions and go from one office to another without counting on anything. When eventually he did get issued with a temporary passport, it was hard to believe it was being accepted at the check-in desk and he was being handed his boarding pass. The ground steward had even smiled and wished him a pleasant flight. But, as he looked down on Cuba from a height, the main thing on his mind was the utter unpredictability the assault and robbery had exposed, an unpredictability usually obscured behind expected supports.

He opened the window to let in air and looked out over roofs, their lines marking off the city from the sky. A cooing, agitated, joined by others, just as agitated, in a growing chorus. He looked down, but in the dark couldn't see anything. It had to be from pigeons on a ledge, perhaps woken into nervous reaction by the window he had opened. The cooing subsided into the muted backdrop of traffic, and with it the last of his anxiety seemed to leave him.

Again he thought of being out there on the street. Now the meaning of "here we go again" seemed to have emptied of frustration into something accepted as implacable, into a phrase from a Greek chorus pointing out the role of fate to the audience. Experiences were fated to be his, what more of any consequence could be said? He shook his head: was he showing his age? Was he just tired? What of Pindar's call to become what you are? Are you not a protagonist in your own small drama? The questions went unanswered, and their meaning drained away, leaving him in the awareness of standing in a hotel room looking out over city roofs at the sky. Then the awareness itself began to make its presence felt. Awareness without particular focus – its breadth seemed limitless. He had felt this awareness before, but not to the same extent. It seemed to have seeped into the emptiness after the day's anxieties had gone, or simply become apparent in the absence of any other thing preoccupying him. It lay around him, perhaps a basic orientation, for it seemed it could be at hand regardless of what he would do or what would happen. Perhaps in the awareness an intimation of *the logos* Heraclitus claimed existed, the dynamic element pervading all change, plurality and conflict, and that by virtue of its pervasiveness could be experienced as oneness. He caught hold of the drift of his thoughts: speculation was superfluous. Experience of the awareness all that mattered. From now on he could try to connect with the awareness around his intentions and responses, looking on them as the immediate need and impulse to give its presence particular focus. He could try to have it there round a gesture, to observe the gesture figure its surface. And he could listen for it in an appropriately even tone, one in which the weight of a situation, insofar as it could be measured, had entered.

Manus Charleton lectures in Ethics, Politics and Morality & Social Policy at the Institute of Technology, Sligo. His book, Ethics for Social Care in Ireland: Philosophy and Practice, *was published by Gill and MacMillan in 2007.*

TRÍ DÁNTA

Simon Ó Faoláin

AG CÁITHEADH

Seo linn ag iarraidh
féidirtheachtaí éigríochta an tsaoil
a scaradh ó
na cúinsí teoranta ab áil linn.

Ag an dé deiridh
n'fheadar aoinne againn
cioca é
an cháith nó
an gráinne
a scaoileadh le gaoth.

WINNOWING

Here we go, trying
to separate
the infinite possibilities of life
from the limited circumstances
we prefer.

At the last breath
none of us know
whether it was
the chaff
or the grain
that flew off in the wind.

AN BANAOIRE

Oíche Dhomhnaigh aimsir Chásca,
Ag siúl abhaile ar bhogmeisce,
Chualas an monabhar doiléir
Ón ndorchadas ar dheis.

Cé nach raibh brí le baint
Ón achar san
D'aithníos tú ó fhuaim is friotail.

Léimeas an claí is chuas
Ar aghaidh ag scaipeadh caorach,
Ag fágaint limistéar oráiste
dearbh na soilse sráide.

Thuigeas thar mo dhóchas buan
Nach sídhbhrúgh a bhí romham.
Fós b'ábhar díomá dhom,
Ar theacht go lár an ghoirt,
Aimsiú an raidió chiontaigh
Clúdaithe i mála plaisteach.

Bhís ann ag sileadh as:
Máthairtheanga.

Cé nach baintear leat go hoscailte
Níos mó in Íochtar Acla,
Fós níl tú gan d'áisiúlacht:
Bí id' fhoraire ar na huain,
Sciath in aghaidh an mhadarua.

Ach cogar, ná dearúd:
Ar éirí gréine is do chúram déanta
Agus cnaipe casta amach

Fág trén gcúldoras go balbh.

THE SHEPHERDESS

A Sunday night, Eastertide,
Walking home quite drunk
A low and constant murmur heard
Floating out of darkness.

No grasping meaning from that distance,
Yet I knew you,
Knew your flair, your intonation.

Vaulting the fence and onwards,
Scattering sheep,
Leaving the safe and certain
Orange circle of the streetlight,
Aware, despite my constant hope,
No spectral palace lay ahead.

Still disappointment stabbed
On finding the guilty radio
Wrapped in a plastic bag.

You were there, pouring forth:
Mothertongue.

There is no open truck with you
These days in lower Achill,
Yet you're not without your uses,
Stand sentinel over our lambs,
A shield against the wily fox.

But listen,
When night ends
And your work is done
And the dial clicks to OFF
Depart – mute – through the tradesman's entrance.

THIAR

An chúinne seo den mbaile fearainn
Mar nach bhfuil na páirceanna néata, dronuilleogach
Le clathacha comhthreomhar,
Ach iad beag, neamhrialta, breac le boirneoga,
Ar nós chnuas de chealla ailse i bhfíochán sláintiúil,
Nó a mhalairt iomlán de scéal.

In áirde, teaspánann rian fiarlán an bhóithrín glas,
Sall is anall ar scáileán an chnoic,
Go bhfuil cuisle inti, croí ag bualadh fós,
Nó tá dul amú orm.

Ní chorraíonn bád nó coit sa chuan thíos,
Bíodh ráthaíocht nó – is minice – faic.
Ní hé an t-uisce amháin áta ina léinseach,
Nó tá léinseach ’na luí ar na haon ghné den mhír.

B’fhéidir go bhféadtar an rún seo a fhuascailt,
An ortha a bhriseadh, dá mbeadh na focail cuí ann,
Agus fios ar ord cheart na n-uimhir,
Cosúil leis na méarchláir chróime
Ar chuaillí gaineamhchloiche na ngeataí,
Ach tá tost toll laistigh agus tost amugh.

BACK WEST

This corner of the townland
Where the fields are not neat and rectangular
With parallel boundaries,
But small and irregular, speckled with boulders,
Like a cluster of cancer cells in healthy tissue
Or the absolute opposite.

Above, the zigzag course of the green track
Back and forth across the mountain's screen
Shows a pulse, a still-beating heart,
Or perhaps I am mistaken.

No boat nor punt stirs the harbour below,
Be there shoaling or – most often – nothing.
It is not the water only which is like a sheet,
For a sheet lies on this scene's every part.

Perhaps the riddle could be untied, the spell broken,
Had we the correct words
Or knowledge of the combination,
Like the chrome keyboards on the sandstone gateposts.
But there is a hollow silence within
and silence has slipped the leash.

Translated by the author.

Simon Ó Faoláin was born in Dublin in 1973 and raised for the most part in Paróiste Mhárthain in West Kerry. He is a professional archaeologist and has written, or co-written, several books and articles on the subject. He holds two degrees from University College Galway. He spent various periods working and living in Galway, Wales and Achill Island, but has now settled again in West Kerry. His first collection Anam Mhadra *(*A Dog's Soul*) was commissioned by Bord na Leabhar Gaeilge and published by Coiscéim in 2008.*

ALLELUIA, BELOVED

Maureen Duffy

It's not rational. It's not wise. It just is.

This morning, as I gather leftover mail and books for my ex, I think of the question I've been tripping over lately, the one I keep coming across in even the simplest Buddhist texts; the one whose answer, they say, is the only thing that matters in the end: *Did I love well?*

Before today, I would have answered *yes* without thinking, and maybe even, *of course*! Wouldn't you? But if I agree with this assertion, and intuitively I do, then for me, what will the answer really be? And am I the one to decide? If so, can I be trusted? What if I've been misled? Or if I've been the one to mislead, what will the answer be then?

As I dress to meet my ex, I pause: *Did I love well?*

I decide to wear the white linen blouse and black skirt – it's August and it's hot in Berkeley. I slip on new sandals and flashes of worry skip through me: what if I burst into tears when I see him? Or yell?

Just relax, I think. If I cry, so what? And would I really yell? In a public place? Besides, what could I say that hasn't already been said? Something snide, I think.

I walk across campus to the café, through the cool, fragrant eucalyptus grove. It's been over a year since we've divorced. Peter lives in Cambridge now. The one in England, I say, when people ask. I don't say I miss him. Each morning I step into the kitchen to make tea and a slight ache moves through me. I place the kettle down and it's gone. I don't think of him; I think of Jasmine and Russian Caravan.

And lately, I think of Hitchcock. This has happened before – more than once. When I realize I've been wrong about something or someone in my life, the initial feeling of disbelief triggers my memory of an interview I'd heard, of Hitchcock discussing the opening scenes of *Psycho* – the ones where the camera focuses on Janet Leigh's body and the money she's stolen from her employer – she wants to start a new life with her lover; the ones before she steps into the shower at the Bates Motel; the scenes that lead an unsuspecting audience, like me when I saw the film for the first time, to pay attention to the wrong details and to mistakenly believe, at first, that the film is about the affair and the money; the scenes that mislead, and mislead, and mislead again.

And again, on this Sunday morning, as I dress to meet my ex, I think of those scenes from the film, and I wonder: what had I been paying attention to that led me away from my life with Peter?

At the café, Peter rises to kiss my cheek and my eyes do tear, but if I look away from him, I'm fine; no words of any kind enter my mind. His European-cut jeans are tighter than the ones he wore when he lived here and I've never seen this jacket before – a silky grey chenille. He's tall, angular, still at ease with himself. He gestures to the pot of tea on the table. "It's Irish Breakfast." He holds his hand to his chest. "In honor of the occasion." But I'm American, I think, and my jaw tightens.

I let it pass; he's simply trying to make conversation – my name and face are Irish – but since he has said so little about why he moved out and why he filed for divorce, everything he says now takes on too much meaning. And the way his body stiffens when he says the word, *Irish*, as if the word itself is irreverent and closer to fairy life than real life, makes me think: that's the reason why that he tells himself.

He's German. He grew up in Hamburg and speaks English with a soft British accent. Once, when I asked him what he was laughing at, he looked up from the paper he'd been reading and said, without irony, "Do you know classical Greek?"

The line to order moves slowly and Peter steps in front of me. "What can I get for you?" he asks. He insists. "Iced tea", I say, and it seems almost rude to order something so different from what he's having – unfriendly somehow. "And a glass of water."

The café is painted the same shade of green as the leaves on the rug I have at home: celadon, or sage, depending on the angle of the light. I bought the rug long before I met Peter and I still have a picture – somewhere – of him sitting cross-legged on it, wearing the bicycle helmet that he hadn't bothered to take off before sitting down to play with my friend's baby.

At the café, Peter brings the tea and water to me and tells me that his mother in Hamburg says hello and his great-aunt in Essen has a new boyfriend. She's ninety-six. Give them my love, I say, as if this is possible.

It's my turn to share family news and I pause: I want to tell him the latest news that worries me, that my sister – the one he got along with best – spent the night in jail, and my niece spent a day in the emergency room, but I can't – these stories are too intimate now. "Everybody's doing really well", I say. I don't offer any details. I smile. "Glad to hear it", he says and I think, his mother didn't tell him to say hello.

I had expected to feel some pain today – an ache in the chest or the head; perhaps a bit of nausea. But not this pain that I feel as we sit across the table from each other, saying whatever nonsense comes into our heads. This pain feels as if rays of light are moving through me and around the two of us, and everywhere my body meets the light – the edge of my collarbone, the tips of my elbows, the top of my left hip – the pain flares. It's intense – and it's everywhere; it's specific – and it radiates.

And the words that flow in a ribbon through my mind aren't snide or bitter epithets, but rather, *I am my beloved's, and my beloved is mine.*

"So," he says, "anything new with you?"

I don't tell him.

He crosses one long leg over the other and rests his left hand on his knee; he's not wearing a ring.

"What are you doing here?" I sound more puzzled than I expected.

"Beavering away at my old lab", he says, and I manage not to smile – his use of slang had never been well-informed.

"You aren't moving back, are you?"

"No." He tries to give me a withering look, but I think I've embarrassed him. Perhaps he had been thinking about moving back. His three-year fellowship to do AIDS research and to teach pathology to medical students at Cambridge would end soon enough – and then, where will he go? I don't ask.

He'd lived here for ten years. He never applied for a green card, though. He would gather the forms, fail to fill them out, and then, just before his visa expired, he'd panic and leave the country for a day. When he'd return the next day, he'd get a fresh date of entry stamped into his passport and extend his visa for just a little bit longer.

"How are the med students?" I ask, shifting the conversation back to his life in England. I don't need to know if he wants to live in the States again.

"Lovely", he says, but he looks away from me as he says it and I think: he'll never settle anywhere.

"I need room to think", Peter said the day he told me of his plans to move out of our apartment. He'd just returned from a trip to visit his mother in Germany and he still hadn't told me everything that had happened. He'd gone with the intention to relax and to take day trips with her to the North Sea and Köln – places they both loved.

In the end, he cancelled everything and stayed in Hamburg. When he arrived at his mother's apartment, he found her mailbox overflowing and her curtains drawn. Although she'd sounded lucid over the phone whenever they'd spoken, it turned out that she hadn't stepped outside of her apartment in weeks. Or bathed. Or eaten. She'd been living on cigarettes and alcohol and the fear in his voice over the phone when he called me from his hotel and told me a few details triggered my own worries that my husband would get sick as he tried to take care of his mother. He'd been exhausted when he left to start what should have been a vacation, and now he sounded completely spent. My first instinct was to reach out for professional help in Hamburg, but even over the phone I sensed Peter's body stiffen at such a suggestion. He was the one who knew how to take care of her, he said.

Even now, as he sits across from me drinking tea and asking about my family, it feels as if he hasn't forgiven me for saying this, for not seeing her as he does, as she was when he left home at eighteen: healthy, stable, sane.

"I just need room to think", Peter said that day. Our tiny apartment had one bedroom and a galley kitchen, but if I stepped out on the patio, the Bay filled the horizon. And the fireplace worked. Before that moment, we'd light it at night and fall asleep on the pull-out couch, watching the flames rise and fall.

Before that moment, I'd never begged for anything: I begged him to stay.

Peter moved into a smaller apartment, without a fireplace, in a building a few blocks away that looked out on a busy street and reeked of mold. He'd set it up to look like the apartment he'd had when I met him four years before. Every photo of me had been packed away; every book I'd given to him had disappeared from his shelves. I'd been erased.

What had I been paying attention to?

Peter looks over the dessert tray at the café and asks me if I'd like a slice of apple *streusel*. His accent on the word from his childhood triggers a wave of longing in me for our once-future life together. I miss hearing him with friends speaking German, a little French, and beautiful Italian.

I shake my head. The pain hasn't dissipated and the tips of my ears burn where the light touches them: *I am my beloved's and my beloved is mine* continues to sound in my mind.

I watch Peter's mouth as he talks about the paper he hopes to finish before heading back to England. He doesn't smile when he speaks, so everything he says sounds more serious than it is. His new lab in Cambridge is working with the Berkeley lab on this project, and they hope to finish it this month. Since he's single and doesn't have children, he says, it's easy for him to come here.

He's single and doesn't have children. I tell myself to breathe slowly. Is the pain exquisite? Would it be less so if I wasn't also single and had no children? I touch the well-worn table and tell him about my own work on a case where the plaintiff had forged his documents.

"If the documents *were* forged," Peter says, "why did the attorney take the case?"

I shrug. "He believed his client – until we pointed out the different colors of ink."

"But how did he miss that?" Peter says. "Was he color-blind?"

I feel my cheeks grow hot. I don't know why I'm embarrassed; we won the case. "People believe what they want to believe."

"I guess." Peter takes a bite of his apple streusel. He holds his fork in his left hand, now. He looks elegant, I think, efficient. Different. Why are we, Peter and I, Europeans and Americans, so different about something as basic as how to hold a fork?

"My mother's doing well now", he says. "She came to Cambridge ..." he continues, but I stop listening. I don't believe a word he's saying. Every trip we'd planned for her to visit us in the States or England had fallen through. After the second cancelled trip, I accepted this fact – she couldn't travel; Peter always insisted that she could. In the end, we only saw her in Germany.

We're both quiet as he finishes his dessert. The café hums around us. I'm not a scientist, but after living with Peter, I know that "T-cells" and "markers" are important words and I ask a question using both. He's handsome when he smiles. With his dark hair and lovely eyes, he doesn't look German to me.

What do I look like to him? I hold my hair up off of my neck for a moment to cool off. I have let it grow long for the first time, and I've colored it a dark chestnut brown. When I arrived at the café, Peter seemed to notice that I looked quite different from the last time he'd seen me – or did he? He didn't say anything. Perhaps to him, I look exactly the same. I don't feel the same. I feel like a singer who's just received, finally, a favorable review from a fierce critic.

Peter has a beautiful voice and choir directors like to fight over him. The first time I heard him sing was on the first New Year's Eve we spent together. He sang vespers with a small chapel choir. *Deus, in adiutorium meum intende*, the choir sang, as if they knew what the words meant: O God, reach forth to my aid. That night, Peter and I sang our favorite phrases as I drove us slowly through the fog to an inn by the sea.

After Peter moved out, the thought of lying in bed at night alone, listening to our upstairs neighbors fighting, felt intolerable, so I moved out too. I put everything I owned into storage and sublet a furnished apartment down the street. I didn't put up any photographs of Peter and I put everything he'd given to me, along with the small envelope of ultrasound photos, into a drawer I never opened. He'd been erased.

I liked living in someone else's apartment for a few months. The carpet, walls, and furniture were a creamy white. I used one cup, one plate, one fork. The leafy green of the sycamores filled the bay window looking out on the quiet street – Holy Hill. Seventeen seminaries and twenty-seven churches surrounded me. Monks in brown robes and nuns in blue, crisscrossed the courtyard outside my kitchen window.

One Saturday morning, Peter asked to visit me there. We were still married. He arrived on time and a bit out of breath. He'd ridden his bicycle, but that wasn't unusual: he'd never owned a car. Our apartment had been at the top of a steep hill and he'd ride up it several times on any given day.

He wore what he always wore: grey dress slacks, an oxford shirt and a blue sweater. It didn't matter if he was going to work or going to the beach; he wore the same clothes. And his wedding ring.

He took a seat on the white bamboo chair and repeated his refrain of the past few months; he still needed time and space to think. But he wanted me to know that he'd started dating a woman he'd recently met at Quaker Meeting.

I didn't strike him. I didn't throw a snow globe at his heart. I looked at his ring. I couldn't remember what I'd had engraved on it.

I'd taken mine off.

He mumbled her name when I asked. "It sounds German", I said. He shrugged.

"Is there anything else you want to say?"

"No", he said. "I just wanted to be the one to tell you."

I held the door for him and waited. He hesitated before rising to leave and I had the sense that this hadn't turned out as he'd planned, though I could not imagine what he'd expected. If he had looked happy and glowing, then I might have felt a spark of jealous rage or even a weird voyeuristic curiosity. But he looked like hell with his pale skin, hair stuck to his forehead with sweat, and blood on his neck where he'd cut himself shaving. And he looked completely lost.

I didn't kiss him goodbye. I stepped back as he passed and gently closed the door behind him.

It didn't occur to me to ask her age.

I knew Peter had dated older women before he met me and I assumed this Quaker woman with the German-sounding name was about my age, forty-five. Or his, thirty-nine.

On the following Monday, I closed the door to my law office and googled her name. She was nineteen years old, a freshman at UC Berkeley and she lived in my neighborhood. She'd been president of her high school Latin club the year before.

I called my friends Marc and Simone, and they agreed: if she'd only been secretary of the Latin club, Peter wouldn't have bothered.

A few weeks later, I saw them standing together in front of a dress shop, talking. By chance, I had parked my car in the spot right in front of them. I'd been so focused on finding a parking space, I hadn't noticed them until I turned off the engine. They didn't notice me; they were looking at each other.

I'd planned to go into the shop, but I stayed in the car. Even at nineteen, she didn't look like a co-ed; she looked maternal. She wore sweatpants and a lumpy sweater, and I guessed she wasn't looking her best. Peter looked sad. He said something and she took his hand in a gesture of comfort.

I checked for cars before I pulled away. It had never occurred to me that comfort could be the one thing I couldn't give my husband.

Our baby miscarried in the fifth month, well after we'd watched with wonder the beat of the heart and been told that everything looked fine; our doctors were happy and gave us the go-ahead to tell the world we would be parents soon.

When the word got out that we were pregnant, everyone wished us joy, and they too seemed to feel joy. Again and again we heard how romantic and inspiring it was. I was forty-three and he was thirty-seven. Neither of us had children. I'd never been pregnant before. It felt delicious and sexy – which surprised me. He felt ecstatic – which surprised him. Peter had never met his own father – he'd left Peter's mother before he was born. But now Peter couldn't wait to be a father, to meet his own son. Or daughter. We didn't want to know and chose names for either possibility.

Peter broke up with the former president of the Latin club when our divorce became final. Then he moved to Cambridge. The one in England, I say, when people ask.

Peter asks the server at the café counter for more water for his tea.

"I'll have a solo on the recording, too", he says. The choir at his college is scheduled to record Britten's "Alleluia" when he returns to Cambridge. The same one I'd recorded years before.

"Can I get a copy of the CD?" I ask, not thinking of how it might feel now to listen to him sing. *"Come to me, bend to me",* Peter would sing at recitals. He'd dedicate the song from *Brigadoon* to me and we chose the name Fiona, from the same play, if it was a girl. William, or rather, the German, Wilhelm, if it was a boy. I didn't have the heart to tell him that no one in the States, including me, would call the baby Wilhelm. It would morph into William, then Will, and if the child turned out to be athletic, Billy.

"Are you sure you want a CD?" Peter asks. He knows me better than I want to give him credit for. "It's no problem if you do, but –"

"You're right." I smile. "I don't really want one."

Neither of us speaks, but it's an easy silence. The server asks us if we'd like anything else and we both say no. Neither of us makes a move to leave.

"We sang for a memorial service a few months ago", Peter says.

"Was it for someone you knew?" I expect a simple yes or no in response, but Peter's cheeks flush and he shifts in his chair. "It was for one of the deans of my college." His voice sounds forced and I wonder whether this dean had been the one who had helped him get the Fellowship. "I never met him," Peter says, as if he can read my thoughts, "but I'd heard great things about him." He presses his hands on the table to steady himself. "Everyone loved him", he says and his eyes tear. This is rare. This is not about the dean. "The church was packed." His voice wavers and breaks; scenes of the memorial service we held on the beach for Fiona Wilhelm flash through my mind and it feels as if Peter is thinking of this too. How long ago was it? Does it matter? We'd written down our wishes for the baby's spirit and threw them into the ocean, hoping the waves would carry them away, but the tide came in and the slips of paper kept washing up at our feet. Finally, we asked a homeless man to let us toss the paper into his small fire. He seemed to understand what we were trying to do and left us alone as we stood and watched the flames rise and fall with the wind.

At the café, two students covet our table, but we ignore them. We're in no hurry to leave. We have nowhere that we have to be.

I drink the last of my tea. We rise and my hand brushes the soft chenille of his jacket. He rests his hand on my shoulder and draws me close to him. We don't kiss. We don't need to. We both know we may never see each other again, and that feels right.

I walk home the way I came. The campus feels empty now. I cut through the small woods and breathe in the tang of eucalyptus and cedar; with each step away from the café, the pain dissipates. I have no desire to be with Peter. And no clarity that we should have ever married. I just love him. It's not rational. It's not wise. It just is. I could make nuanced, well-supported arguments as to why I should not love Peter, and the list of reasons why he shouldn't love me is infinite. But that list is to be tossed and burned, and I make no such arguments. I pay attention to my heart.

At home, I call a friend and invite him over for dinner. The evening fog will cool the air and the apartment; I have more than enough salmon and blackberries to share. I pin up my hair and slip off my blouse before I rinse the berries. The juice stains my fingers.

Did I love well? I place a berry into my mouth and expect it to be sweet. Yes, I say, yes, *my beloved. Alleluia.*

Maureen Duffy was born in 1959 in Illinois and studied English at the University of Iowa. She also holds a law degree from the University of Michigan and an MFA in Writing from Bennington College. For many years she was a practising attorney, specializing in employment law and litigation. She is currently working on two books: Witness, *a memoir of a deceased friend, and* When It Was Zaire, *a work of non-fiction on village life in the mid-1980s in what is now the Democratic Republic of Congo. She lives in San Francisco.*

MURMURS FOR REMCO CAMPERT

Michael Augustin

MURMURS FOR REMCO CAMPERT

1.
The Indonesian moon:
so much warmer
than the sun over here.

2.
But how shall we
understand the frogs
if they make so much noise?

3.
Samalona Island:
surrounded by water
like a pond by land.

4.
The little trees
between the tracks
follow their own timetable.

5.
In Cognac forever,
so it doesn't break:
Chopin's heart.

6.
The living:
easy to get rid of.
But with the dead
you have to live.

7.
At our table:
someone dead
pretending to be alive.

8.
For her entire life
Darwin's turtle believed
that it was God
who had made her out of clay.

9.
Even in black and white
still colourful:
the Irish rainbow.

10.
To be in the slipstream
of snails rushing ahead.

11.
A United Nations High Commissioner
responsible for humour.

12.
What, however, is
a poem about Bordeaux,
compared to a bottle of Bordeaux?

13.
Only drunks know
that twins
consist of four people.

14.
It's not me who is bad,
it's my conscience.

15.
You suffer from writer's block?
Then, you should write about it!

16.
In the fridge
two cans of beer
and a humming sound.
the humming remains.

17.
Would you prefer
a bit of freedom
or a bit of marzipan?

18.
A springtime thought
sharp as a knife:
this is the autumn
of my life.

19.
Man:
a sack filled
with water and calcium
waging wars
and writing poems.

Translated, from the German, by Sujata Bhatt.

This poem is included in a forthcoming anthology of poems in celebration of Remco Campert's 80th birthday.

One of Holland's foremost poets, Remco Campert was born in 1929 in The Hague. He is the son of the actress Joekie Broedelet and the poet Jan Campert, who was murdered in Germany in 1943 in the Nueuegamme concentration camp, where he was imprisoned for aiding the Jews. He is the author of over 60 books of poetry, fiction, journalism and children's stories. His most recent collection of poetry in English translation is I Dreamed in the Cities at Night *(Arc Publications, 2007).*

Michael Augustin was born in Lübeck, Germany, in 1953. He studied Anglo-Irish Literature and Folklore at University College Dublin and the University of Kiel. He is the author of many volumes of poetry, short drama and short prose – most recently, in English translation, Mickle Makes Muckle *(The Dedalus Press, 2007) – as well as numerous translations of English-language poetry and drama. He lives in Bremen with his wife, the Indian poet Sujata Bhatt, and works for Radio Bremen.*

FIVE POEMS

Sam Gardiner

ANGLING

Grey weather was better, with a dimpling
of raindrops and maybe a wind
to roughen the water. If nothing more
dangerous came along I went with
the Bad Hand gang, the four of us:
Errol and Mac, and Herb who swapped
his book token for a fishing rod.
But I hoped we'd catch nothing,
pull no perch or roach, or even pike,
flapping out of its world and into ours
and have to tear the hook from its mouth.
Watching them die was part of the sport,
or turning away to admire a reel
or float, or to prime the next bait,
not letting the fish spoil the fun,
nor the parents who told us that fish
could feel no pain, and left no gap
in the water. We knew they did.
Looking death in the gaping mouth,
in the dazed eye, and watching
the thrashing around fighting for breath,
must be necessary for growing up,
like making sure my asthma inhaler
was on standby, deep in my trouser pocket.

MEASLES

I watched the sun stroll from flower to flower
across the wall and shared my knowledge
with two staring adults that it was the world
that moved. "You'd better not forget",
the measled me shrilled from the bed,
and cringed when they nearly kissed me.

Looking up their noses into the darkness
where they hid their brains, I knew, just knew
that she would tittle, he would shally
and together they would prove that two
take twice as long as one to get to the shop
and back, with my Beano and sweets.

I watched from between the curtains, stood
on a chair to see over the hedge, first on one leg,
then the other. A flurry of cherry blossom
across the window included butterflies,
but not many, hardly any at all. Just one or two.

Ten more minutes dragged themselves past,
and a bluebottle landed on the glass and wrung
its hands. Strolling up Lisnisky Lane they came,
arm in arm, sharing a joke, much happier
now they knew it was the world that moved.

SOME DAYS ARE

Some days are always with you,
as when your mum oversteps her domain,
delineated by thin blue skirting boards,
and sees you off. She makes sure you pay
half fare, smiles lovingly and waves
at completely the wrong window
as you accelerate away, maybe for ever,

on the front seat of the upper deck,
ducking each time a tree reaches out
to brush your hair or slap your face.
A thousand stops later and a schoolgirl,
one of a supervised group, stumbles up
on a pair of mismatched, misshapen legs
and plumps down on the seat beside you.
"I'm happy", she says, loose smile
widening to emit a trickle of drool. "Guess
where I'm going. I'm going to the seaside.
Are you happy too?" she asks, as if
there must be a perfectly simple answer.
But I smile anyway. We all end up smiling
at completely the wrong window.

RIFT VALLEY POLKA

Things we should apologize for are:
Rift Valley settlement; the slave trade;
logical positivism; iambic pentameters;
the invasion of Iraq; being one of us
instead of a bold Sam Hall, goddam us all.
Lilacky blossom is an ambush, a bush
for a dancing smother of butterfly kisses.

What the heart wants is to deceive
its short-lived self and be long deceived.

Love lies radiating heat back into space.
Her handbag gapes amazed at her side
and buddleia butterflies, debauched
by perfumes well beyond their means,
climb the air for a drunken glissade,
a colourful turbulence that fools the soul.

So much deception, so many men lost.
Someone should apologize for this.

CHARITY CLAY SHOOT

Scant pants are not for Farmer Pillow's wife,
who, like Curley's missus, has no name
of her own. She wears hot cinnamon slacks
of especially generous cut across the seat
and drives her 4 by 4 Suzuki Scoundrel
to creative sugarcraft and belly dancing
classes at St Helen's Church Hall.
Here she was once heard telling
the girls' room mirror that "When I think
how beautiful I am I feel quite orgasmic".
Men, she muses, gaze up their telescopes,
and down their microscopes at a universe
where nothing is as wonderful as I am.
They fear me because my looks defeat
their logic, my touch stupefies them,
my scent induces dizziness beyond diagnosis,
and my kisses cause rigor mortis.

But as she drives home, to a massacre
of clay pigeons, she can tell that many
a peaceful herd of Holstein milkers,
and many a gold-leafed maple and field
of summer wheat feels equally luscious.
Lie heavy, Martha Pillow, darling,
give the earth back every ounce you've got.
The stone that will bear your name lets the sun
go down, but holds back the heat for slow
release in the cold hours before dawn.

Sam Gardiner was born in Portadown in 1936. He was educated at Portadown College and apprenticed to an architect's firm in Lurgan, Co Armagh. At the outbreak of the Troubles, he emigrated to England, where worked as an architect until retirement. He is the author of two collections of poems, Protestant Windows *(2000) and* The Night Ships *(2007), both from Lagan Press. He lives near Grimsby, Co Lincolnshire, England.*

THE SPORTS OF EASTER MONDAY

John Gray

All history is local.

Now group on group is seen to follow far,
Like to a Persian army in array;
On foot on steed, coach, jingle, cart, and car –
Tow'rds the high Hill of Caves they wend away ...

Thus William Read in his "Hill of Caves" describes huge crowds advancing to the Easter Monday fair of 1818 on the Cave Hill above Belfast. The twenty-three-year-old army officer, ultimately Lieutenant Colonel of the Royal Down Rifles, was a minor poet with a penchant for the epic, but, in six pages of his otherwise lengthy and ponderous poem, gives us the earliest detailed account of the Cave Hill fair. It is closely observed and he must have been there.

The "Persian army" was poetic license, yes, but Read did not exaggerate the multitude. Take the *Northern Whig's* account of "Easter festivities" in 1825 which was entirely devoted to the Cave Hill gathering:

> The dark lanes and gloomy alleys of our town were emptied of their tenants at an early hour. Foul and fair, young and old – fled as from "the wrath to come", from city to country: each decked with speck and span new suits of finery – the lasses to captivate. The cliff crowned Hill of Caves, being from long custom, the annual resort at Easter, it early presented a living panorama of "real life" and "raree show".

So great was the turnout that by 1830 it rated inclusion in Philip Dixon-Hardy's *The Northern Tourist*, where he noted that "on Easter Monday, vast crowds of people from Belfast, and the surrounding country, ascend this mountain, as far at least, as the first or lower cave, and enjoy themselves in various sports and pleasures".

When and how did this vast assembly originate? Read in 1818 had "not met any person who could explain whence the sports and festivities practiced here on Easter Monday had their origin". Thus the fair preceded living memory stretching back at least to the 1760s. In 1825 *The Northern Whig* had spoken of "long custom", and in 1855 J.B. Doyle in his *Tours in Ulster* described the fair as one carried on "in accordance with immemorial usage".

During the celebrated Cave Hill rights-of-way case in 1859, two aged veterans, James Hamilton and Abraham Whelan, gave evidence of their own knowledge of the fair back to the beginning of the nineteenth century. It first surfaces in newspaper coverage in the *Belfast News Letter* of 27 April 1810 which reported that "two children lost their lives and several persons were much hurt at the Easter revel held on the Cave Hill".

By then the fair had a prominent place in the public imagination. Later in 1810, Maywood (probably Robert Campbell Maywood, later celebrated for his "Scotch character" acting) performed his song, "Cave Hill or the Sports of Easter Monday" at the Belfast Theatre. According to the nineteenth-century theatre historian, W.J. Lawrence, this "grew very popular". In 1812 Easter Monday was marked by "A Dance and a View of the Cave Hill", and in the following year by a ballet dance, "Easter Monday; or the Humours of Cave Hill". This may have reappeared as "the favourite interlude" entitled simply "The Humours of Cave Hill" in 1818, and may indeed have been re-enacted in 1820, although described then as a "new ballet dance".

Read speculated about the origins of the fair, presuming "the usage to be some remains of superstition which survived as a custom, when no longer a rite". He may have been suggesting pre-Christian origins: what Estyn Evans has described as "the periodic assemblies of early Celtic Ireland held on hill tops", and indeed Evans refers to the Cave Hill fair in this context. Dunnanney Rath below neighbouring Carnmoney Hill is interpreted by O'Laverty, writing in 1880, as "The Fort of the Aenech [or of] the fair or public meeting". The practice of "parles on hills" was to last far longer, as an alternative, indeed a form of resistance, to the new order with its towns and authorised markets.

Read would certainly have been well aware, in his time, of the continuing observance of "pattern" (pardon) days reflecting the co-option by Christianity of older practices. These often involved an ascent to a high place or well associated with a particular patron saint, and equally often combined religious observance with revelry, a conjunction noted with various degrees of pious disgust by nineteenth-century travellers. The most notable survivor today, though stripped of drink and disorder, is the annual pilgrimage to the summit of Croagh Patrick in County Mayo.

The difficulty in suggesting any continuity between these practices and the Cave Hill fair is that Chichester's original seventeenth-century conquest of Ulster "extirpated" the native Irish population in the Cave Hill hinterland. There can have been very few left to hand on ancient practice to a new settler community, and one principally of the Presbyterian faith. According to the compilers in 1838-39 of the *Ordnance Survey Memoirs* for the neighbouring and overwhelmingly Presbyterian parish of Carnmoney, there was "scarcely a tradition in the parish". Yet Evans tells us that Presbyterians did have a tradition of "sacrament Sabbaths", popularly known as "holy fairs".

In the era of the United Irishmen we can indeed find them engaging in their very own form of "parles on hills", and on the Cave Hill. Thus the informer Edward Newell was able to relate to government how, on the anniversary of the fall of the Bastille in July 1796, "a few hundred assembled on Cave Hill, made bonefires, talk'd a good deal, ate and drank still more and then retired to complete the night in drunkenness and debauchery". They were hardly assembling on the Cave Hill to sanctify the high-flown re-designation of the hill by more literary United Irishmen as "The Cap of Liberty", but the hill provided a natural arena for "a revel" justified by an auspicious anniversary. It was not the Easter Monday fair, but there were similarities.

Certainly Easter was a time of central importance to all of Christianity in Ireland, marked by fasting and atonement for the death of Christ, and by celebration on Easter Sunday and Monday to mark his resurrection. Ulster Presbyterians who disregarded Christmas placed greater emphasis on the Easter holiday, and were to do so throughout the nineteenth century – thus the Belfast theatre offered an Easter pantomime rather than a Christmas one. Even today the most important day in terms of visitor numbers for Belfast Zoo, on the slopes of the Cave Hill, is Easter Monday.

By the time the Cave Hill fair surfaces in recorded form there is no evidence of any religious focus. It nonetheless shared the ascent to a high place practiced elsewhere in Ireland, for example in the Mourne Mountains, though usually on the Easter Sunday rather than on Easter Monday. Elsewhere in Ireland Easter Monday was the more secular of the two days, featuring local markets and fairs and drink-fuelled entertainment.

The strongest argument for some link, however tenuous, between the Cave Hill fair and much earlier Irish and religious practice was its actual location around "the tent rock" in the hillocky terrain immediately below the caves and the summit crags. On all practical grounds this was a venue utterly unsuited to such an assembly. It lay 700 feet above sea level and, on Easter Monday the climate could be unforgiving as fair-goers found "the climate as they rise grow breme – [and] keen cutting winds assail th'unsheltered frame". On occasion the event had to be abandoned because of "virgin snow". As Evans has aptly noted, "for climatic reasons – great gatherings have been largely confined to the summer half year between May and November". Here was an exception in the colder north-east and most of the way up a mountain, and one principally patronized by Presbyterians.

Just getting there was a significant undertaking. Francis Joseph Biggar, writing in 1923, gave a succinct description of the route for would-be revellers from Belfast up until the construction of the Antrim Road in the 1830s. It was "a whole day trip, beginning hours before noon and ending only with sundown". Fair-goers came out along the Shore Road to Greencastle, and only from there did they make the direct approach to the Cave Hill up what is today's Gray's Lane but was then "a rough enough road". Crossing the line of what was later to be the Antrim Road the unremitting ascent continued to the Volunteer Well some 400 feet above sea level. As the last point with an ample supply of water, and also the last point which wheeled vehicles could reach, this was an obvious resting point for people, most of whom had already managed "a good three Irish mile trake".

From there the path was rougher still:

> With laugh, and jest, and antic feat they rise
> The mountain's side; but many a grievous trip
> Doth send more woeful music to the skies,
> From luckless wight foredoomed to slip;
> Whilst youthful imps the giddy pathway skip,
> And gibe at those whom time hath tardier made;
> Too fat to climb, with bottle at the lip.

The practicalities must have been more formidable still for those laying on the entertainment. The one surviving illustration of the fair is a poor newspaper photograph of a painting once owned by Biggar. One can see here a substantial tented encampment, or almost an encampment of marquees. In 1859 William Bryce described how he was employed as a carpenter in their erection, and they would have had wooden floors to facilitate dancing. All this infrastructure had to be manhandled up the hill. Carts could have reached the Volunteer Well, but above that point, loads would have had to be strapped to the back of horses or ponies. Even if the carriage was successfully accomplished, the scarcity of flat ground around the "tent rock" must have caused further problems. For these reasons the Cave Hill fair can never have served as a market involving the buying and selling of cattle and horses, or any wide range of produce.

Although the fair was progressively co-opted by the populace of the growing town of Belfast, the town alone was too small to provide Read's "Persian army" of 1818, or even the 20,000 reported as attending by *The Northern Whig* in 1845. We need to bear in mind that Belfast was a late developer with a population of only 37,277 in 1821 and still only of 75,308 in 1841. As the old and infirm, or the very young, could not have made the arduous journey to the fair ground, and many of the able-bodied would have chosen not to go, it is evident that the crowd must have come largely from the still densely populated rural hinterland, and the further we look back the more certain it is that the impetus behind the event was rural rather than urban. The revelry and excess associated with the fair were surely an example of what Evans has described as the "moral holidays [which] are a feature of many societies which have not been greatly influenced by urban ways and values".

The importance of the rural context is borne out by references in the *Ordnance Survey Memoirs* where, almost as a matter of routine, the Cave Hill fair is mentioned as the major social event of the year for ordinary people in surrounding districts. Thus in neighbouring Carnmoney, "On Easter Monday and Tuesday numbers from this parish flock to the Cave Hill".

Thanks to the rights-of-way trial in 1859, we know the identities of a handful of people who were involved in the fair, or who attended, and this tends to confirm its rural nature. Thus Adam Thomson of Boghouse in the neighbouring townland of Ballygolan was the owner of a tent and employed William Bryce, son of a tenant on the high slopes of the hill, as a carpenter to help erect it. Patrick McHale, variously a labourer and herd, lived with his wife at the Volunteer Well, and, as we shall see, they supplied refreshment both there and at the first cave. Other elderly locals who could remember attending the fair were James Hamilton who lived at Greencastle at the foot of the hill, but whose father had lived "above the White Well", and Abraham Whelan from the neighbouring townland of Ballaghaghan.

An exception to this picture of an event patronized by country folk of modest status and Belfast's growing working class is provided by the Grimshaw family of Whitehouse, the dynasty who pioneered cotton manufacture on the shores of Belfast Lough. George Benn in his *History of the Town of Belfast* recorded that "on an Easter Monday fete on the Cave Hill – the Grimshaws were represented that day by 40 individuals of the name". Their attendance suggests an identification with their chosen communities of Whitehouse and Greencastle, rather than with a Belfast axis, and also a willingness, at least on one day in the year, to view the entertainments of many from their own workforce.

They had other interests on the Cave Hill too. The oldest member of the third generation of Ulster Grimshaws, James Grimshaw, had married a daughter of John Templeton, Belfast's pioneer naturalist, and pursued those interests himself as a founder of the Belfast Natural History Society, and author of a pioneer *Flora of Cave Hill*.

A spirit of adventure of the kind which took some gentlemen to concealed balconies in Belfast's singing saloons, may have encouraged others to sally forth to the Cave Hill fair, but we need not doubt that, Grimshaws and proto-bohemians apart, this was overwhelmingly an affair of the common people.

What remains striking, and always remembering the relative inaccessibility of the locale, is the range of refreshment and entertainment that was available. The marchers to the hill would certainly have been both hungry and thirsty, and:

> Full many a well heaped basket lines the way,
> Where tempting fruits, and witching liquids spread.

We have to rely on Biggar for an exhaustive list of edibles. He offers "pigs' feet, soda farls with wedges of butter and boiled beef, slim cake and oat cake, dullies and willicks with a pin thrown in, treacle and dough-nuts, yellow man and fancies, – ginger bread dolls, cockles and mussels from Greencastle strand, [and] liquorice babies". Some may have brought their own provisions and halted at the Volunteer Well, where Patrick McHale "sometimes did little kindnesses for them. I boiled water, peas and beans for them".

Many clearly put liquid refreshment at the top of their list of priorities:

Behold that graceless slave with shirtless back,
Shoe down of heel, and kibe betraying hose,
Hat void of rim, surtout like tattered sack,
All blood shot eye, and purple spotted nose.

It comes as no surprise when this character in Read's poem goes

To yonder jar, which burning liquor fills,
And down his throat a brimming bumper throws,
Till at his heart like liquid flame it thrills …

As to the contents of "the brimming bumper", Biggar refers to "a good run on local poteen, for the Belfast mountains harboured many a still", and we know that, in the 1820s, Mrs McHale moved from her usual station at the Volunteer Well and was "up in the caves selling whiskey" at the Easter Monday fair. This was certainly the bottom cave, though given the difficulty of getting into this cave today even when sober, this may seem unlikely. In fact, viewed on a sunny early morning, one can see the mark left by the original early nineteenth century ground level only a couple of feet below the lip of the cave; it is subsequent erosion that has made access more difficult. J. Dixon-Hardy, writing in 1830, merely described how "many of the elder regale themselves with copious libations of the 'mountain dew', or native whiskey".

Fed and liquored, many fair-goers turned to dancing, and music there was aplenty. According to Read "the fiddle's flourish, and the bagpipe's grunting" encouraged dancers to "Hibernia's planxties, [and] Caledonia's reels". Then as now their talents varied:

Some lightly springing, seem to leap on air,
Some beat the earth with iron studded heels …

Bigger gives primacy to the dancing:

> Dancing was the favourite pastime, reels, jigs, hornpipes, accompanied by fiddles, pipes and flutes – when there were boarded floors as often happened, the noise rose to a general hub-bub and the plaudits were loud and frequent, especially when a favourite "tuk the flure" or danced down a strenuous rival.

Then from high above from McArts Fort came music from one of the last of the blind harpers:

> The dance is oe'r – but hark! The plaintive tone
> Of minstrel string is breathing in the wind;
> There sits neglected on the grey cairn stone
> His country's latest bard – poor – aged – blind ...

The harper and his companion already symbolized a vanishing age for Read:

> Couched at his feet an Irish wolf-dog lay –
> Last, like himself, of once a valued race ...

To these differing musical traditions, Biggar added singers performing songs such as "T'is Sweet to be in Ballinderry", "Barbara Allen", "The Irishman", and, most site specific, "T'was on the Belfast Mountain I Heard a Maid Complain". He also records "the sad story of the shipwreck in Dublin Bay, when so many young Belfastmen lost their lives". Ballad sheets were on sale at 1d a time.

There were the gambling games which offered nothing but peril to one anxious father who

> The glittering trash – observes with anxious eye,
> The freaks of Chance upon the chequered board;–
> He tempts her frown – a week's hard wages fly!

Read doesn't spare us the moral:

> His urchin son doth see his wealth's decay –
> Right sad to think how hunger, by and by,
> Shall pinch —-

Bigger too refers to gambling games such as thimble-rigging and Aunt Sally, but there were other more innocent entertainments provided by fire-eaters, jugglers, and Punch and Judy.

For children there was that most innocent of all Easter pastimes: rolling "the snowy egg". Read, as was the custom with epic poems of the time, even provided an explanatory footnote: "Among the juvenile sports of Easter Monday, rolling hard-boiled eggs, stained in a variety of colours, is one of the principal". Dixon-Hardy described rather more vigorous "hurling and tossing about [of] hard-boiled eggs" and the compilers of the *Ordnance Survey Memoirs* also recorded "rolling coloured eggs".

As the Lenten fast involved abstinence from eggs as well as meat, and a surplus of eggs was available by Easter Sunday, it was natural that they featured largely in the feasting of that day, and in a variety of customs throughout Ireland. Children were given eggs as presents, and the practice of dyeing eggs was widespread. "Trundling eggs" seems to have been more specific to the North of Ireland, where Mason in his *Parochial Survey* of 1814-19 described it as an "amusement which is common at Easter" and one pursued "in the vicinity of Belfast".

At Holywood, Co Down, on the opposite shore of Belfast Lough, "it was usual with the women and children to collect in large bodies for this purpose". His description of the actual practice closely matches those we have for the Cave Hill fair: "The sport consists in throwing or trundling them along the ground, especially down a declivity, and gathering up the fragments to eat them". Mason also observed that "it is a curious circumstance that this sport is practiced only by the Presbyterians", and thus, if he was correct, they can lay claim to at least one aspect of Easter Monday tradition, and perhaps one of Scottish origin.

Teenagers and young lovers had less need of the organised entertainment than others. Rough flirtation was very evident even on the march up, with the "maids screaming out, for men are most insulting". Relationships might develop on the dance floor where

> – the sly maid her taper leg reveals,
> As though unwitting, to the graceful knee.

Or romance which had first stirred elsewhere might blossom further on the hill:

> Yet *now* the youth may boldly grasp at bliss –
> (Lovers like chiefs should choose a favouring day,)
> Faint with fatigue she rests her arm on his –
> And through a half feigned frown, smiles at the stolen kiss.

There was a less romantic side to the fair. After all, the earliest report of all, that in the *Belfast News Letter* for 1810, was a reference to deaths and injuries. Violence did not always occur: in 1825, according to *The Northern Whig*, there was "scarcely a discordant note to create a crash", but the very fact that absence of trouble was felt worthy of report suggests that violence of whatever kind frequently occurred, indeed the following year the *Whig*, apart from recording two accidental broken legs, added that "several individuals received severe contusions on the head by quarreling". Given the size of the assembly and the surfeit of drink this was hardly surprising, indeed typical of such assemblies elsewhere in Ireland, where faction fights were also a common occurrence.

There was, however, a developing and very northern dimension to tensions on the Cave Hill. This was evident in 1828 when on Easter Sunday Dr Crolly, Catholic Bishop of Down and Connor, warned his parishioners not to go the Cave Hill the following day as he had been warned that an attempt "to excite a party riot would be made". *The Northern Whig* was again on hand to report what occurred. Just as the crowds were beginning to leave the hill;

> An Orange lodge, headed by a fellow in a scarlet cloak, and armed with a musket and fixed bayonet, ascended to the level space below the lower cave, playing the usual party tunes, and calling, with the wonted accompaniment of oaths and blasphemy for the "face of a papist". Every possible attempt was made to excite a riot: and among the most active on the occasion, was a sergeant of Dragoons, dressed in his uniform.

The Belfast Commercial Chronicle added additional information which made it clear that the Orange intervention had local origins involving "20 or 30 fellows pretending to be Orangemen from the Carnmoney Lodge, No. 1725", a point confirmed because "their master [was] a labourer in one of the lime quarries". Small numbers did not lessen the danger because he "was armed with a gun and bayonet [and] others had pistols and swords; they had a flag which at intervals, on the hill, they waved as in defiance and fired several shots". The *Chronicle* concluded that it was fortunate that Catholics had by and large obeyed their bishop's advice to stay away, otherwise "there is reason to fear that that lives would have been lost". Not all Catholics did stay away because that evening Dr Crolly and the police magistrate, Mr Skinner, went to "the Whitehouse Road for the purpose of persuading the Roman Catholics who were in the crowds by which the way was covered, to retire".

Why should Orangemen demonstrate in this way at the Cave Hill fair? It was certainly a tribute to the continuing importance of the occasion, which was accordingly seen as a suitable locale for rank and file Orangemen to demonstrate their defiance of the ban on the organization that had been in force since 1823. Their arrival also reflected new sectarian tensions in Belfast, and perhaps in Greencastle, where a new mill village had sprung up, attracting a tide of workers many of whom "have come from the counties of Tyrone and Derry", and many of whom were poor Catholic immigrants. The old demographics of an overwhelmingly Presbyterian world were changing, and we may assume that the same was true of participants at the Cave Hill fair.

The Orange challenge was still present in 1833 when "a party of Orangemen held themselves in readiness" but for *The Northern Whig* the effects of "John Barleycorn" provided an equal threat amongst the "absolutely astonishing" numbers. In the event "no serious riots" occurred.

In the long term a more serious threat to the fair came from rapidly changing social attitudes. All the main churches were manifesting a new severity with regard to social conduct, and a growing imperative, indeed anxiety, in the arena of social control. As early as 1829 the Catholic hierarchy, concerned at the riotous conduct associated with Easter Monday gatherings, successfully petitioned the Pope to remove it from the list of days of religious obligation, and hence to make it a normal working day.

In most of Ireland where Catholics were employers, this had the desired dampening effect, or at least displaced former Easter Monday activity to Easter Sunday. However, in the North, major employers were almost exclusively Protestant and Easter Monday remained a rare public holiday.

There were other ways in which the new moralism of the churches in Ulster impacted on the Cave Hill fair. Father Mathew's temperance campaign made a rapid impact on the Catholic community from 1838 onwards, and, unusually for the times, was admired by other denominations. Presbyterians, once so tolerant of alcohol, even at Sessions Meetings, foreswore the old ways, and evangelicals within the Church of Ireland were establishing their own temperance societies. It was the latter who took the initiative on the Cave Hill.

Thomas Drew, Rector of Christ Church, noted how "it was customary for multitudes to resort on Easter Monday to the Cave Hill, when with folly and riot the day was wasted". From 1834 onwards he, and his associates, set about organizing counter measures "to this scene of disorder and peril" by "collecting the schools together on this day and giving them an annual feast, with an excursion into the country".

By 1841 they were ready to take on the Cave Hill itself for the new puritanical order of things. *The Northern Whig* described an assembly very different from the traditional one, as the members of the Teetotal Society "marched out in regular order to the Cave Hill". Once there they listened to "eloquent speeches in praise of sobriety, and total abstinence from all intoxicating drinks". There was also a total abstinence from the old and varied traditional musical fare; instead "the band played several enlivening airs". The crowd seems to have been satisfied with both music and speeches as "frequently the caves were made to resound with the cheers of the assembled multitude". The meeting closed with three cheers for the Queen, three for Father Mathew, and, rather incongruously, with three for "the publican who owned the field".

One can see parallels here with the growing campaign to bring an end to the notorious Donnybrook fair outside Dublin. There were differences: the Donnybrook fair was established by thirteenth-century charter, and was a market for a variety of goods, though by the late eighteenth century it had become a byword for dissipation. As the nineteenth century advanced it became a focus for moral outrage, as with the Cave Hill fair, though because of its formal status as a market, it was possible for a syndicate to buy out its charter and abolish it in 1855.

On the Cave Hill it briefly appeared that the intervention of the teetotalers had achieved the same effect. If we are to believe *The Northern Whig* they had the Cave Hill to themselves in 1841. In 1842 they planned to repeat this success but faced competition, not from traditional drunken revellers, but from Orangemen. Evidently, even under teetotal control, the Cave Hill assembly was still sufficiently significant to be worth muscling in on and accordingly the following placard appeared on the streets of Belfast;

> We the members of the Protestant Association, seeing an advertisement stuck on the corners of the various streets, announcing a procession denominated teetotalers, to walk from this town to the Cave Hill on Easter Monday, but very wisely, without party colours – we finding that they are considered by the authorities, to be perfectly legal (from no attempt having been made to prevent them), see no reason why we should not meet our brethren, from Carnmoney and its neighbourhood, at the Cave Hill

> at 12 o'clock; but it is particularly requested, that no music or party colours be used on the occasion.

Orangemen were once again seeking to use the Cave Hill to test the ban on the organisation, hence the very cautious nature of their poster. It was sufficient to put the teetotalers off: they cancelled their demonstration. It did not fool the authorities, who drafted 150 additional policemen into Belfast, and the Orangemen in turn decided that discretion was the better part of valour; indeed it is not clear who, if anybody, marked Easter Monday on the Hill in 1842.

Meanwhile, yet another pressure was being brought to bear to ensure that the old festivities were not revived. In 1844 the author of the "Annals of Christ Church" noted with approval that:

> The proprietors of land in the neighbourhood, witnessing the great decrease of visitors, have refused admittance to those who may still present themselves, so that this noted place is likely to be no more defiled by such exhibitors as disgraced our community for many years.

Such hopes were premature. Both the access route to the fair and the "tent ground" were owned by Andrew Nash, who, although not a publican, as opponents of the fair had previously suggested, was a rare Catholic landowner on the hill. He may have been less than enamoured by Protestant evangelical stridency, and, as something of a *bon viveur* himself, may have had a sneaking sympathy for the fair-goers. As a man living beyond his means, he may also have received some income from the owners of the fairground tents. In any case he continued to permit the erection of tents.

More immediately, the question arose as to whether there was life left in the fair in its old form after the hiatus of 1841-42. Evidently so: in 1845 *The Northern Whig* described how "a continuous and never ending mass thronged the outlets of the town in the direction of Cave Hill numbering in all probably 20,000 people". Again in 1847 the *Belfast News Letter* was able to report that the "Cave Hill, as usual, was visited by large numbers" but suggested that this was now the venue for an older generation with "the roads leading to this favourite venue – thronged by well dressed elderly persons". Herein lies a suggestion of incipient decay. The "elderly" enthusiasts of 1847 contrasted with "younger members of the families" of

Mallusk who "anxiously looked forward" to the fair in 1838-39, according to the *Ordnance Survey Memoirs*.

As late as 1854 J.B. Doyle in his *Tours in Ulster* describes a continued scene "of the greatest festivity" carried on by "the middle and lower classes from the town and surrounding country". The tented encampment is still there but there is a greater emphasis on informal activity as "happy groups of both sexes are to be seen in every direction, dressed in their holiday attire: – some perched upon the dizzy precipices, others reclining in happy circles upon the green sward". The old moral pitfall is still in evidence: "were it not for the occasional intemperance inseparable from such scenes of jollity, it would be exceedingly pleasing to contemplate", but the emphasis has shifted from the former all-pervading role of alcohol, to the exception of the "occasional".

By the 1850s the Cave Hill had, however, faded from newspaper reports of Easter Monday goings-on. Biggar in 1923 noted the allure of other attractions. You could go to see whether "a balloon went up (or did not) in the Botanic Gardens, or trains were run to take people further afield". He might have added the Museum which offered special rates on Easter Monday from 1845 onwards, or the Bangor Boat, but the most significant successor was the Pleasure Park on Queen's Island which opened in 1849. Thus the organized and easily accessible entertainments of a developing urban world were taking over from the essentially pre-industrial and more informal pleasures of the Easter Monday fair on the Cave Hill.

Meanwhile the old rural hinterland that had been the original mainspring of the fair was changing out of all recognition. The hand-loom weavers with their small holdings and history of conviviality had been eliminated by industrialization. The *Ordnance Survey Memoirs* recorded 800 of them still hanging on in Carnmoney in 1838-39. They were nearly all "small farmers" and their wages were "very small". Their progressive shift into the mills dampened enthusiasm for popular entertainment: "the taste for amusement with the people of this parish has declined as the pressure of the times has increased – their utmost energies being required to ensure a support for themselves and their families".

On the Cave Hill itself, George Wilson, an elderly witness in 1859, recounted how "all the people who lived at the top of the hill, are all gone", and these were people who had been at the heart of the fair. By then marginal upland livings that had once been possible no longer sufficed.

In 1858 the Cave Hill reappeared sensationally on the public scene as *The*

Northern Whig declared that "a demonstration is threatened". The threat arose because three years earlier Joseph Magill, Andrew Nash's son-in-law, had closed off the traditional route of access to the Cave Hill. In 1855 and in the two following years no fair had taken place.

The potential challenge in 1858 arose as a new Rights of Way Association commenced legal action against Magill for closing the right-of-way onto the hill, but no impetus was now available from would be revellers. As *The Northern Whig* ruefully commented, "had the hill visitors mustered in anything like the force or spirit which formerly characterized Easter Monday's assembly at the Cave Hill, from Belfast, or, more especially from the Whitewell or Carnmoney districts, a speedy issue would have been come to – for the day at least – on the right-of-way question".

Instead it was left to a very different class of person: that of gentlemen and well-to-do seekers after fresh air, and of would-be botanists and geologists, to take on Magill. The battle when fought was dramatic enough, but it was in a new field – the law courts. They won a famous victory at an appeal hearing in 1859, but they did not open the way for the return of the Easter Monday revellers. Thus the demise of the Cave Hill fair occurred in 1855, exactly coinciding with that of the Donnybrook fair.

In 1861 McComb in his *Guide to Belfast* consigned the old fair to an already distant past:

> Formerly the hill was a favourite holiday resort of young people from Belfast and the surrounding country on Easter Monday, and the scene of much festivity and hilarious revel. For such purposes, however, it is now deserted on the return of the joyous season.

John Gray was born in 1947 and educated at Campbell College, Belfast and Magdalen College, Oxford. He is the author of City in Revolt: James Larkin and the Belfast Dock Strike of 1907 *(Blackstaff Press, 1984). He served as the Librarian of the Linen Hall Library, Belfast, from 1982 to 2008. He continues to live in Belfast, and is currently working on a book devoted to Cave Hill in all its aspects.*

THE DOMINANCE OF AN ORACULAR HOME

David Fitzpatrick

MacNeice & Son.

Prologue

Louis MacNeice's family is a powerful, often disturbing, presence in his poetry and prose. Like so many more or less rebellious "Thirties" poets, he was the son of a clergyman. Childhood memories of industrial Carrickfergus, where Frederick John MacNeice was rector from 1908 to 1931, provided essential imagery (often bleak, sometimes menacing) for a writer intensely responsive to the sounds, colours, and smells associated with urban life. In various autobiographical writings, the squalor of its streets is juxtaposed with the Norman grandeur of the castle and church, and the middle-class stuffiness of the rectory (somewhat redeemed by its garden sanctuary). Such evocations of place in MacNeice's work intermingle with references to his father and family. For Louis MacNeice, childhood was a source of occasional nostalgia and recurrent nightmare, fuelled by his mother's early death, his father's remarriage soon followed by the ten-year-old's removal to boarding school, and other signs of rejection by family. His poetic treatment of these themes mellowed over time, evolving from angry rejection of his father's morality in 1930 towards acceptance of their essential affinity by the 1940s. MacNeice's exploration of family in verse and prose intensified after his father's death in 1942, contributing to a faltering and uncompleted return journey towards the faith and moral certainties of his "oracular home". My intention here is to apply an historian's eye to eight familiar poems, which together offer a kaleidoscopic view of MacNeice's response to the lives and deaths of his three parents and to the "values" that they embodied. In many cases, the obvious and accepted interpretation of key passages may be undermined by looking closely into the local and personal contexts of their creation. The poems may therefore be read in two registers, either as straightforward and disarmingly candid declarations of feeling and fact, or as coded intimations of a reality largely hidden from the world beyond Protestant Ulster.

The Eight Poems

I	"The Prodigal Son, or, The Dog Returns to his Vomit" (1930)
II	"Auden and MacNeice: Their Last Will and Testament" (1936)
III	"Carrickfergus" (1937)
IV	"Autobiography" (1940)
V	"The Kingdom", VII (1943)
VI	"The Strand" (1945)
VII	"Autumn Sequel", Canto XXII (1953)
VIII	"The Truisms" (*c.* 1961)

I

"The Prodigal Son, or, The Dog Returns to his Vomit" was published in an Oxford magazine in May 1930, a few weeks before Louis's marriage to Mary Ezra. He had spent the previous Christmas at Carrickfergus "under clouds of parental disapproval", partly stirred up by his *fiancée*'s exotic background. As his father complained: "The thought of an engagement to a Jewess is dreadful. If she is a religious Jewess it will be awful, & if she is an indifferent one it will be no better". This "shocker" of a poem, as William McKinnon remarked in the *Honest Ulsterman* (1983), is "surely the high-water mark of his anti-father, anti-religion, anti-family attitude". The unrepentant Prodigal's target is not "Him" but "Them", so implicating his stepmother in "the dominance of an oracular home" with its "imbecile kindness". But the most scathing jibes are reserved for the rector, who sits in judgement over the sinner, his moral code reinforced by "the morons", his words a "ghastly pack of comedy cards". This poetic rant is deliberately subverted by its manifest unfairness, culminating in the impotent protest that, as a believer in the forgiveness of sins, his father had taken "my ultimate salvation for granted". Ostensibly an appeal for the respect due to an errant adult, it is essentially a howl for attention from an anarchic adolescent. Louis wisely omitted this revealing but truly nauseating diatribe from all collections of his work.

II

More than six years elapsed before Louis's next depiction of his family in verse, in "Auden and MacNeice: Their Last Will and Testament". This jocular by-product of a memorable visit to Iceland coincided with Mary's remarriage to Charles Katzman, a year after her abrupt desertion of Louis and their infant son Daniel. Dissolution of the unwelcome marriage was rapidly followed by reconciliation with his father, who had become Bishop of Down and Connor and Dromore in 1934. Louis's new-found "admiration" for a father who had "fixed/His pulpit out of the reach of party slogans" was doubtless prompted by news of the bishop's celebrated attempt in summer 1935 to counteract sectarian conflict by an ecumenical crusade involving all but one of the major denominations in Belfast. The "armoured cars" were possibly the Lancia "Cage cars" used by the Royal Ulster Constabulary (eventually aided by the army and part-time "B" Special Constabulary) when endeavouring to suppress the spiral of reprisals and counter-reprisals occasioned by attacks on Orangemen and loyalists celebrating the Jubilee and "the Twelfth".

His stepmother no longer appears as an accessory in moral repression, but as an efficient if "placid" household manager who is "rich" in delight as well as wealth. Ever generous, she bought a fine car for Louis and Mary in 1931 ("£135, sliding roof, for £114"), later willing her profligate stepson the income from a bequest of £2,000, to be set aside in trust for his lifetime. Louis expressed his gratitude in "Death of an Old Lady", written soon after her funeral service in Carrickfergus on 11 April 1956, which Louis attended. Though old and tired (in her eighty-fourth year), her approach to death was "calm and slow", just as, two decades earlier, she had reigned "calm in the circle of her household gods". In his obituary poem, Louis likened Beatrice's dying to the destruction of the *Titanic* in 1912, an unexpected comparison which Jon Stallworthy (in *Louis MacNeice*, 1995) attributes to a "subconscious association" with "the loss of his mother (to a psychiatric institution) in the same year, 1912". Since Lily was not admitted to her first hospital until March 1913, it seems more likely that the metaphor was inspired by the well-publicised anniversary of the fatal collision on 14 April. It is worth noting that publication of the death notice for Beatrice MacNeice coincided precisely with a broadcast on "The Sinking of the Titanic" over the BBC's Home Service.

In "Their Last Will and Testament", "L." not only left his father "half my pride of blood", but specified his Sligo rather than Connemara ancestors when declaring the origins of his own "peasant vitality" and "peasant's sense of humour". His sister Elizabeth, when discussing a draft of *Apollo's Blended Dream*, McKinnon's study of MacNeice published in 1971, recalled that "when my father first read Louis' tribute to himself (which he liked) in

Letters from Iceland he said to me 'There is just one mistake in it'. When I said 'What is that?' he said to me 'The MacNeices were never peasants' and said 'Oh well you know, I expect Louis would rather think that they were'". Having investigated their Sligo origins, Elizabeth concluded that Louis had been deceived by the apparent poverty of some descendants whom they had visited in 1927. They were in fact "small farmers, and for that matter, a great deal more prosperous even than Louis thought". She surmised that any "peasant characteristics" were "probably from our mother's side of the family", which provided "some real Connemara peasant ancestry" with earthy values helping to counteract the "fecklessness" of some of the MacNeices. Though Louis toured Connemara as well as Sligo with his family in September 1927, the climax of this atavistic visit was his father's birthplace, Omey Island (where Frederick's missionary parents kept a school), not his mother's native Killymongaun. This was the townland slightly eastwards of Clifden where his maternal grandfather, the convert Martin Clesham, had farmed some thirty acres of extremely arid land. The MacNeice holding in Ballysodare, though slightly smaller in area, consisted of relatively fertile land six times as valuable as the Cleshams' farm in Connemara. Louis's misleading account of his Connaught origins reflects the dominance of "forefathers" rather than foremothers in his personal myth of origin. Despite Louis's lifelong grief at the loss of his mother when he was barely seven years old, he remained profoundly ignorant of her background in what he romantically termed "the West of Ireland".

III

"Carrickfergus", perhaps MacNeice's most widely quoted work, was the declamatory opening salvo in *The Earth Compels*, published in 1938. Here, his father is treated not as a living being but as a factor in the poet's social conditioning: "I was the Rector's son, born to the anglican order, / Banned for ever from the candles of the Irish poor". It would be easy to assume, given Louis's frequent and disparaging references to impoverished devotees of the Blessed Virgin, that the "Irish poor" signified candle-venerating Roman Catholics, segregated in a ghetto from which the Protestant majority was absent: "The Scotch Quarter was a line of residential houses / But the Irish Quarter was a slum for the blind and halt". For Fran Brearton, in *The Great War and Irish Poetry* (2000), this passage indicates that "past invasions are responsible for the divisions and inequalities of the present", still redolent of the conflict between the "invader" (epitomised in "the anglican order") and "his slave" (the "Irish poor").

This inference is more blatant in John Banville's burlesque, *The Untouchable* (1997), where "Victor Maskell" (an uneasy hybrid of MacNeice and Anthony Blunt) defies his upbringing by undertaking nocturnal rambles in forbidden territory:

> When I was a boy in Carrickdrum I often ventured at night into Irishtown, a half acre of higgledy-piggledy shacks behind the seafront where the Catholic poor lived in what seemed to me euphoric squalor ... I would creep up to Murphy's Lounge or Maloney's Select Bar and stand outside the shut door, my heart beating in my throat – it was known for a fact that if the Catholics caught a Protestant child he would be spirited away and buried alive in a shallow grave in the hills above the town.

Banville's rigmarole is paraphrased from a graphic passage in *The Strings are False*, in which no reference whatever is made to religious distinctions:

> We rarely went into the Irish Quarter and I used to hold my breath till I got through it. There was a dense smell of poverty as of soot mixed with porter mixed with cheap frying fat mixed with festering scabs and rags that had never been washed ... And in Irish Quarter West there was a place which I knew was bad – a public house with great wide windows of opaque decorated glass.

MacNeice's autobiographical account refers exclusively to divisions of class rather than religion, and would have been so interpreted by anyone familiar with the social geography of Carrickfergus. By the early twentieth century, all trace of the ethnic origins of the seventeenth-century "Irish" and "Scotch" Quarters, apart from their names, had been eradicated. Examination of the unpublished enumerators' abstracts of the 1901 census reveals that less than one-fifth of the 800-odd residents of the two Irish Quarters (South and West) were Catholics, only slightly above the proportion for the entire town, whereas two-fifths adhered to the Church of Ireland, easily the highest proportion for any sector of Carrickfergus. Though undoubtedly poor, most of the cripples, shopkeepers, and drinkers of the Irish Quarters were Protestants, half of them Frederick MacNeice's parishioners. Presbyterians accounted for only two-fifths of the 300 inhabitants of "residential houses" in Scotch Quarter, being greatly outnumbered by Protestants of other denominations.

By no means a preserve of the rich and powerful, as superficially suggested by the image of the Chichesters kneeling in marble in the north transept of St Nicholas's parish church, "anglicanism" in Antrim embraced all classes, the mercantile and professional élite being disproportionately Presbyterian and Methodist as in most of Ulster. The Church of Ireland laity in urban Ulster was far humbler than its southern counterpart, whose ever tinier congregations were indeed dominated by the residue of the fallen "Ascendancy". In Carrickfergus, as in "Carrickfergus", most of the "candles of the Irish poor" illuminated Protestant hovels rather than the "garish altars" or "garish Virgin" ridiculed in "Autumn Journal", XVI (1938) and "Belfast" (1931). The contrast between the candles of the poor and the rectory's oil lamps is explicit in "Country Week-End" (*c.*1961), which evokes the comforting association between the dim, steady light of oil lamps and "Bustling dead women with steady hands, / One from Tyrone and one from Cavan / And one my mother'. The lamps offered

> Assurance, not like the fickle candles
> Which gave the dark a jagged edge
> And made it darker yet, more evil,
> Whereas these lamps, we knew, were kind.

Far from symbolising an idealised Catholic Ireland from which MacNeice was unfairly excluded by his upbringing, the candles of the poor betokened the menace of an underclass latent within his father's own flock. Since Louis MacNeice was a stickler for the literal truth, adept though he was in deluding the uninitiated through studied ambiguities, the term "anglican order" must refer not to the laity, but to the clerical order that his father had entered in 1895. For the historically alert reader, "Carrickfergus" encapsulates the profound class divisions within twentieth-century Ulster Protestantism rather than some eternal contest between Protestant invader and Catholic slave.

IV

"Autobiography" is one of eleven poems that MacNeice composed during a week's convalescence, from peritonitis, on a Connecticut island in August and September 1940. As he self-deprecatingly informed his recalcitrant

American muse, Eleanor Clark, it is "a naive-seeming kind of little ballad with refrain". The poem crystallised the painful memory of his mother's illness and death which he had recently explored so powerfully in *The Strings are False*, and to which he would return in his final (posthumous) broadcast, "Childhood Memories". The rector appears as a forceful, almost frightening figure, who "made the walls resound,/He wore his collar the wrong way round". By contrast, his mother eludes specific recollection, leaving the the bereft seven-year-old of the poem to clutch at straws: the colour of a dress, a vague aura of "gentleness". His sister Elizabeth, more than four years older, cast some doubt on this "naive-seeming" failure of precise recollection when she remarked that "his memories of her before that time [1913] were fragmentary and shadowy, at least so he said". Her own memories were of "warmth and love and vitality", expressed through Lily's creation of "a placid, orderly kind of household" abounding with pets, rituals, and games, and also through her gaity, love of dancing, and emotional responsiveness. But Elizabeth also recalled elements of "tension" arising from Lily's dislike of "the Ulster atmosphere" and the first signs of physical breakdown and "mental disturbance" that culminated in a successful hysterectomy, followed by unsuccessful treatment for depression.

Louis, like Elizabeth, must have been aware that Lily "developed ideas of having committed unforgivable sins and was inclined to talk even to the children about Death and Judgement, Hell and Heaven and kindred subjects". As Elizabeth makes clear, the images of Hellfire that may have intensified Louis's "black dreams" are more likely to have emanated from Lily MacNeice than either her husband or poor "Miss Craig" (Margaret McCready) from Co Armagh, the reputedly Calvinist (in fact anglican) "mother's help" on whom Louis heaped so much probably undeserved odium. By vilifying his substitute mother in prose, and poetically contrasting his father's forcefulness with Lily's "gentleness", Louis did his best to cleanse his memory of the more alarming maternal images recorded by Elizabeth. Yet, even in "Autobiography", there is an undertone of anger in the refrain, "*Come back early or never come*". It was not his mother's help or father that failed Freddie as he shivered in the dark, but his mother. It was "the dead" that "did not care", that were not there, that did not reply, that left the child to "walk away alone". While the music of the poem wraps his mother in a protective layer of sentimentality which reproaches those that survived her, the syntax conveys unrequited anger against the mother who had betrayed her child by dying too early.

V

Frederick MacNeice's death on 14 April 1942 unleashed a rich sequence of positive filial memories, beginning with an affectionate post-funeral tribute incorporated in "The Kingdom". As in 1930 and 1936, the years of his first marriage and divorce, Louis's poetic treatment of his father was clearly influenced by major changes in his personal life (as an astrologer might put it). If Frederick's opposition to his marriage to a Jewess added rancour to "The Prodigal Son", while divorce facilitated the renewed goodwill expressed in "Their Last Will and Testament", the bishop's death released Louis from the risk of an equally negative paternal response to his second marriage (to Hedli Anderson), which occurred on 2 July. No longer a threatening or awesome figure, his father in death had become as gentle as a mother and as vulnerable as a child: "All is well, said the voice from the tiny pulpit,/All is well with the child". The "child" of the biblical text appears to be dead, but subsequently returns to life in an emblem of resurrection (II Kings, iv: 26).

The voice from the pulpit was that of Richard James Clarke, archdeacon of Connor, who delivered "a short address" to mourners at St Patrick's Church, Drumbeg. The preacher was indeed "very old" (in his eighty-sixth year, with a decade yet to come), and had played a crucial part in Frederick's advancement in the Church. As rector of Holy Trinity (1894–1903), Clarke had first engaged him as his curate and later welcomed him back to the parish as his successor, deeming him a man of "ability, energy, and a sympathetic mind". Preaching at his consecration as Bishop of Cashel at Christ Church Cathedral in 1931, he had depicted MacNeice's election "as a sign from Heaven, as something tending to bind together the whole Church of Ireland". At the election for the new Bishop of Down in December 1934, Clarke's intervention had helped to persuade the synod to hold an additional ballot after the inconclusive outcome of earlier rounds, so ensuring that the synod rather than the bench of bishops would determine the result and enabling MacNeice to secure the required majorities. Like his protégé, Clarke was a Trinity man with an unremarkable academic record, from a "Southern" background (Virginia, Co Cavan), who adjusted to Belfast conditions by becoming an active Orangeman. He was not merely his "friend and colleague" but, in several senses, his brother in spirit.

The "generous puritan" of this poem gained his serenity from authentic faith, as "One who believed and practised and whose life/Presumed the

Resurrection. What that means/He may have felt he knew". According to a sermon delivered in Carrickfergus in 1925, MacNeice adhered to St Paul's teaching "that there will be a resurrection of the body, but that there will not be a resurrection of flesh and blood". The "raising" of the "Spiritual" body referred "to the whole career of the same personality, beginning with the birth, through death into that spiritual order in which each, according to his capacity, will be able to share in the unexplored and inexhaustible wealth of the world to come". This doctrine, literally interpreted, allowed Frederick to pay so little attention to the fate of the physical body that he neglected to reserve any plot for his own burial, bishop though he was. The survival and rebirth of his "personality" was achieved, irrevocably, in the poetry of his agnostic son.

VI

In "The Strand", Louis evoked his father not as a disembodied "personality" but as a fully visualised physical being, though the force of his faith is obliquely fixed in the image of "a square black figure whom the horizon understood" (the horizon being itself understood as "the line at which earth and sky appear to meet"). The memory of his father "Carrying his boots and paddling like a child" echoes Frederick's own account of a visit to Omey in 1930: "Bea and I crossed Omey strand, carrying our footwear". The poem, however, emerged from a visit with Hedli to Achill Island in 1945, which re-enacted the presumably fraught family holiday, sixteen years earlier, in which Louis's unsuitable *fiancée* Mary Ezra had spent nearly a month getting to be known by his father, stepmother, and siblings. They had rented the Old Rectory at Dugort, once the headquarters of Edward Nangle's celebrated Protestant "colony" which the Irish Church Missions had attempted to revive in the 1850s. Though none of his "fathers" had dwelt in Mayo, its mountainous terrain and Atlantic seaboard gave it enough in common with Ballysodare, Omey, and Killymongaun to serve as an outpost of the generalised, far-away "pre-natal mountain" of "Carrick Revisited" (another product of the summer holiday in 1945). "Slievemore/ Menaun and Croaghaun" were rugged Achill surrogates for the Twelve Pins outside Clifden, or Knockalongy a few miles to the west of Ballysodare.

Beatrice's diary of the earlier holiday suggests that the rector ("Derrick") was indeed intoxicated, if not "fulfilled", by the island's mountainous challenge. Their third Sunday in Achill was a

> *Lovely day*. Service 11.30, Dugort. Derrick & I had walk after tea towards Keel – I came Home alone & he went up Slievemore – not Home till 11.15 p.m. – I was anxiously looking out for him.

Next Sunday, he kept the family waiting for an hour at the Bull's Mouth before returning from "the Island service" on Inishbiggle, while they watched a "beautiful sunset behind Slievemore". These rambles allowed possibly welcome escape from domestic tension at the Old Rectory, where Mary plied them with lobsters spirited out of Keel while Beatrice countered this display of Oxford hedonism with a homely macaroni cheese. Consumption of the lobsters was postponed, perhaps unfortunately, till the following lunchtime. Frederick, Beatrice, and William returned briefly to Achill in the following summer, without the company of Louis and his new wife, and once again the rector made for the mountains. As he noted in his holiday diary (one of those "account books of a devout, precise routine" which failed to conceal "something in him solitary and wild"):

> We attended service in Dugort Church. – There were about 50 persons present. It was about 1.45 before we had lunch. After lunch we drove to the entrance of what is known as "Captain Boycott's place". Bea remained there and William and I essayed to climb Croaghaun. It was a perfect day with a cloudless sky.

After some faltering, they reached the summit (2,192 feet) before collecting the patient Beatrice on their way to supper at the Slievemore Hotel.

VII

The association between his father and ascent reappears in "Autumn Sequel", no longer as a symbol of fulfilment but as a premonition of death in "the worst of my dreams". In "The Strand", the poet traces his father's sturdy steps along the seashore; in "Autumn Sequel", written eight years later in 1953, both father and son seem older: "he could not keep/Up with me, being heavy", while "I began/To feel I had never been young". Yet the dream originated in his time as a pupil at Marlborough College, six or seven years before that first holiday in Achill. For two years after his promotion as a fifteen-year-old to Upper School and "C. House", he had slept in a dormitory of the former Seymour mansion clearly identifiable as that "high long panelled room from the time of Queen Anne". Though the poem's setting is in Wiltshire, the "steep dune" with its sinister hidden amphitheatre does not belong to the English landscape of "Woods" (1946) – each "moored/To a village somewhere near" – which his father had found so "tame" by comparison with the West of Ireland. In the dream, there is no reprieve (as in "Woods") from "the neolithic night", as the poet feels his "mind/Crumble and dry like a fossil sponge" and his body "curl like a foetus". The poem draws a theological fable out of his grotesque vision of the funfair, the "holiday throng", and the "newspaper scraps" that "capered around the foot of three tall black crosses". For the boy who has lost his faith, these images of Armageddon inspire sheer fear of death; for his father, faith in salvation makes the imminent collapse of the world a triumph rather than a catastrophe. As so often, the poet's imposed interpretation fails to conceal a still more alarming undercurrent: the possibility that Louis's scepticism, the very spark of his creativity, might eventually succumb to the certainties of his father, "still coming up, coming up" behind him.

VIII

Eight years later, this possibility was made manifest in "The Truisms", which portrays a world-weary son welcomed by tokens of his dead father's approval. Unlike "The Prodigal Son" of 1930, whose challenge to "the dominance of an oracular home" had "passed unnoticed", he remembers how to bless his father's home. In response, he too is blessed: "The truisms flew and perched on his shoulders/And a tall tree sprouted from his father's grave". Through some enchantment, the son seems ready at last to embrace his father's long-discarded moral precepts and so reclaim the lost "home". The very term "truisms" suggests, deceptively, that the character of these precepts is self-evident: presumably the plain Christian virtues which, according to "The Kingdom", "made him courteous/And lyrical and strong and kind and truthful". Conspicuous among those virtues, according to the prevalent view, were courage, tolerance, hatred of violence, and rejection of sectarianism. On closer inspection, as I argue elsewhere, Frederick MacNeice's worldview appears less liberal, more complex, and altogether more interesting. The truisms that "perched on his shoulders" were, in my view, slightly unsettling. The apparent theme of the poem – redemption – is further subverted (for literal-minded historians) by the fact that no tree shelters the grassy plot at Drumbeg where John Frederick MacNeice, "Bishop", lies buried.

Epilogue

As a person and a writer, Louis MacNeice never escaped the formative influence of his family, and his father in particular. Admittedly, few of us do escape our origins, however hard we may try. What marks out MacNeice is his lifelong and obsessional interest in his childhood, and the extent to which childhood dramas were re-enacted and embellished in his later life and work. The bequest of childhood and upbringing is equally obvious in the pious little boy; the rebellious adolescent (a protracted phase) rejecting his father's temperance, prudishness, and Christian morality; and the troubled adult embarking on the "Quest" for certainty, virtue, and redemption. The psychological consequences of losing his mother and blaming his father were not only far-reaching but the subject of relentless reflection and Freudian self-analysis, as one would expect of a Thirties poet. Yet, even as a rebel, Louis maintained close contact with his family, writing affectionate letters to "Daddie" and "Madre", staying with them at home or on holiday, entertaining them in England, borrowing their money, and accompanying his father to rugby matches and the Dublin University Club as well as church. Frederick left a strong imprint on Louis's likes as well as dislikes: his intellectual curiosity, love of manly games, social radicalism, distaste for Roman Catholicism, unwillingness to surrender his political independence to the Communist Party or any other, and (sometimes appalled) intoxication with exotic cultures. Frederick's influence was also evident in Louis's long head and wide mouth, his lack of an Ulster accent, his initial reticence with strangers, and his warmth with trusted friends. These affinities do not imply that Louis was his father reincarnate: Frederick was too grave, Louis too playful to swap personalities at will. Yet, as Louis observed in "The Strand", there was something in his father (as in himself) that was "solitary and wild".

As a writer and master of language, he was also strikingly indebted to his father. Both were precise and logical, avoiding high-flown phrases and epigrammatic swagger. Though self-consciously dismissive of his own facility in Greek, Louis too relished command of an esoteric medium giving access to a secret world. Like Frederick, he resisted flaunting his classical education through arcane allusions, preferring to utter complex thoughts in everyday words. For initiates, layers of less accessible resonances and references cushioned the surface banality of so much of his poetry and prose. Louis was conscious of the likeness between poems and sermons, properly conceived, with their expository and didactic functions and their amalgam of intellectual, emotional, and moral elements. As he declared in *Modern Poetry: A Personal Essay* (1938): "The poet is primarily a spokesman, making statements or incantations on behalf of himself or others" – someone trying to convey to others what excites him in his own life and experience. The didactic strand is dominant in discursive works such as *Autumn Journal* (1939) and *Autumn Sequel* (1953); whereas the lyric poems, with their flashes of revelation and subterranean tremors, share the clergyman's mission to jolt the congregation into some sense of mystery and transcendence.

The alternation between commonsense and inspiration, so characteristic of Louis's poetry, has much in common with the structure of Frederick's finest sermons. Though not a linguistic magician like his son, he was capable of dramatic changes of register when pointing out the alarming implications of actually loving one's neighbour or turning the other cheek. The unsuspecting listener or reader is first lulled by familiar truisms, then guided towards something novel or disconcerting, finally calmed by a second flurry of truisms. Both, in short, were expert practitioners of scholastic (and Ciceronian) rhetoric, in which the audience of a speech or letter is won over by an informal, conversational style. The impact of the "petition" is enhanced by a preliminary "exordium" (such as a proverb or passage from scripture), and a "narration" providing context for the crucial appeal or exhortation that follows. Frederick, like his son, was a truth-teller who had no compunction in guiding his readers or listeners towards false but beneficial inferences from his carefully chosen words. For father and son alike, words were tools serving a higher purpose, though only Frederick had a clear and consistent sense of what that purpose was.

Frederick MacNeice's influence on his son's outlook and writing was anything but static, reflecting profound changes in his own situation. His puritanism and missionary zeal were constants, but his place in Ulster society was transformed during Louis's lifetime. At the time of Louis's birth in 1907, he was an impoverished minister in an inner Belfast parish, without any of the benefits of inherited wealth or status enjoyed by most clergymen of the "anglican order". Remarriage to a rich spinster gave access to an ever-widening circle of influential relatives and friends, without whose support he could scarcely have contemplated becoming a bishop and a formidable figure in the Church of Ireland. Frederick's social advance was accompanied by gradual retreat from active involvement in unionism and Orangeism, though (contrary to common belief) he never truly became a nationalist.

His struggle against the Anti-Christ was redirected from popery to secularism, in keeping with his conviction that the alliances and antagonisms shaping humanity had been transformed by the disaster of the Great War. The security conferred by wealth and influence made him in some respects a rebel rather than a conformist, enabling him to become a fearless opponent of sectarianism, a passionate internationalist, and a dogged advocate of the autonomy of the Church of Christ when imperilled by political interference.

These changes in Frederick's public persona entailed suppression of certain facets of his earlier career, a process in which Louis willingly colluded. This is evident in Louis's strange and contradictory utterances about nationalism and Orangeism, and the loyal manner in which he asserted and backdated his father's liberal credentials. As he came closer to Frederick in later life, Louis took an active and imaginative part in recasting the family narrative into the plausible and attractive form now generally accepted by MacNeicians. He had become his father's protector.

Further Reading

The best edition of the *Collected Poems* is that edited by Peter McDonald (2007). Several autobiographical essays, edited by E. R. Dodds, were published as *The Strings are False: An Unfinished Autobiography* (1965). Edna Longley's *Louis MacNeice: A Study* (1988) is a perceptive introduction to his poetry, illuminating its offbeat but pervasive Irishness. The only major biography is Jon Stallworthy's zestful *Louis MacNeice* (1995). For my own interpretations and their documentary basis, see "'I will acquire an attitude not yours': Was Frederick MacNeice a Home Ruler and Why Does This Matter?" in *Field Day Review* (2008); and *Solitary and Wild: Frederick MacNeice and the Salvation of Ireland*, to be published by the Lilliput Press, Dublin.

David Fitzpatrick was born in 1949 in Melbourne, Australia. He took degrees at the University of Melbourne and Trinity College, Cambridge. He is the author of several works relating to Ireland in the period of the Great War and subsequent revolution, including Politics and Irish Life, 1913-1921: Provincial Experience of War and Revolution *(Gill and Macmillan, 1977),* The Two Irelands, 1912-1939 *(Oxford University Press, 1998), and* Harry Boland's Irish Revolution *(Cork University Press, 2003). He is currently preparing a history of the Orange Order in Ireland, to be preceded by a biography of Louis MacNeice's father, in which the personal impact of the war on a pacifist clergyman is a major theme. He is Professor of Modern History, Centre for War Studies, Trinity College Dublin, and lives in Belfast.*

BEES OF THE INVISIBLE

Harry Clifton

Autumn in Paris.

The Rond Point, in mid-September, sits on the fault-line between summer and autumn, with the roar of traffic through Porte d'Orleans outside. The chairs are unstacked, the tables are busy. The Aveyronais proprietor, back from *la France profonde*, has his best shirt on. Regulars from the neighbourhood are in for their Sunday lunch. The waiters, cummerbunded, white-aproned, fuss around the elderly. The very old, who drool over their food, are gently placed at the end-tables. The widows who live around the corner are shown to small tables with a bowl placed underneath for their dogs to eat out of. A man in blue peaked cap cleans oysters, winkles, crabs for a seafood platter. A waiter with a glass of beer on a tray is weaving through traffic to the man with who sells *France Dimanche* at the kiosk. Great black skies are building up. The trees, unearthly yellow in sun and shadow, belly and heave in the breeze, but no leaves fall. It is September, the city has resumed, but the weather still hesitates.

"At Versailles", the widow beside me states, "there is a Motor Show. *Beaucoup de voitures.*" She has no more interest in it than I do, but it might pass the time, like a public hanging. "Today is the last day." The remnants of a bad meal are scattered in front of her, with a half-drunk glass of Pepsi Cola. She talks to herself, she talks to the dog under the table. Occasionally she talks to me. I am eating, to her amazement, a plate of kidneys, my favourite dish here and the reason I come in the first place. Served with steamed potatoes, pieces of fried bacon. A local Aveyronais dish, smuggled on to a Paris menu by a homesick owner, then taken off again when no one wanted it. It is not there now. I have to ask for it specially. Shame of origins, or the taint of offal from the demolished abattoirs of the fifteenth district, a few minutes away.

Al Hocevar, our friend from Slovenia, is due any minute. He lives and writes in Paris, but only for the autumn. His spring semesters are spent in America, teaching. Now, in September, he is back again. The air temperature is right now, for the reflective species to dwell on itself in plexiglass cafés and drink its cocktail of past and present. Careful of each other, territorial as cats. The Americans and the Poles, each with their chosen corners. Jewish writers with the extinct volcano of Europe to look into, the ashes of the recent past. Arabs, Slavs, out of Palestine, Bosnia, explaining their case to the world. Prominent names like Edmund White, C.K.Williams and Adam Zagajewski, away for half the year in American universities. Shadowy names like myself and Al, banished into the suburbs. And the recently dead, who were there all the time, whose books are now unread, who outlived their hour of exile and glamour to wander disregarded through the streets and gardens of an adopted city. Al Hocevar, Deirdre and I, we are all part of that delicate species, the contemplative, seeking an ecological niche in the meta-life of Paris.

"I borrowed an idea from you", he says when he arrives. "That French intellectual life is too theory-based while Irish intellectual life is too lyrical, and both have something to give to the other. For my Stockholm lecture. I hope you don't mind."

Al is eminent, higher on the food-chain than I am myself. We pretend to respect each other, our malice is friendly, professional. I have read his stories and his autobiography which charmingly avoids anything relevant, such as how he left Slovenia in the difficult years, or fetched up in Paris with a French wife, in the wealthy suburb of Billancourt. He is difficult to place, as I think he wishes to be, though of course he would say the same about me. Meanwhile I contemplate his wonderful white shovel-beard, which always seems to me the beard of a prophet without prophecy, a mariner who has never been to sea.

"How was Schloss Solitude?"

"Schloss Solitude", he says, "was good. We had three weeks there, my wife and I. It was a kind of holiday."

"You got no writing done?"

"A little", he says carefully. "A critical essay. There is so much criticism in the air I can't escape it. The same in Paris. I need to get away."

From Schloss Solitude, the writers' colony in south Germany, they crossed by car through Austria into Slovenia. Slovenia, which is free now. Disconcertingly, his suitcases were stolen and he had to outfit himself from head to toe in local wear, a matter of some importance for Al is a snappy dresser, whose Paris clothes are of the best labels. They stayed with his ageing mother, and went to see the house they have bought on the outskirts of Ljubljana where Al hopes to retire, after twenty years in Paris, with the aura if not the actuality of a former dissident. A big fish in a very small pool.

"And you", he asks me, "are you writing anything?"

"A prose text. Interleaved chapters, present and past. A study of ancestry."

Should I tell him he is in it already? It hardly seems necessary, in a realm where everyone uses everyone else. As it is, I consider him in debt to me anyway, for the Stockholm lecture.

"John Silverman", he says, "is still there. He won't be back in Paris until the end of September."

"Which rooms did he get?"

"The Beethoven suite. I was stuck with the Schumann. The desk is in a cloakroom, between bedroom and bathroom."

"Hopeless."

"But better than the Stravinsky suite, where they shoved the poor Russian. A kind of scullery, behind the kitchen. All he could hear was pot-lids, day and night. Still, he was very grateful."

John Silverman, a mutual friend, also frequents Schloss Solitude. He is up there now, with all the other bees of the invisible, as Rilke described them, turning the honey of existence into inwardness. Others, on flowered balconies above Lake Garda, write and ponder. A knock comes on the door. Would they like lunch brought to their room, or a picnic to take to the shore? In Switzerland, above dark lakes, in old Scottish castles, Provencal retreats, colonies of contemplatives rarify life into writing, in an end-of-the-century air. Everything is turning into thought.

Al Hocevar brightens suddenly. My wife has come in. He kisses her on both cheeks. Women, at least, are still real.

We walk with Al up the Avenue Leclerc. There is an afternoon matinée he wants to see, at Denfert Rochereau, in an hour. A small cinema, specialising in offbeat films.

Often he sits in there, on empty afternoons, clearing his head. Films, bad, good or indifferent, have that effect, he says. Or maybe it is the velvety smooth darkness of the small auditorium, the few heads dotted here and there, watching. I suspect Al is bored with Paris. After twenty years frequenting concerts, bars, expatriate libraries, having his books translated, coming and going from the States, flirting with strange women, the law of diminishing returns has set in. He is preparing, in his middle fifties, to bring his life full circle again.

"This one," he says nostalgically, "is about an East European conductor who never agreed to record, but only existed in live performance.

Principles. No compromise."

Paris, of course, is all about compromise. John Silverman, for instance, lived for decades off a private income settled on him by his father, whom he later described as a monster in one of his novels. Now, with a French wife and the novels at the bottom end of the American bestseller lists, he crosses the Atlantic each January with Al, his oldest friend in Paris, to a midwest teaching stint. Two grey-haired men, taking the same plane to the depths of American space.

"The flea market", Deirdre says, "is on at the Avenue du Maine."

"Will it rain, do you think?"

"Not for an hour yet. Let's take a look."

Shutters slam in a gust and canvas flaps on the half-dismantled stalls of the Place d'Alesia, as the foodsellers pack up. Stacks of orange-crates, loaded with unsold produce, are rolled back up the tailboards of waiting lorries. Grapes from the Burgundy harvest, *cepes* and *chanterelles* from the far south-west. The produce of autumn, in all the markets now. In the open backs of refrigerator vans, whole sides of animals hang, and a whiff of stacked cheeses insinuates itself between metal grilles. The vendors are inside the neighbouring café and stand at the back counter drinking. Young teachers, at the front tables, do their corrections for Monday. On the other side of the rue d'Alesia, African women and children in traditional dress stream through the entrance of an evangelical church. Weather and habit, the daily rites of Paris on a Sunday, are back to normal.

On the Avenue du Maine, the pavements are wide. A fresh breeze, so rare in the windless streets of the city, makes walking a pleasure. Any other Sunday, Al, who loves exercise, would be racing his bike down the poplared avenues outside Paris. For his age, he is a fit man, but the city pools where I swim, with their crowded changing-rooms and ancient plumbing, are not to his taste. I feel there is a great deal he has gone beyond already, in his unplaceable life that I do not inquire into, and that one day soon he will be gone from Paris as so many have come and gone, and that already I am seeing him, and Paris itself, through the eyes of memory.

"The city", he says, "is emptying its pockets for autumn."

In the square of the fourteenth *arrondissement*, stalls are selling furniture, old cutlery, glass and linen, the disembowelled living of half a century, from the buildings in the neighbourhood. Old bric-a-brac interests me very little, having grown up in Dublin, where the past cluttered the present. But Al, whose past has cluttered his present far more than mine, lifts from the midden a silver champagne bucket.

"Old marriage", he says.

It is one of those days when Paris throws itself open to its own public, in a grand revolutionary gesture. Everything for the people. All over the city, citizens are walking through inner courtyards normally closed off to them, among box hedges, gravel, topiary. Garden Sunday, it is called. In a week or a fortnight it will be the turn of the observatories, the hospitals, the Senate, the Presidential Palace and the art collections to present themselves for inspection by their own populace, on whom the taxes are levied.

"Bread and circuses", Al says. "They expect it, considering how much they pay in rates."

I do not ask Al how much he has bought into this system, out there in Billancourt where he lives, and he does not ask me. Outsiders, we watch the French admiring themselves in their own national mirror.

On rue Daguerre, Al ducks into a bookshop. I recognise the gesture, an occupational disease of authors everywhere – checking to see if his work is on the shelf. Seconds later, out he comes again.

"You look around these places", he says blackly, "and then hang yourself."

We leave Al outside his little cinema, around the corner from the metro entrance at Denfert Rochereau. He will pass an hour in there, performing sophisticated mental operations on himself, as authors do in a city where literature now is the self screening itself in dark solipsistic space. Not dishonourable, but hard on a Sunday afternoon when you have been around too long and life goes on without buying what you write.

"Till later in the autumn", he says, embracing us both, "when John Silverman gets back."

The skies are about to open. By the time our bus leaves Porte d'Orleans for the suburbs, gusts and sheets of steely rain are moving on invisible curtain-rods across the public spaces. Through bangs of thunder and the flash-photography of lightning on the tossing trees, the bus moves slowly. Below, the traffic on the *peripherique* moves in blurred lines as we cross into Malakoff, where old men wait in doorways, with dogs asleep at their feet, and flasks of cheap wine.

The other Paris, of tramps, Muslim immigrants, North African *sans papiers*. We swish through it, past the drenched trees and tenements of the Avenue Pierre Brossolette in the rain, uphill into Chatillon.

Madame Dacquet leans from a ground-floor window. Scaffolding strains and canvas flaps in the wind and rain. A smell of wet brick-dust hangs in front of the building where the stonework has been water-blasted all last week. The facelift is under way.

"*Ca ne changera rien*", she says, weeping.

Her sister-in-law has just died, suddenly, of a brain haemorrhage, at the age of fifty-four. Death has taken someone else away. Time is passing, bland and grey as a Sunday afternoon. Nothing, not even the facelift of our building, will hold our little world together.

"*Ca ne changera rien*", she repeats.

Her boyfriend, a dour little man in his late seventies, lets himself out the front door. We have met him before. He knows we are Irish.

"In Ireland", he says darkly, "riots, bombings, war. Like Corsica. Or North Africa. Or the Middle East." France, he would have us believe, is an island of peace and freedom in this sea of barbarism.

"The world is going mad", he adds, getting into his car.

In the dank vestibule, a couple of prams are bunched against the wall, with the wet boots and sweaty socks of tomorrow's workmen. Buckets, flex, electric drills litter the muddy floor. A pungent smell of cabbage and steamed fish leaks from Jesus Lopes' apartment, below our own. It will creep through the floorboards and stink the place out for days. Raised voices sound, on the first landing. Alberique, the house manager, is arguing with Carlos, the concierge who works up the hill. About costs, as usual, the quality of the work being done. I could do it myself, Carlos shouts, and do it better. There is a smell of white port.

"Je ne paierai pas … ."

"Pas de menaces! Je ne suis pas responsible. Je ne serai pas jete dans le merde!"

"Je m'en fou!"

They work their way down the stairs and out into the dank, dripping garden at the back, still arguing. *Pas de menaces!* I close our own door and the voices grow shrill and distant, the wives joining in through the back windows, supporting their wronged husbands, half-angry, half-attracted by the energies of a quarrel. I put a record on the turntable our friend and landlady Arlette left behind. The needle squitters across the vinyl into silence. The ancient tapedeck, too, is useless.

A mood descends. Everything, rooms and projects, the house itself, is doomed to fall apart. Who are we anyway? Poets, writers, caretakers – obsolete trades, soon to be swept away by the New. I press a button on the disc-player Alberique has lent us, and a Bach organ toccata fills the room. A little art, to offset reality. Off in the garden the voices diminish, drift in again from the rain. There are steps on the stairs, and a knocking, ever so gentle, on the door.

"Excuse us", says Alberique in English, "for all of that ..."

He is ashen, exhausted. In the background, through the open door of his own apartment, two small children crawl on a chequerboard floor. Aurelie, his wife of Polish extraction, drags at a mop and bucket. He clutches the air with both hands, in a mock-throttling gesture at the world in general, and goes inside. There is silence again on the stairs, the rattle of canvas in the wind, the drip of rain on catwalks outside the windows.

"Spleen-weather", Deirdre says. "The weather of Baudelaire."

But the next morning, it is fine bright autumn again. Life is bearable, effort is still worthwhile. The masons' mallets tap at the stone façade outside, the traffic passes below and Paris again has a working air. On the wooden stairs, there are steps and protests of children going to school. Through the open window, in the distance, the slow cranes revolve, the changes go on. From the garden, a smell of compost-fires drifts in, and the yard is littered with ash-keys. Madame Dacquet strings washing on the line. Alberique, a cigar in hand, checks his plum-tree for dead branches. We are glad of Monday. For us, the weekends are hardest, because least innerly directed.

"... to work", a voice on the radio is saying, "from the area of damage inside yourself ..."

Any minute now, in the din of repair and reconstruction, we will go inside to our separate rooms. Carlos clumps past on his way to caretaking in the new buildings up the hill. Madame Garnier, her mind far away in Réunion, drags a shopping trolley down the stairs. In our honeycombed apartments, Al Hocevar and ourselves, Zagajewski and Williams and all the others all over Paris, the bees of the invisible, are settling in to write, to deal with the past.

"Bees of the Invisible" is the third chapter of an unpublished Paris-based autobiographical text, The End of Exile.

Harry Clifton was born in Dublin in 1952 and has travelled widely in Africa and Asia, as well as Europe. He is the author of six collections of poems, most recently Secular Eden: Paris Notebooks 1994-2004 *(Wake Forest University Press, 2007), and two prose books,* On the Spine of Italy *(Macmillan, 1999) and* Berkeley's Telephone *(Lilliput Press, 2000). He currently lives in Dublin.*